Praise for the Second Edition of Coaching

"In *Coaching: Evoking Excellence in Others*, James Flaherty brilliantly dissects both the art and science of coaching—one of the more difficult and least understood roles in organizations. Beginning with theories, concepts, and models, he shows their application to practice and empowers any aspiring coach to be more effective in helping people achieve their goals. A better book on this subject just doesn't exist."

—**Jerry I. Porras**, Lane Professor of Organizational Behavior and Change Emeritus, Graduate School of Business, Stanford University and Co-Author, *Built to Last*

"As the field of coaching finds its way to becoming a mature discipline, James Flaherty's dedicated field research, study, and sound articulation offers a definitive ground and a sensibility of genuine care. At the core, this book offers a way of thinking about human beings that makes action and practice central to learning. This is a no-nonsense, generous, pragmatic book that belongs on the shelf every coach, novice or veteran."

—**Richard Strozzi-Heckler**, Ph.D., Founder of Somatic Coaching and author of *The Anatomy of Change* and *Holding The Center*

"At long last, a book on coaching that moves beyond 'advice from the sidelines.' James Flaherty convincingly shows that the only way to truly help people grow is to help them in developing new practices and new language, and that the only way to coach effectively is to enter into a reciprocal relationship where 'coach' and 'coachee' engage in a dance of mutual influence and growth".

—**Peter M. Senge**, MIT and Society for Organizational Learning

D1166184

"This extraordinary book clearly represents James Flaherty's ability to insightfully enable the self-generating and self-correcting capacities of his clients. His clarity and candor engage the reader to more deeply examine the opportunities to live a more integrated and holistic life."

—**Michele Goins**, Vice President and Chief Information Officer, Imaging and Printing Group, Hewlett-Packard Company

"James Flaherty focuses on the commonly overlooked fact that a coachee is a 'human-being.' He effectively emphasizes that this is the most important aspect that a coach should always have in mind, something that many of us tend to forget. It was this tact that he applies toward coaching, as well as many other brilliant insights, that helped me make the decision to publish *Coaching* in Japanese and apply its lessons in my practice."

—**Mamoru Itoh**, President, Coach21 Co., Ltd., Tokyo, Japan

"James Flaherty frames deep questions about how humans operate across a series of interconnected domains such as the mind, body, and emotions, which will give both new and experienced coaches pause to reflect. He frames crisp distinctions about the coaching process which will generate new perspectives on the role of the coach. He leaves a trail of deeply researched threads that the reader can explore after reading to deepen their knowledge and understanding. All of this is done in a crisp and quietly elegant dialogue which makes you believe he is present as you are inspired to explore, with profound curiosity, your own beliefs on what we are as human beings and how we should show up as coaches. As you read and digest his coaching metaphors, analogies and questions, there are inexplicable possibilities that crystallize, fresh insights that emerge and a renewed commitment to explore oneself and the coaching we strive to master."

—**Craig O'Flaherty**, Director, Centre for Coaching, Graduate School of Business, University of Cape Town, South Africa

Coaching: Evoking Excellence in Others

(Third Edition)

James Flaherty

Routledge
Taylor & Francis Group

LONDON AND NEW YORK

First published 1998 by Butterworth-Heinemann
Second edition 2005
Third edition 2010

Published 2014 by Routledge
2 Park Square, Milton Park, Abingdon, Oxon OX14 4RN
711 Third Avenue, New York, NY, 10017, USA

Routledge is an imprint of the Taylor & Francis Group, an informa business

Library of Congress Cataloging-in-Publication Data
Flaherty, James.
    Coaching: evoking excellence in others / James Flaherty.-3rd ed.
    p. cm.
    Includes bibliographical references and index.
    ISBN-13: 978-1-85617-816-7 (alk. paper)
    ISBN-10: 0-7506-7920-4
1. Mentoring in business. 2. Employees-Training of. 3. Employees-Counseling of.
4. Employees-Counseling of. 5. Executive coaching. I. Title.
    HF5385.F55 2010
    658.30124-c22

                                                                    2009053514

British Library Cataloguing in Publication Data
A catalogue record for this book is available from the British Library

ISBN-13: 978-1-85617-816-7 (pbk)

"Talent neglected or misguided, investigations into the nature of things not completed, what is right understood but not acted upon, and the lack of energy to rectify what is wrong—these are the things which pain my heart, which I exist to remedy."

—KUNG-TZU (CONFUCIUS)

Contents

Foreword   xi
Preface to the Third Edition   xv
Preface   xix
    How to Use This Book   xx
    Limits of the Text   xxi
Acknowledgments   xxiii
Orientation   xxv
Introduction   xxvii

1.   The Foundation for Coaching   1
    Why Coaching Now?   1
    What Is Coaching?   3
    Operating Principles of Coaching   9

2.   Basic Principles   15
    What Is a Human Being?   15
    Language, Observation, and Assessment   23

3.   The Flow of Coaching   31
    Stage One: Relationship   33
    Stage Two: Openings   34
    Stage Three: Assessment   35
    Stage Four: Enrollment   36
    Stage Five: Coaching Itself   37

4.   The Coaching Relationship   39
    Mutual Trust   40
    Mutual Respect   42
    Mutual Freedom of Expression   44

5. Openings   51

     Habits   51
     Social Identity   53
     Openings   55

6. Assessment Models   59

     Model One: Five Elements Model   62
     Model Two: Domains of Competence   70
     Model Three: Components of Satisfaction and Effectiveness   73
     Using These Models   76
     Applications of the Models to Our Case   78

7. How Things Really Get Done   83

     Speech Act Theory   83
     Requests   86
     Promises   90
     Offers   91
     Assertions   93
     Assessments   95
     Declarations   98
     Conversation for Relationship   100
     Conversation for Possibilities   101
     Conversation for Action   102

8. Enrollment   107

9. Coaching Conversations   115

     Types of Conversation   116
     Type One: Single Conversations   117
     Type Two: Several Conversations   120
     Type Three   132
     Assessment Exercise   144
     Self-Observation Exercise   145
     Practice Exercise   146

10. Stuck   151

     Client Being Stuck   151
     Program Being Stuck   153

11. Getting in Condition for Change   157

What's Necessary for Change   158
Assessing the Client's Readiness   159
What To Do with What You Find   161

12. Track Two: Working with Ourselves   169

Truing Questions   170
Self-Development Process for Coaches: Skills and Qualities   170
The Process: Working with Yourself   174
The Process: An Example   175
Definitions   178
How Bob Turned Out   178

Conclusion   181
Appendix A: Self-Observations   183
Appendix B: Practices   193
Bibliography   205
About the Author   213
Index   215

Foreword

On its surface, James Flaherty's book looks to be a *how-to* text for a rapidly emerging set of disciplines and practices called *Coaching*. Don't be misled. This book is a lot more than that, although you can read it for no other reason, and it will help you improve your practices as a coach (or as a client, a customer of coaching).

Not long ago, coaching meant training athletes, performers, and students. Recently, the use of the term has been extended into the worlds of management, leadership, entrepreneurship, and performance in other domains of life. I remember my initial reaction to hearing Fernando Flores propose in the early 1980s to bring the skills of basketball coaches to management teams and the boardroom. I was surprised at this unexpected appropriation; and, it made a lot of sense. In retrospect, I think that it made particular sense to me because of what I knew about how difficult it is to learn the practices of managing and leading. It is extraordinarily difficult to observe and improve one's own performance in the challenging roles people face in taking responsibility for the future—especially managing and leading.

The discipline of coaching puts the center of its attention on the question of how a person can help other people develop new capabilities, new horizons, and new worlds of opportunity for themselves and those around them. Put this way, we can begin to see that this role—coaching—will be especially relevant for the coming era. This book is about building relationships among people who are continuously learning about the changing environments in which they live and work, intervening in and moving to set aside ineffective and counter-productive habits, and building new skills, practices, habits, and platforms for collaborating in this ever-changing world.

In the 20th Century, we built enormous organizations around the world in which people were employed as special kinds of irritating and expensive interchangeable parts. Those organizations changed the face of the planet, bringing both valuable and wasteful practices everywhere they touched. To get more efficient and effective we centralized, decentralized, cut costs, outsourced, down-sized, right-sized, and automated. We coordinated manufacturing and logistics through "ERP" systems and dealt with our customers with "CIS" and "CRM" systems. (Don't worry if you are not familiar with those acronyms; that underscores my point.) Coaching was not an essential capacity in that world; it was not necessary to re-shape the skills of most individual employees. People were trained to perform in roles that had been designed to serve the purposes of the enterprise, and they adapted or they were replaced. We trained people to remember and repeat "information" and follow rules. It was only in the last decades of the 20th Century that various features of the world began to call for the kinds of capacities to deal with the continuously changing environments that this new kind of coaching was invented to address.

James has put the client in the center of his interpretation of coaching in a way that is worthy of our attention. One reviewer says that James does not forget that those who are coached "are human beings." What does he mean by this? No one would dispute the proposition that coaches work with human beings. But James has very particular interpretations about the kinds of beings he is training to coach, and about the beings that they, in turn will coach. He has worked for many years to develop these interpretations, and they are fundamental to what is so helpful about this book. There is no way to sum them up; you must read the book and make your own sense of what James is doing. However, I want to point to three interpretations that James is writing from that I would not want the reader to miss.

1. Human beings create themselves in language, continuously shaping and re-shaping the narratives in which they make sense of their worlds. If you would make sense of another human being, pay close attention to the language and narratives in which s/he interprets him/herself.
2. Human beings are biological creatures all the way down. They invent, carry, and express their moods, what they care about, and how they understand the world in their bodies. If you would make sense of another human being, pay close attention to their body, and to how they attend to it themselves.
3. Human beings are paradoxical, at once far more creatures of habit than most of us like to think, and at the same time far more malleable. For James this paradox is a bottomless source of wonder, appreciation, inquiry, and amusement. This is a serious book, but you will see James's humor here too.

These distinctions arise from James's study of many disciplines. For example, it will be obvious to the reader that he has thought deeply about human language and the ways that we invent ourselves and our worlds in language. This is one of the most distinctive features of the book. In this, he stands on the shoulders of great philosophers and shares their work with the reader. Finally, he includes learnings from his Buddhist practices, the biology of Humberto Maturana and Francisco Varela, and his work as a Certified Rolfer (which he did before becoming a coach and developer of coaches) and makes what he has learned available to the reader in direct and indirect ways.

In the book, James presents ingenious maps for thinking about the multi-dimensional space in which two human beings come together to produce a shift in the world(s) of one or both. He calls them "models." The models that the commonsense world gives us for thinking about these questions are, for the most part, bad maps. On her College Board Test, for example, my daughter is asked to write about this question: "Are people more often motivated by money or fame, or by personal satisfaction?" On reflection, it is easy to see that this is a bad question that shares the structure of the old joke, "When did you stop beating your wife?" Don't be misled when James says that the models he presents are not terribly important. He warns against mistaking maps for territories, and calls those who would label people using models, simply, "lazy." Here he is speaking in the philosophical tradition of Wittgenstein, who said, "My propositions serve as elucidations in the following way: anyone who understands me eventually recognizes them as non-sensical when he has climbed out through them, on them, over them. (He must, so to speak, throw away the ladder after he has climbed up it.)" [1] In the end I agree that you will be wise to discard the models James offers, but before that, they are enormously useful as "ladders" to access new terrain.

At this turning point of history, far too many of our leaders, managers, designers, and others in positions of responsibility for our communities and enterprises have come to take for granted that it is possible to *manage* and *lead* other people without attending to questions that sit in the middle of this book: how to intervene in situations in which people are "stuck" in old habits and badly understood situations, how we observe the world around us, and how people learn.

When I am training designers, I often remind them that if they are not skilled and confident in their capacity to diagnose and intervene in the human messes of the world, they will make important mistakes. They will design features for a new world constrained by the limits of their own ability to understand the capabilities of people. Similarly, confidence in your own capacity to be an effective coach is an essential ingredient for making a better team, business, service, and world. As you read *Coaching: Evoking Excellence in Others* and begin to practice what it offers, I predict you will find yourself experiencing expanding possibilities for yourself and those you interact with, along with growing ambition and confidence that you can take on and succeed at projects and goals that before were not possible.

Chauncey Bell
Managing Director
Pacific Northwest Financial Services
Seattle, Washington

---

[1] *Proposition 6.54 from the Tractatus Logico-Philosophicus. See http://www.public-domain-content. com/Philosophy/Ludwig_Wittgenstein.shtml and http://pd.sparknotes.com/philosophy/tractatus/ section13.html*

Preface to the Third Edition

After over twenty-plus years of coaching, my understanding of it is still evolving. This seems to me to be a very good thing, because every time I sit across from a client is a fresh moment to discover what is possible and to let go of what has worked before.

Of course for someone who is beginning coaching what I just said is not so helpful and might even be anxiety producing. When we first start any activity, it is important for us to have norms, rules, procedures and standards. All of us have encountered this when we took up driving or skiing or typing. The more mechanical the activity, the more rule-based it is. So for example in learning to type, we don't have to worry about the keyboard changing between practice sessions. Unfortunately this steady-state, mechanical way of knowing that is important in the early stages and that fits permanently with particular activities has been extended to a way of knowing about everything forever.

I'm saying that, for example, the beginner way of knowing about management where someone learns to set goals, hold people accountable, give frequent feedback, and so on, won't work for everyone and won't even work for the same person over a period of time. We all learn this from our own experience of attempting to apply a rule in a situation where it doesn't hold up. Sooner or later, in other words, we begin to understand the importance of context and tuning into an individual's situation. At that point, we face our own anxiety because we cannot rely upon a structure to inform us or justify what we do. Once we move beyond strict routines, we must rely upon our own experience and skill.

There is no shortcut to what we learn through experience. No amount of reading about driving a car replicates what it feels like driving down a foggy, mountain road in the middle of torrential rain. Experience is what shapes our understanding so that we can know at a glance what the appropriate action is. We do this everyday, walking into a meeting or stepping into the middle of a situation at home. No one has to stop and explain to us what is going on. We immediately recognize it because we've experienced something similar many times.

At this juncture, careful readers might be seeing a paradox in what I'm saying. At once I'm claiming that each moment is fresh and that we have to rely upon experience to know how to respond beyond rules. How can both be true?

If we hold to experience, aren't we attempting to recreate a past situation? And if we abandon experience, aren't we simply lost or rote in our response?

These questions could be provocative for you to enter into and answer for yourself and I certainly invite you to do that. Here is a simple way of working with the paradox. Once our experience is broad and deep, our response will never be rote. You can see this directly yourself by attending a performance by any skilled jazz ensemble. The musicians will have so much experience in playing and listening and creating music on the spot that they can be spontaneous and fresh in each measure of playing. So in this way of looking at it, experience provides a huge repertory that we can draw upon as necessary.

Sometimes when people read about experience, they imagine that it somehow happens on its own. Yes, it's true that every moment we have experience, but that's not what I'm pointing to here. To take up the jazz example, all of these players have the benefit of experience based upon thousands of hours of practice. Experience with watching sunsets or enjoying rare wine won't help so much when it comes time to respond to a changing rhythm or chord progression during a performance. Practice as presented in the book has a structure and standards and requires great persistence. It's the only way though we can become proficient at an activity and remain freshly creative. In other words, experience is not just a matter of doing something over and over again. We must engage in the activity with a clear intention to improve our competence and continuously correct ourselves as we go. Lacking this intention, repeated activities are not practices but, instead, recurring situations that wear us down. To see what I'm talking about, please see your local Department of Motor Vehicles or other governmental bureaucracy where people for the most part are not freshly meeting each moment but have been instead dulled by repetition.

Central to any practice are distinctions, particular ways of talking, that let us operate within the given activity. We must learn the language of brake, accelerator, steering wheel, rear-view mirror and so on before we drive. Essentially this book is a collection of such distinctions, meant to orient you to the world of coaching so that you can become more and more competent as a practitioner.

This third edition has two new chapters of distinctions that have been added from my experience of training thousands of coaches and working with hundreds of clients. The topics of these new chapters get to the heart of what has coaching succeed or not.

The chapter called "Getting in Condition to Change" addresses what to pay attention to at the beginning of a coaching engagement. The central concern at this juncture is whether the client is in a condition to take on change. No amount of circumstance or concentration of will power will prolong or overcome a lack of readiness. For serious lasting change, clients must have enough freed up attention and energy to observe their life, put down unhelpful habits and take up new practices and new relationships.

As we all know here early in the 21st century, nearly everyone we meet is too busy. In fact the usual response to "How are you?" is "I'm busy." In the midst of this busyness—which is not only behavioral but cognitive and emotional as well—any seed of change will quickly be paved over or die of neglect. Have you noticed this? Many coaches at that juncture abandon their clients or attempt to cheer them on to a more willful effort. As the chapter shows, these methods are at best short-lived and leave the client unable to continue progressing on their own at the end of the coaching program. Instead, the chapter presents ways of assessing the client's readiness for change and appropriate remedies when that is found not to be the case.

The other new chapter, "How Things Really Get Done," addresses the central and usually hidden topic of coaching: language. The only thing that coaches ever do is speak and listen. For many readers, this may be an obvious point but coaches sometimes forget in our contemporary world that almost all our clients do as well is speak and listen. The quality of work that anyone does follows from her ability to listen deeply to what is being asked, engage in a conversation to clarify the intended results and then continuously converse as the project unfolds until everyone involved is satisfied. This competence appears everywhere in work. And its absence is the main cause of breakdowns, waste, and loss of business.

Not only our work life but our relational life as well hinges upon our ability to build rapport, explore possibilities, and coordinate action. Like all competencies, this one has its own list of distinctions, which are presented in detail in the chapter. The good news is that almost everyone can learn to speak in a way that moves action forward, that opens up new possibilities and that builds relationships. It is not so much an innate ability as a learned skill.

As you read these new chapters and the rest of the book as well, please allow what's said to affect you. I wrote this book as a series of distinctions that point to a way of understanding and working with people that is satisfying for both client and coach. Please do not get caught up in the words themselves, but instead find what they are intended to bring your attention towards. Steadily practicing in the way described in the book will over time lead you to a high level of competence. You will be able to be of great assistance to others and be able to live a life of deep fulfillment yourself.

Preface

Probably what's at the core of working with people as a manager, teacher, coach, or parent is our basic understanding of people. Do we believe that human beings are attempting above all else to avoid pain and seek pleasure? Have we concluded that everyone is trying to get ahead himself, regardless of what happens to others? Do we think that people are biocomputers that have been programmed by life circumstances and have very limited possibilities for change? Do we imagine that people are small particles in a vast, unstoppable mechanism of historical forces that leave the individual as helpless as a cork in the ocean? Or do we have the opposite view, that the individual is the captain of his fate, one who can fully determine what happens, bend circumstances to his will, overcome all circumstantial obstacles? Until we can reveal to ourselves what we understand human beings to be, we cannot coach them. Without this understanding, it's as if we are attempting to build a structure with materials that we aren't familiar with. We don't know what will bear weight. We don't know what will be water resistant. We can't tell what might be insulating. Probably no intelligent person would go ahead with such a project unless forced to by circumstances. But many of us go ahead and work with people without coming to grips with this fundamental question.

In fact, many authors and experts do not address the topic at all and work instead with an assumed theory that is never revealed. Perhaps this is because there doesn't seem to be a need to talk about it. After all, we've gotten this far in management theory and education theory without such discussion. Why bring it up now? The reason is because of the most pragmatic conclusion possible—what we're doing is not working. There is no need here to cite statistical evidence for this assertion. What is probably more interesting is people's response to it. We tend to do more of what we've already done in the past, rather than to rethink what we're doing. Without this new thinking, all we can do is continue to repeat the actions we've already taken, which will of course lead to the same outcomes that we already have.

Repackaging the same actions in a program called *coaching* is just another version of the same mistake, as is trying to shorten the amount of time taken to perform the same actions. This book, then, is meant to ask some fundamental questions, and as such it will not be an easy-to-apply collection of tips and techniques. It's more like showing people how to design a building on strong foundations than like teaching them how to apply spackle to the cracks in the wall as they appear. The difficulty with fundamental questioning is that it's uncomfortable and takes time, and consequently many people don't do it. Reading this book is a chance to take some time out and rethink the way you work with people.

HOW TO USE THIS BOOK

There are many different ways to read through this book. Some readers will start at the beginning and go all the way through, reading all the texts, charts, summaries, references, and bibliographies. Others will just glance through and read the summaries at the beginning of each chapter. Some people will look through and read the charts and try to make sense of those. Still others will read the table of contents and the index, and then will make some conclusion about the book. Instead of doing what you habitually do when reading a book, take some time to consider what it is that you want to accomplish by reading and working with this book. And then ask yourself what is the best way to do that. Intervening in habits is very important in coaching and you can begin to coach yourself by asking these questions. Each person, of course, will end up determining for himself what he does. The question remains, though—what is the basis for this action? Is it the most efficient and quickest way, or is it a proven methodology that is continually measured against outcomes? Coaching, you see, is not telling people what to do; it's giving them a chance to examine what they are doing in the light of their intentions. So if you read this book looking for someone to tell you what to do, you won't find it.

In any case, there is a particular organization to the book. Each chapter begins with a brief summary of its content, followed by a text that is the theoretical basis for the topic. Following are reference notes and bibliographic information. The text is deliberately simple and straightforward. You'll find grounding for the ideas presented and references for further study in the annotated bibliography at the end of each chapter. You can use the book as a coaching tool if you allow yourself to use the distinctions presented as a way to look at your own world. What you find will be useful or not according to what you are up to. On the other hand, trying to think of exceptions to what's presented or arguing with the book will leave you with what you already knew before you started. Yes, it does make sense to question and to struggle with a text, but dismissing it out of hand without a sincere attempt to take its notions into life will assure that we continue to remain only as capable as we are already. The proof of coaching is in action, not in argumentation. Taking the book into action will give you a chance to assess its value to you much more than arguing with it will. As a coach, you'll find yourself taking the same tack, asking your client (the person you're coaching) to take what you're saying into action as a test, rather than arguing with you in an abstract way about the truth of what you're saying. Naturally this takes trust, and in real life this must be in place before coaching starts. For you to get the most benefit out of this book as a reader, you have to give it the benefit of the doubt.

LIMITS OF THE TEXT

If you've looked through the table of contents, you've seen that this book takes on some formidable topics: subjects that have been the topic of philosophical, sociological, and psychological discussion for centuries. Naturally, the book is not meant to be the definitive word on any of these subjects, but is instead intended to be a spur to reveal to yourself your thoughts on the subjects. Actively reading the book will mean watching your reactions to the ideas presented, because it's in this reaction that you will see where you stand on the subject matter. In a sense, your understanding of life is like light that can only be seen when it is reflected off something else. This book can be such an object, in which you can see your own thinking reflected, if you are open and looking for it. Your particular problems or situations may not be explicitly addressed, but you can take the notions presented and apply them to yourself and your own life, resulting in a new awareness. This awareness can be a chance to see in a new way what is happening, to form a new relationship with the situation, and to take new action. The book is not a cookbook that tells you what to combine in what preparations, how to cook it, and for how long. It is only when someone tosses away a cookbook that he or she can be a truly great chef. Similarly, we can never become very great coaches by following a step-by-step procedure that someone else gives us. Yes, it's true that beginners need structure and instruction and those are included in the text, but they are meant to be only the preliminary steps—steps that you take only to build your competence and then throw away as you design your own steps.

Acknowledgments

Fernando Flores provided my foundation and orientation to language and coaching. For this I will always be grateful. The work of Humberto Maturana underlies all the ideas presented here. Simon Turkalj, Amy Carroll and Janique Gascoigne worked for many hours in their dedicated and careful way to make this book possible. Many clients and colleagues, especially Melissa McNair, have contributed to my work and have been open to it—allowing me to learn. All of you have my gratitude. My parents always believed that I could do it—thanks. My wife Stacy and daughter Devin inspire me each day with their love, support, and insight.

More recently, my colleagues Pam Weiss, Sarita Chawla and Craig O'Flaherty have made instrumental contributions to the work presented in this book. Norman Fischer, my Zen teacher, continues to inspire me with his profound compassion and insight into the human condition. Numerous others have made significant contributions to my development; they include Ken Anbender, Keith Bailey, Chauncey Bell, Linda Ruth Cutts, Michael Salveson, Ada Shedlock, Mary Ellen Stanke, Rosanne Annoni, Sara Hurley, Eugene Cash, Dale Sides and Larry Johnson.

Orientation

Probably everyone at one time or another has wanted to help someone else improve at what he or she was doing. Parents watching their children grow, teachers working with students, supervisors and managers on the job, friends supporting each other in a common endeavor, and countless other examples show our basic human desire to contribute. This book (and my life) is directed at the questions, "How do I do that?" and "How do I contribute to someone's competence in a respectful, dignified, and effective way?" If you find yourself asking these or similar questions, then this book definitely has something to say to you.

Introduction

The challenges in writing a book on coaching are the same as those one faces when beginning to coach:

- How to say something distinct enough to foster change and yet familiar enough to be understood.
- How to say something linearly (the organized form of nearly any book) that can only be fully understood holistically or systemically.
- How to show something meant to evoke a paradigm shift in a way efficient (cogent) enough to maintain interest.

In other words, how to be heard saying something well beyond quick techniques in a world clamoring for them. The list could go on, as you well know if you've ever attempted to evoke excellence from someone else—if you've ever tried to coach someone. However, the job of a coach is always to speak about/show what can happen and to do so in a way that frees people to take action.

We are all too familiar with constraints in our world. In fact, it often seems that the more aware/experienced/informed we become, the more convinced we are that it will take more awareness, experience, and information before we can overcome constraints, be fulfilled in our work, and bring meaning to our lives (see Figure I.1).

And of course, the circle, frequently vicious, as you've probably noticed, is at first about ourselves only, but later, it becomes a constraint to our coaching of others.

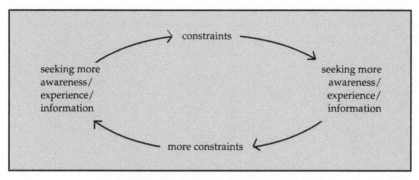

FIGURE I.1   The Constraints of Learning

Doesn't it seem that the more books we study, the more we self-diagnose as having whatever the syndrome is that the author describes? For the same reason, reading medical textbooks is much more frightening than reading Edgar Allan Poe or Stephen King.

Keep this in mind as you read the following chapters. Do you find yourself more constrained? Are the distinctions showing you more reasons why something cannot happen? Or, are you finding yourself more free to take action? Of course, these are the same questions to ask when you're coaching someone.

When you find yourself constrained/confused/in disagreement, I invite you to ask yourself the following questions: "What way of seeing this topic am I attached to or defending?" and "What would happen if I saw it this new way?" Keep working with yourself in this way as you read this book and you'll find yourself more competent by the end.

1

The Foundation for Coaching

Here are the basics, the building blocks for everything that follows-the funda-mentals of coaching. They're presented simply, directly, and concisely with few examples or elaborations. The presentation gives you maximum room for your own thinking and creativity. This book doesn't tell you what to do. Instead, it gives you distinctions, ideas, models, and principles from which you can design your own actions. Some readers will be annoyed by this, others will feel informed and liberated. In either case, regardless of initial response, the question remains-what will leave you, the reader, with the greatest chance to be an excellent coach who can self-correct and self-generate your own innovations? The following is my response to that question.

"Our chief want in life is someone who will make us do what we can."

—Emerson

WHY COACHING NOW?

Maybe as you select a book about coaching you already have in mind the situation in which you want to use coaching. Perhaps you're a manager in some kind of organization who is trying to improve the performance of someone who works for you, or maybe you are someone attempting to mentor a young promising person. Alternatively, you might be a team leader on a software development task force attempting to build the proficiency of your team. You could also be a parent who wants to provide the best possible upbringing for your child. The possible scenarios could go on and on, and it's the purpose of this book to give you an introduction to coaching in a way that allows you to apply it to the wide range of situations we find ourselves in these days.

The common thread running through these circumstances is the intention of the coach to leave the person being coached, whom we'll call the client, more competent in an activity that is of mutual interest to coach and client. Since many of the people reading this book are probably interested in how coaching applies to business, here are some reasons why coaching is important in the world of commerce today:

1. The need for innovation is endless. Businesses must keep reinventing not only their products and ways of delighting their customers, but also the way they organize themselves; communicate so as to coordinate activities; and stay current with changes in technology, demographics, politics, government regulations, and so on.
2. Because of relentless downsizing and reengineering efforts, the traditional relationship between organization and employee has been changed in a way that is probably irreparable. Consequently, even outstanding performers do not anticipate staying with one organization for their entire career and are always working with the knowledge, at least in the background, that their current position is temporary. Organizations have to find a way to retain such people as long as possible by providing both attractive compensation and a chance to continuously learn.
3. Organizations by necessity are having to work in multicultural environments. This happens when organizations recruit or market in other nations as well as within the United States, as our demographics evolve from the historic Eurocentrality.

It is one of the central tenets of this book that command-and-control organizations cannot bring about the conditions and competencies necessary to successfully meet the challenges holistically. For the most part, organizations know this and have attempted to reorganize themselves using the principles of total quality management and reengineering. The usual problem with these interventions is that they are implemented by and end up reinforcing the command-and-control structure. Here's my objection to that: command-and-control organizations are based on the premise that a power and knowledge hierarchy is the most effective way of structuring an organization. People at the top make the decisions and people further down implement those decisions, changing them as little as possible. The process is slow, expensive, and has as its core belief that people cannot be trusted and must be closely monitored. As long as those beliefs are in place any organization will have tremendous difficulty flourishing in today's world. Of course, what I'm saying here is not a new statement. What I'm offering in this book is an alternative to working in a command-and-control environment by beginning with new premises. It's been my experience that organizations must be dedicated to allowing people to be both effective and fulfilled. Organizations are the ongoing creations of the people who work in them. Treating organizations as if they were huge machines, as is done with command and control, badly misunderstands the nature of the phenomenon. To sum up and simplify what I'm saying, coaching is a way of working with people that leaves them more competent and more fulfilled so that they are more able to contribute to their organizations and find meaning in what they are doing. I hope that reading this book will convince you that this is possible and that you will experiment with the ideas presented here. That is the only way you can find out for yourself that what I'm saying here is worthwhile.

WHAT IS COACHING?

Perhaps one of the most powerful ways of understanding coaching is from the end. If we know what we are intending to accomplish, we can correct ourselves as we go along and be able to evaluate our success at the end. These products are meant to distinguish what we mean about coaching from other interpretations. We present coaching as more than being an accountability partner that supports someone in reaching her goals or as a disciplinarian who changes someone's unwanted actions. Instead we claim that coaching occurs in a bigger frame that sometimes includes these two modalities but goes well beyond that.

The Products of Coaching

Long-Term Excellent Performance

This means that the client meets the high objective standards of the discipline in which coaching is occurring. Standards are objective when they can be observed by any competent person. For example, hitting a home run in baseball is an objective standard, as is a checkmate in chess; however, we must know something about each game to be able to observe these outcomes as favorable.

Self-Correction

Well-coached clients can observe when they are performing well and when they are not and will make any necessary adjustments independently of the coach. By keeping this criterion in mind, coaches can avoid the big temptation of becoming indispensable and, instead, work to build the competence of their client.

Self-Generation

We can always improve, and well-coached people know this and will continually find ways on their own to do so. They'll practice more, or they'll watch others perform, or they'll learn an activity that will strengthen them in a new way that improves their competence (see Figure 1.1).

Let me give you an example that will illustrate what I'm saying and will perhaps make these ideas more clear. I coached a man named Bob at a major oil company in California. Bob was referred to me by my friend Nancy, who worked as an internal human resources consultant. He was a competent and well-regarded accountant who traveled to various sites

- Long-term excellent performance
- Self-correction
- Self-generation

FIGURE 1.1   The Products of Coaching

worldwide and audited drilling operations. But Bob had greater ambitions. He felt as if he were trapped by his own success, that management would never let him move on because he was doing such good work. At least that is what he told me.

As I got to know Bob better I saw that he was missing a whole set of competencies to move ahead in a large organization with powerful political forces at play. Bob's initial assumption was that by doing good work he would get noticed and promoted. When this didn't happen he blamed management for their shortsightedness and selfishness. This explanation left Bob powerless; there was nothing he could do to change the thinking of his managers.

Of course, this is where a coach comes in. A coach is someone who builds a respectful relationship with a client and then researches the situations the client finds himself in, with particular emphasis on the client's interpretation of the events. When I did that, I saw that Bob would be captured in the vicious circle of his thinking until he saw the situation in a new way, developed new competencies, and created a new identity for himself in the organization.

I'll continue to tell you the story of Bob as the book continues, but for now I want to talk about the products of coaching in terms of this scenario. For Bob to be a long-term excellent performer, he had to be known as someone who could deal effectively with the bigger issues facing executives in the company and not merely skillful dealing with problems at his level. He had to know how decisions were made and power was brokered. He needed to learn to build alliances, share concerns, and present himself as executive material.

To be self-correcting, Bob had to be able to alter in midconversation or midmeeting what he was doing to bring about the outcomes he intended. He had to learn about his own habits and how they might get him in trouble, about the subtle communications clues he had been oblivious to in his environment, and he had to be able to keep learning without either being too harsh on himself or too lax.

To be self-generating, Bob had to have more than a list of tasks he was going to accomplish during his coaching program. He had to locate the resources in himself, in his relationships at work, and in the wider community that would allow him to continuously improve. He had to develop the capacity to renew himself, question his premises, let go of assumptions when they no longer were helpful, and do all this while maintaining his well-being, family life, and closely held personal values.

Perhaps from this example you can see that coaches have to address both a short- and a long-term view. Short-term in the sense that they must support their clients in reaching their goals, but long-term in the sense that the client will always have more challenges later and must be left competent to deal with these situations as they arise, while simultaneously conducting a fulfilling life.

An Alternative Model of Coaching

The hundreds of times I've described the products of coaching in classes or with individual clients I've always had people agree that they were terrific, worthwhile, and desirable. After all, who wouldn't want to leave people as long-term excellent performers who were self-correcting and self-generating? I found that nearly everyone agrees with the products. Problems arise though, when people attempting to coach work to bring them about.

The heart of these problems is the assumptions coaches make about people. When attempting to bring about changes in others, many of us employ what I call the amoeba theory (see Figure 1.2).

You may recall that amoeba are single-cell protozoa. Perhaps you studied them in high school biology. It's easy to change the behavior of an amoeba. We can either poke it to get it to move away or entice it to move in the desired direction by giving it sugar. Poking and sugar work very well for amoebas, who never wake up and say, "Today I will ignore the sugar." Day after day they

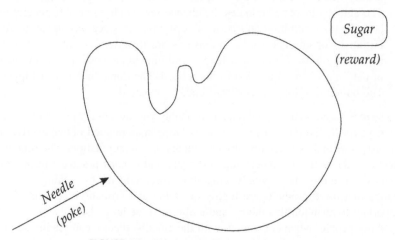

FIGURE 1.2   The Amoeba Theory of Management

predictably respond to the stimuli presented. All of this was useful and powerful learning that was brought to the world through Pavlov, Watson, and Skinner. The only problem, as far as we're concerned in this book, is that the amoeba theory becomes management theory. For the most part, managers and coaches attempt to bring about changes in others by figuring out how to poke them or give them sugar.

The vast majority of psychologists have abandoned the amoeba theory, which is more properly called behaviorism, because they made an amazing discovery: human beings are more complicated than amoebas. It's unfortunate that many managers and many coaches act as if they haven't made a similar discovery. In fact, one of the most well-known coaching books by Fournies proposes that the only way to coach is to use behaviorism in its most blunt and stark form.

I can assure you that using the amoeba theory will never bring about the products of coaching. Here's why:

1. Nothing long term can come from the amoeba theory; as soon as the stimulus ends, the behavior ends.
2. People are more clever than amoebas and we learn to get the reward without doing the action. Many of us have learned, for example, how to get top grades in college without really learning much, and organizations are full of people who have mastered looking good, while not accomplishing anything of use.
3. The amoeba theory eliminates the possibility of people being self-correcting because they are merely responding to stimuli and not correcting according to principles, desired outcomes, or values.
4. The amoeba theory weakens people every time it's applied because it habituates people to taking actions only when someone else provides the stimulus. This is terrific when we want passive, nonthinking drones, but deadly when we expect initiative, innovation, risk-taking, and creativity.
5. The amoeba theory eliminates the chance for people to be self-generating because their ambition and curiosity are crushed, since any unauthorized initiatives or unsanctioned relationships are thwarted. All attention must be on only those actions that lead to the immediate cessation of the pain or the immediate acquisition of the reward. The immediate is worshipped. The building of long-term competence is thwarted.

These reasons could go on and on, and probably you can come up with plenty of them yourself. Everyone I know resents being manipulated either overtly or covertly and that is what the amoeba theory is—manipulation. The amoeba theory is also a theory underlying command-and-control practices in organizations. Since this theory won't bring about the products of coaching, and we realize that these products are highly desirable and probably necessary, it is important to abandon this theory and embrace something else.

Many people, when confronted with the amoeba theory, can readily see its limitations and pernicious aspects. Nonetheless, under pressure that's what many of us employ. Coaches need a lot of discipline and practice over an extended amount of time to stay out of the amoeba theory and to employ instead an alternate theory that makes it more likely that the products of coaching will occur (see Figure 1.3).

This alternate theory must be respectful of people, flexible enough to include the vast differences among people, allow the coach to understand the client and design and conduct coaching programs that result in a client who is a long-term excellent performer who is self-correcting and self-generating. Simultaneously, the theory must also be a blending of academic rigor and everyday, commonsense experience. Absent this blending, any coaching theory will lack the robustness necessary to actively engage both coach and client.

The theory I'm proposing is drawn from phenomenology, a school of modern philosophy centered on the way phenomena actually show up in people's lives, as distinct from metaphysical schools of philosophy in which events and experiences are categorized by pre-existing distinctions. By explaining the theory with some examples I hope to make clear exactly what I'm saying.

The coach must account for behavior because behavior leads to outcomes. A coach whose work does not affect outcomes will soon find himself unemployed. The question then becomes how to account for behavior. I recommend that we account for behavior by understanding it as what follows from the way the world is showing up for someone. In other words, it's not events, communication, or stimuli that lead to behavior, it is the interpretation an individual gives to the phenomenon that leads to the actions taken.

To use an example drawn from the work of Perls (1973), imagine that three people are coming to the same party. The celebration is a typical one with music, food, drink, and people engaged in conversation. It's important to understand in this example that although the actions of the three people described are different, it's not because the environment they are in is different. Each person finds himself in the middle of a different interpretation of the environment and his actions come from that interpretation. The first person who comes to the party is an artist who has sold a work of art to the family hosting the party. What action does this artist take? He begins to look for where his art is hung, and he wonders aloud when he discovers it whether being placed above the toilet is really the best possible location for his work. The second attendee is

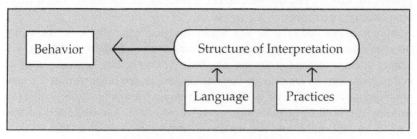

FIGURE 1.3 The Premise of Coaching

an alcoholic. You can probably easily predict that his first action is to find out where the alcohol is, and like the first partygoer, everything else—food, people, and music—fades way into the background. You might need a little more imagination or memory to predict the actions of the third person. He is madly in love with someone he is meeting at the party. Can you remember being head-over-heels in love with someone and the moment when you spotted your beloved? It's as if time slows down, sounds other than the beloved's voice quiet, and the loved one's presence stands out as if lit by a huge spotlight. For our third partygoer, everything besides his beloved—the food, the music, the other people—becomes transparent.

Here is my major point; if this becomes clear for you everything else in coaching will fall from it. Each person's actions were fully consistent with the interpretation he brought, an interpretation that will persist across time, across events, across circumstances. Our job as coaches will be to understand the client's structure of interpretation, then in partnership alter this structure so that the actions that follow bring about the intended outcome. As coaches we do this by providing a new language that allows the client to make new observations. For example, we cannot find chartreuse unless we have the language for it. We can't find the brake pedal in our car unless we have the language of driving. We can't observe what we're feeling if we don't have the language of emotion. We can't tell if we are communicating effectively if we don't know what to look for.

Providing language that allows for new observations is not sufficient but it's surely necessary. The second vital element the coach provides is practices that allow the language introduced to become permanently part of the client's structure of interpretation. No one can learn to drive a car simply by learning the language of automobiles and traffic laws. After learning that language we must get behind the wheel, spending many hours practicing driving. It's only by this continual, focused, intentional practice that we become competent drivers. Practicing without knowing the language may leave us able to drive, but we will be powerless when breakdowns occur or when we have to coordinate our driving with other people, say at a crowded urban intersection.

To connect the importance of language and practice to the products of coaching, language is what allows the client to be self-correcting and self-generating, and it's practice that makes it possible for the client to be a long-term excellent performer.

Maybe it has occurred to you while you read this why it is that many interventions we attempt to improve the competence of others fail. Either we simply attempt to employ the amoeba theory by judicially applying rewards and punishments, or we provide language inadequate or inappropriate for new observations to be made. Or we don't know how to design practices so that the learning can become permanently a part of our client. The remainder of this book is an explanation and demonstration about how to do all of this.

OPERATING PRINCIPLES OF COACHING

Interventions in competence to improve the actions of others can be called coaching when they adhere to these five principles (see Figure 1.4). You can use these five principles as a way to design your coaching or correct it when it's not working.

Relationship is the first principle and the most important one. We will speak about the coaching relationship in detail later in the book. So let me say here simply that the relationship is the background for all coaching efforts. The relationship must be one in which there is mutual respect, trust, and mutual freedom of expression.

The second principle is that coaching must be pragmatic. Pragmatism is America's contribution to philosophy. Its central tenet is that what's "true" is what works. Practical outcomes replace theoretical constructs. Coaching is not a collection of techniques to apply or dogma to adhere to, rather it's a discipline that requires freshness, innovation, and relentless correction according to the outcomes being produced. In other words, it's invalid for a coach to say, "I did

Relationship

- Mutually satisfying
- Based on *mutual respect*
  mutual trust
  freedom of expression

Pragmatism

- Outcome-based
- Relentless correction based on feedback loop

Two Tracks

- Both client and coach are engaged in learning
- Breakdowns may occur in either person's commitment or competence

Always/Already

- Human beings are always/ already in the middle of something
- Not empty vessels
- Each has their own immediate concerns
- Each has their own commitments

Techniques Don't Work

- "If . . . then" scenarios are limited
- Manipulation
- Undermine dignity of people
- Foster resistance and resentment

FIGURE 1.4 Five Principles of Coaching

everything right, but the coaching didn't work." My view is that a coach who makes that statement wasn't correcting as he went along, and instead followed a rote routine that may have worked before.

The rigor of pragmatism requires that as coaches we continually undo our conclusions, and face each coaching situation with a willingness to learn anew and find out that what we learned last time does not apply now.

Coaching is a learning experience for both coach and client. I refer to that in the principle called "two tracks." Track one is work coaches do with clients. Track two is the ongoing work coaches must do with themselves. Unless we question our assumptions, abandon our techniques, and vigilantly correct from the outcomes we're producing, we will soon fail as coaches.

Often coaching fails because of the blindness, prejudice, stubbornness, or rigidity of the coach and not because of the "uncoachability" of the client. Many life situations, such as managing in large organizations, teaching, or parenting, do not provide us with the luxury of selecting who we will coach. Coaches in sports have the chance to cut players from the team or bring new people aboard, and it's unfortunate in a way that the word used to describe the activities of someone working to have a team or individual succeed in sports is the same term we're using to describe the efforts of someone dedicated to the excellence of someone else.

Nonetheless, we continue to use the word coaching even though it may for some readers bring to mind what is done in sports. I hope that as you read through this book the distinctions between sports coaching and coaching to evoke excellence in others will become more and more clear.

Many times the antics, pressure, and force of athletic coaches are held up as models for what coaches in organizations, schools, and families ought to be doing. These situations are vastly different. But you will be on safe ground if you follow the premise of coaching as presented earlier and the five principles in this section. These notions have been developed by both academic research and practical application over many years in the world of organizations, schools, and families.

Athletic coaches rarely take the stance that they can learn something from their players, and perhaps that makes sense given the situation they're in, but I assure you that as coaches elsewhere in life, we must keep ourselves learning as an integral part of our coaching. Central to this learning is engaging ourselves continually in asking how we might be getting in the way of the coaching's success. A later chapter in the book will recommend ways to develop the skills and qualities necessary to coach.

The fourth principle is that clients are always and already in the middle of their lives. When coaching adults, our interventions must always fit in with their structure of interpretation. They are already in the middle of their lives and always have views, commitments, possibilities, and concerns. Five-year-olds who come to school don't brush off the teachers by saying, "I don't need to learn how to write the alphabet, I already have my own method." But when coaching adults we must recognize that it's likely that the clients already have their own way of doing things, and given the stability and momentum of habit, our coaching has to be adapted to fit individuals.

That techniques don't work is the final principle. When I say techniques don't work, I mean to bring about two outcomes. The first is to challenge the routinized, mechanical way we may be doing coaching, and the second is to warn that clients quickly catch on when techniques are being used on them and react with resentment. This happens, for example, when the boss returns from the latest training class and begins to apply the techniques she learned there. Usually people wait for this surge in enthusiasm to die off, and in the meantime shield themselves from the effects of any new procedures.

Perhaps it would be more fair to say that using only techniques won't work, since there are probably fundamental techniques that each coach has to use. The difficulty in using techniques, besides what I've already said, is that the coach has to know when to use what technique, even proven ones. It is also dangerous for coaches to imagine that the use of any technique, however powerful, will allow them to escape engaging fully with the client with openness, courage, and curiosity. Techniques cannot replace human heart and creativity in coaching.

It's my premise that coaching is a principle-shaped ontological stance and not a series of techniques. By that I mean that I consider any activity to be coaching when the ontological stance is as described earlier in the chapter, or is the equivalent; the listed operating principles are in force; and the intended outcomes are long-term excellence, the competence to self-correct, and the competence to self-generate. Beyond that the coach is free to create any form for the work. This book is meant to be an example of a particular form that can be used and that has proven to be effective. It's not intended to be "the answer" to every coaching situation. I expect that other coaches will create their own forms and I look forward to learning from them.

SUGGESTED READING

The list below is the longest for any chapter. That's because, similar to the chapter, the foundation of coaching can be found in these volumes. If you haven't read philosophy before, perhaps the *Passion of the Western Mind* by Richard Tarnas can give you a friendly introduction to the domain.

If you're interested in reading only a few books, I suggest the following in this order:

1. *Being-in-the-World*, Hubert Dreyfus
2. *Understanding Computers and Cognition*, Fernando Flores and Terry Winograd
3. *The Tree of Knowledge*, Humberto Maturana and Francisco Varela

All of the books, however, are worth your time and effort.

Barrett, William. *The Illusion of Technique*. Garden City, NY: Anchor Press/Doubleday, 1979.
   A slice through the modern history of philosophy focusing on the topic of the title. Well written.
   Terrific orientation for coaches.
Becker, Ernest. *The Denial of Death*. New York: Free Press, 1973.
   A book that, with its title alone, defines our postmodern culture. An anthropologist uses the
   insight of depth psychology (especially Rank) to show us the source of our suffering/confusion
   and a way beyond it.
Boss, Medard. *Existential Foundations of Medicine and Psychology*. New York: Jason Aronson,
   Inc., 1983.
   Provides a model that considers physical, emotional, mental, and ontological factors that are
   always occurring simultaneously and contribute to or diminish our health.
—. *Psychoanalysis and Daseinanalysis*. New York: Da Capo Press, 1982.
   The author was analyzed by Freud, was a neighbor of Jung, and was a long-term friend and
   student of Heidegger. He presents an alternative to psychoanalysis that can be called dasei-
   nanalysis. He shows its power with several amazing examples. Very useful as an entry to a new
   understanding of people.
Dreyfus, Hubert L. *Being-in-the-World*. Cambridge: MIT Press, 1991.
   An explanation of Being and Time, *written by a top professor who's been studying and*
   teaching Heidegger for decades. The book has charts, summaries, and good examples.
   Sometimes you didn't understand Heidegger (you'll learn in the text) because he was unclear
   or self-contradictory himself.
—, and Paul Rabinow. *Michel Foucault: Beyond Structuralism and Hermeneutics*. Chicago:
   University of Chicago Press, 1982.
   Even if you don't understand the title, the book is worth reading. When you read it you'll
   understand the title, and you'll be introduced to how and why Foucault wrote scathing
   critiques of modern cultural practices that determine our reality.
Flores, Fernando, and Terry Winograd. *Understanding Computers and Cognition*. Norwood, NJ:
   Ablex Publishing Corporation, 1986.
   The authors combine (in a rigorous and concise style) many seminal ideas of twentieth-century
   thought (from Heidegger, Maturana, Habermas, etc.) into their own creative synthesis of what
   it is to be, speak, and work as a human being. Especially useful for people looking for
   a practical application of powerful principles. In that, Flores and Winograd are unsurpassed.
Fromm, Erich. *To Have or to Be?* New York: Harper & Row, 1976.
   The way we respond to the title determines if our lives will be dedicated to greed or to the
   fulfillment of our natures. A powerful work by a profound, compassionate philosopher and
   therapist.
Grossmann, Reinhardt. *Phenomenology and Existentialism*. Boston: Routledge & Kegan Paul, 1984.
   A solid introductory text to these two philosophical schools which, along with pragmatism,
   underlie the theory and practice of coaching.
Heidegger, Martin. *Being and Time*. Translated by John Macquarrie and Edward Robinson. New
   York: Harper & Row, 1962.
   A very challenging book that turned philosophy away from idealism and positivism by showing
   the way we actually live. Along with pragmatism, Heidegger's work provides the philosophical
   foundations for coaching.
Hillman, James. *Suicide and the Soul*. Dallas, TX: Spring Publications, Inc., 1964.
   Don't let the title deter you. Hillman penetrates to the essential issues in being human in our
   times.
Ihde, Don. *Experimental Phenomenology*. Albany, NY: State University of New York Press, 1986.
   An introductory text that gives the reader a chance to experience phenomenology by doing
   a series of fascinating exercises.
Iyengar, B. K. S. *Light on Yoga*. New York: Schocken Books, Inc., 1966.

A liberally illustrated encyclopedia of yoga postures (asanas) written and demonstrated by an influential contemporary teacher. The author's introductory essay on yoga is considered a classic in itself.

James, William. *Pragmatism*. New York: Simon & Schuster, 1963.
In a style that lays out the ideas openly and boldly, James presents the basic notions of a philosophy that suits coaching perfectly.

—. *The Will to Believe*. New York: Dover Publications, 1956.
James's book is so well written, clear, and accessible, you may wonder why all philosophy isn't so available. He wrote and spoke for the nonphilosopher and brought pragmatism to a wide audience.

Kierkegaard, Søren. *The Present Age*. New York: Harper & Row, 1962.
A short book that takes unerring aim at the shallowness and rootlessness of our modern culture.

Kockelmans, Joseph J. *On the Truth of Being*. Bloomington, IN: Indiana University Press, 1984.
An exploration of Heidegger's ontological notions emphasizing the ramifications they have on what counts as truth. An esoteric subject that strikes at the root of positivism.

Levine, Stephen. *Who Dies?* New York: Anchor Books/Doubleday, 1982.
The author has been with thousands of people as they died or dealt with the death of a loved one. Profoundly compassionate and unwavering in its insistence that we come to terms with mortality and live accordingly.

Lowen, Alexander, M.D. *Betrayal of the Body*. New York: Macmillan Publishing Company, 1969.
Accessible book (along with the following two books) for a lay reader in which the author presents the theoretical basis for his work and recommendations for its applicability.

—. *Bioenergetics*. New York: Penguin Books, 1975.

—. *The Language of the Body*. New York: Macmillan Publishing Company, 1971. (Originally published as *Physical Dynamics of Character Structure*, Grune and Stratton, Inc., 1958.)

Maturana, Humberto R., and Francisco J. Varela. *The Tree of Knowledge*. Boston: Shambhala Publications, 1987.
A rigorous, scientific presentation of the biological roots of human consciousness. Convincingly shows the interaction of the biological, social, and linguistic. Founds coaching in the bedrock of fundamental biology. Unravels many of the pseudoproblems of skepticism and other philosophical schools. Changes you as you read it.

Morgan, Gareth, ed. *Beyond Method*. Beverly Hills, CA: Sage Publications, 1983.
It's all very well to say that techniques don't work, but what's the alternative? This book is a collection of essays by managers and academics who have found ways to work successfully in complex environments. Rigorous, useful, and human.

Needleman, Jacob. *The Heart of Philosophy*. New York: Alfred A. Knopf, Inc., 1982; reprint, San Francisco: Harper & Row, 1986.
A powerful antidote for those of us who became glazed and disgruntled in Philosophy 101. Shows that it is questioning that keeps us alive and fully human.

Palmer, Richard E. *Hermeneutics*. Evanston, IL: Northwestern University Press, 1969.
An introductory text to one of the important philosophical movements of the twentieth century. The premise that human reality is always historically shaped interpretation is vital to coaches.

Perls, Fritz. *The Gestalt Approach and Eye Witness to Therapy*. Berkeley, CA: Science & Behavior Books, 1973.
The great therapist's last attempt to make his work clear and accessible. Full of profound wisdom practically applied.

Rolf, Ida P. *Rolfing*. Santa Monica, CA: Dennis-Landman Publisher, 1977.
The author discusses her powerful process for self-development through working to free up and realign the body. Many photographs and beautiful anatomical drawings, and a text that explains the principles and benefits of the process.

Rorty, Richard. *Consequences of Pragmatism.* Minneapolis, MN: University of Minnesota Press, 1982.

Provides a philosophical foundation for designing, conducting, and correcting coaching programs. Rorty's style is lively, thought-provoking, and lucid.

Ryle, Gilbert. *The Concept of Mind.* Chicago: University of Chicago Press, 1949.

A classic text that demystifies a deeply rooted cultural myth—that there exists a mind separate from the functionality it displays. A monument to light, to logical argumentation, and to observation-based assessment.

Searle, John R. *Minds, Brains and Science.* Cambridge, MA: Harvard University Press, 1984.

A series of talks meant to untangle many long-standing philosophical dilemmas. Useful as a model for rigor and insistence.

Tarnas, Richard. *The Passion of the Western Mind.* New York: Random House, 1991.

A beautifully written history of Western thought from the pre-Socratics to the 1990s. Includes a useful timeline of major events and an extensive bibliography. Near the end, the author steps out of his role as dispassionate commentator and recommends a way to confront the current dilemmas of thought and morality.

Taylor, Charles. *Human Agency and Language: Philosophical Papers I.* Cambridge: Cambridge University Press, 1985.

Provides a clear, well-written argument against reductionistic tendencies, and presents practical alternatives in understanding people.

—. *Sources of the Self.* Cambridge, MA: Harvard University Press, 1989.

A tour-de-force historical review of how our modern Western views evolved through political and philosophical discourse.

Vail, L. M. *Heidegger and Ontological Difference.* University Park, PA: Pennsylvania State University Press, 1972.

A rigorous presentation of one of Heidegger's most problematic ideas. By following the argument, the reader will acquire a deep appreciation of what it is to be human.

Wilber, Ken. *A Brief History of Everything.* Boston, MA: Shambhala Publications, 1996.

A tongue-in-cheek title for a shorter presentation of Wilber's central principles. Thought provoking. Many angles, distinctions, views that can shift our world view.

—. *Sex, Ecology, Spirituality.* Boston, MA: Shambhala Publications, 1995.

A title that covers all bases. A long, deep, generous book that passionately argues for a unified view of human development, spirituality, biologically, socially, economically (and many other ways). A huge gift to the world. Amazing breadth. Astounding reference.

Wilson, William Julius. *The Truly Disadvantaged.* Chicago: University of Chicago Press, 1987.

A book that will forever change your understanding of the roots of poverty and class in the United States. Required background for understanding the world of today's U.S. citizen.

Wittgenstein, Ludwig. *Philosophical Investigations.* Oxford: Basil Blackwell, 1953.

A book seldom matched for clarity and cohesion. Precise and elegant. Lays out the insights of Wittgenstein's later work. The basis for a highly original and powerful view of language.

Yalom, Irvin D. *Existential Psychotherapy.* New York: Basic Books, Inc./HarperCollins, 1980.

The classic introductory text. Cogent and clear in its discussion of the ultimately unavoidable human issues—death, loneliness, meaninglessness—and the huge suffering that occurs when we try to avoid them.

2

Basic Principles

This chapter takes on topics that are foundational to coaching yet are almost always ignored in other texts. I'm attempting to concisely present what can be philosophically said about people in a way that's useful for coaching and for understanding ourselves. My point is to show you a deep grounded view of human life without reference to psychology. Although psychology may be familiar territory for many of us, its application to coaching has several drawbacks. First, psychological methods may require personal disclosure beyond what the client is willing to do, and they are too subject to trivialization and clichés. My alternative, based in twentieth-century philosophy, takes work because it's new to many of us but it will, I trust, serve you well as you coach.

"Remember that existence consists solely in its possibility for relationships."

—Medard Boss

WHAT IS A HUMAN BEING?

The heart of my coaching with Bob could be summarized by the quote that opens this chapter. He had to develop new relationships in order to be promoted. The first relationship that had to be addressed was, of course, Bob's relationship with himself. He had to discover the degree of congruence between the relationship he was having with himself and the relationship others were having with him at work. Lack of congruence here would lead him either to feelings of grandiosity in which he felt superior to everyone and beyond the power of their opinion to affect him, or to feelings that he was inept and unworthy and that anything positive said to him was just people trying to be nice. Clearly, either possibility would not lead to what we were intending in Bob's coaching.

Besides the relationship with himself, Bob also had to address his relationship with the people who worked around him, especially those who had a say about his promotion. By attending to these relationships, I don't mean creating a nice warm feeling; rather I mean he had to deeply

comprehend the individuals involved, and from that form a profound trust that would almost inevitably lead to his promotion.

In order to understand people, we must begin with some parameters about what a person is. What are we hoping to understand when we say we are trying to do that? Coaching almost always includes an uncoiling and a reconstruction of the client's notions about being human. In this chapter we begin to take on these topics.

Coaches live in a very different world than other people who are working on improving situations. For example, an auto mechanic who works on Volvos really does not have to be concerned with the individuality of a car that shows up at his garage. Knowing that it will be a 1993 850 Turbo with 37,000 miles is all he really needs to know. Of course, working with human beings is much different. There is not even agreement about what does show up to be coached. Should coaches consider their potential clients to be biocomputers that they need to program, or are they stimulus–response machines that merely need the correct stimulus? Or are they products of historical, political, and economic courses? Or maybe they are a single unit from a complex familial system, or creatures of their own emotional history. If coaches cannot answer the question of what kind of being is showing up to be coached, I wonder how they can prepare themselves. How could the Volvo mechanic in our example prepare if he did not know whether what was going to arrive was a giant clam or a redwood tree or a Trinitron television? That is why it is important to take on the topic of this chapter and make explicit what understanding of human beings is at the basis of our work.

This chapter takes on topics that other texts may not bring up. From my reading it seems that other authors assume that we share a common understanding of these topics or that they're not worth discussing. My view is that we have to have an explicit theory about human beings since they are the focus, center, and subject of coaching. It's as if we are attempting to build an edifice without understanding the tensile strength of the steel employed or the insulating properties of the roofing material. Probably we would not place much faith in an architect or building contractor who could not give us the facts about the materials he was working with. It seems to me that there is an exactly parallel situation in coaching. We must understand the essential constitutive particulars of human beings before we can begin to coach. What I'm presenting here is firmly rooted in academic and philosophical traditions and has been proven to be practically useful in application over the last dozen years. The academic references appear at the end of this chapter. This chapter closely follows the work of Medard Boss's *Existential Foundations of Medicine and Psychology* (1983).

The criteria in coaching have been stated several times and I will briefly summarize them here. The answer must be one that allows for people to change, to become more competent, and to become excellent at performance. Any explanation that doesn't allow for this is by definition excluded, for example, notions that people are fully and finally determined by genetic makeup or by early social influences. Since these notions would make coaching impossible, they are to be rejected out of hand.

The Truth

The American pragmatists James and Dewey have already done a good job of this, as did Rorty in his book *Consequences of Pragmatism* (1982). My presentation closely follows Rorty. To summarize briefly, people have tried for 3,000 years or so in the West and no one has come up with a universally accepted notion of what is "true." For those of you who think science has, I refer you to the work of Karl Popper. How could one tell if what one had discovered was true unless one already had an idea of what one was looking for and the criteria for verification? This is a very abbreviated and simplified version of one of Heidegger's arguments around the issue.

Another difficulty is that the (supposed) answers that have been presented throughout history have so very often increased human suffering, for example, Christian vs. Moslem in the Crusades, the Church vs. heretics in the Inquisition, capitalism vs. communism in the Cold War. It seems through observation that there is no formula, process, procedure, authority, or leader that can wholly solve human concerns or ensure positive outcomes. No doubt you've noticed this. Yet we keep looking for it and despair that we haven't found it, or alternately envy those who supposedly have found it.

How then are we to determine what to do or how to live? My recommendation is that we determine the worth of something based upon its power to alleviate human concern, lessen human suffering, improve how we live together, and free people to take action. When I say human concern and human suffering, this is a shorthand way of saying the concerns that are part of living with and within all the living systems on the planet. Even if we came to a consensus that this is how to determine the worth of something, it still would take a lot of open, respectful conversation in order to determine in each case the course of action to take. With all that as a background, the criteria for answering the question "What is a human being?" in coaching will perhaps make more sense.

As coaches, then, we don't have to deal with "The Truth," we can deal with ways of speaking that fulfill the project of coaching. What follows is a way of speaking about human beings that takes all of this into account. The job is not so much to talk about how human beings become what we are, but to be able to speak about how we are now in a way that allows for coaching to occur. The ideas presented are not in order of importance. Human beings are a whole, and no part is dispensable without changing the whole. It's not possible, though, to say everything at once, so while you read this I suggest that you keep the whole in mind. The quote that began this chapter is the shortest summary of the ideas that follow.

Human Beings as the Possibility for Relating

This section is meant to present an alternative to the usual way we think of people—as a means to an end and/or a collection of fixed properties with desire attached. It's also my suggestion on how a coach can think about relating to human beings. The mistakes in other books about coaching originate here. The authors don't explain what they understand a person to be and completely ignore our biological aspects. What are the consequences of this for coaching? Here are some: the more fundamental the distinctions we address, the more radical, creative, and transforming can be the actions we take or design. For example, if we understand how the eye, pigment, and light come together in our seeing of a painting, then we can take quite different actions than if we only understand how to select a frame to fit a particular room. We can go further and question, "What is painting?" and "What is art?" The works of DuChamp, Neuman, Pollack, Picasso, and so on follow such questions. This leads to different possible actions and designs than asking, "How can I paint the face of my patron on the body of St. Jerome in this painting?" See much of the art in European museums for endless examples of what follows from this type of questioning. In your coaching, are you merely putting a frame on what's been presented to you, having your clients fit in or find a place where they won't disturb many people? Or are you asking and then acting/designing from fundamental principles?

Another way to approach the question "What is a human being?" is to decide if it is an ontological or epistemological issue. That is to say, are humans a being like any other in the world, differentiated from chairs, stars, or frogs only by properties such as chemical makeup, weight, height, and so on that constitute each? Or do humans exist in a way unique to them—a way that cannot be comprehended by a listing of properties, however long the list? Can a listing of properties add up to human existence and account for all that is experienced and created by human beings? Along with Heidegger and many others, I've decided that humans exist in a different way from other phenomena. This section sets forth an ontological view of people that, it seems to me, captures more of our human experience and opens up more possibilities for coaching. Perhaps you come down on the other side and consider the question an epistemological one (e.g., humans are like chairs except that they have X property). Are you confident of your list of properties? Where did it come from? What consequences will result from considering others and yourself in this way? Who gets to add or subtract from the list of properties? And what consequences does that have ethically and politically?

If you're asking where is the empirical research to verify all of this, the answer is that there is none. The more profound questions are perhaps "Why do you claim that empirical research, based upon the formulations of Bacon, Descartes, and Newton, has something useful to say about the individual human being in front of you?" and "Are humans the kind of being that follows the laws of science, developed by studying objects?" If we look at people as subject to the same laws as objects, what do we see? Does what we see further or inhibit coaching? Can we escape by using empirical methods, building a relationship, and knowing our client well? I say no, although some U.S. physicians have tried. Can we learn about general patterns of orientation, stages of maturation, and generalized symptoms of distress by systematically studying large numbers of people? I say we can. What have you discovered?

Human beings enter into relationships with everything that we encounter. We don't have a choice about this. Any phenomenon that we meet in our world appears to us as "something." We relate immediately with this something. We prereflexively interact with the phenomenon, even if the way we interact is to ignore it. All this is said in a different way in the next section on language. What I'm attempting to say here is that our capacity for relating is a constitutive part to the kind of being that we are. Clearly, some of us are more open than others and some people have been so physically or emotionally damaged that the capacity for relating is nearly extinct. We do consider these people to be human beings, however, and many times we continue to speak with them as if their capacity to relate is undiminished. Once someone's capacity to be open is fully diminished, we often call this person a "vegetable." This way of being with other humans is our way of showing our understanding of what a human being is. Probably what we are most open to is being with other human beings. In fact, it's probably impossible for there to be any such phenomenon as a single human being; that is to say, that it's only by being raised in a human community that we become human beings. The many stories in literature about babies being raised by wolves or monkeys attest to this.

Each of us, having been raised in a human community, is by two years of age already a member of the language community. We already are able to make distinctions that separate something from everything else. We can do this before we are able to speak. This relating with language, once it begins, is always with us; even our thoughts are part of the horizon of possibilities that language provides for us. As a member of the language community, we also learn how to relate to other human beings, what's important, and how to act.

Language and Time

Once we are in the language community, we are also immediately in time. It's always the case that we are fulfilling what was begun in the past by taking action in the present to bring about an outcome in the future. In a way, this may be unique to human beings; we exist simultaneously in these three openings in time. Perhaps you've noticed that different cultures seem to emphasize different openings: in some cases, the emphasis is on tradition, in other cases, the emphasis is on the progress that is a valued part of the future. Each of us in our own way exists more in one of these openings than the others. But once we speak a language that has the possibility of past, present, and future, we cannot escape existing in some way in all three openings.

This may seem like an obvious point, but it's a vital one in coaching, because a coach is never able to begin coaching at the real beginning. The coach always begins in the middle. And the outcomes specified in any coaching program are, in some sense, arbitrary, because once something begins it always exists in some form. As human beings, we will always relate to something once we have encountered it.

Language is also what allows us to move through these openings in time, emphasizing one opening at one moment and another at another moment, but still including other people in our world. Including others is a funny way of saying it, because our world is never void of other people, even when they're not physically present. The effect of our relationships always shapes the way we see our world and the actions we take. Anyone who has traveled or been separated from his family knows that physical distance does not necessarily diminish the presence of people who are always close to us. This capacity for being close to human beings and other phenomena, regardless of physical distance, is also important for coaches to remember in learning to understand clients.

Mood

At any given moment, we are not only open, we are open in a particular way. The way that we are open is called *mood*. For most of us, mood means something like the emotion a person is feeling. I mean something that includes this, but also goes beyond. Mood describes what we are open to encountering, our view of the future, and the distance we put between ourselves and the other people, events, and circumstances in our life. We can see this most readily, for example, when people are "in love," probably one of the most intoxicating moods. A person who is in love is close to his beloved even when in the midst of other activities, at a great distance from the beloved, or in a crowd of other people. A mood of resentment is, in a way, the opposite, because it keeps at a distance everything we encounter, even when it is in close physical proximity.

Perhaps the most important element of any coaching program is the extent to which the program affects the mood of the client. Initially, of course, the coach must find a way of speaking to the client so that she is open to coaching. In order to accomplish this, the coach has to take into account the mood of the client—that is, to discern what the client is open to, what she is closed to, what the client is holding close, and what she is keeping at a distance. Studying the circumstances will not tell us this; we can only tell this by studying the client and speaking with the client.

The Human Body

We have not yet spoken about the most obvious component of human beings, and that is that every human being has a human body. I've been assuming in all this discussion that a person has a body that functions well enough so that he is able to interact with the phenomena that he encounters with the full range of human possibilities. A body must have an intact nervous system in order for this to happen. As Helen Keller, Stephen Hawking, and Christy Brown have shown us, with a nervous system intact, almost all other human activities are possible in some way.

Our body, though, is not only a collection of chemicals arranged into a sophisticated system. Our body is also the way we are in the world, and our body will at each moment tell us how open or closed we are and what is the real nature of our concern. Sometimes we try to deny this or ignore it, as when we are meeting someone who is very important to us and our body is responding with a racing heart, while we are pretending to be cool or distant. At other times, our body will be tired and heavy in a way that we cannot explain at first, but upon reflection we discover that we have lost touch with someone important to us or have lost out on a chance to make something important to us happen.

Our body doesn't, in a sense, end at the end of our skin, because, as I said earlier, what is close to us is not necessarily what is next to us physically. So our body extends to wherever and to whenever our concern exists. If you've ever been with a homesick child or someone who is missing his beloved, you will have noticed the effect this has on his body. Physicians who attempt to cure people as if their bodies were only collections of bones, muscles, and chemicals often have a very difficult time healing them. You may have noticed this in your own experience with doctors, when it seems as if they are speaking about your body or a part of your body as if it were a separate and distinct object existing outside of your life. No real healing can occur in this way of understanding the body.

Many therapeutic modalities have focused on the human body as a locus of transformation. Here is a representative listing. Hatha yoga is the most ancient of these (Iyengar, 1966). Postures and breathing exercises have brought strength, balance, and serenity to practitioners for centuries. Yoga can frequently be a useful adjunct to coaching programs, especially for clients who are experientially distant from their body and emotions. The work of William Reich was directed at including the body as both a symbolic representation and container of neurotic patterns. Alexander Lowen brought Reich's work to a wider, nonprofessional audience through his writing and teaching (see Bibliography). Ida Rolf established a school of bodyworkers who assist clients to greater physical and emotional ease through a series of sessions in which the body is realigned in gravity and patterns of chronic holding are released. A coach's familiarity with these and other methods will be of great assistance in designing coaching programs that can include referring a client to the appropriate practitioners. Reading the texts cited will give the coach a better idea of when such a referral makes sense.

Death

Clearly, this discussion could go on and on. However, there is only one more topic that I will address at this point, and that is our relationship with death. Once we find out about death, which we usually do within the first five years of our life, we always thereafter have a relationship with death. Death is the certain ending of the form of relationships we have now. None of us escape, although many of us live as if we will. In fact, many of us lead lives designed to keep us distracted from death. Even our customs of dealing with dead people—for example, putting makeup and new clothing on dead bodies so that they look alive, and sending people to the hospital to die—are ways of attempting to deny, avoid, or keep distracted from this inevitable outcome.

The point in honestly confronting death is not that we become depressed or resigned, rather it's only in such an authentic encounter that we have a chance to really prioritize life. It's only in looking at our lives from the end that we can begin to determine what's really important for us and what is only distraction or waste. The sooner we begin to see life in this light, the better, because at the end of your life it will be too late. There is probably nothing more painful than being with people as they experience remorse, guilt, and regret at the end of their lives because of what they did not fulfill as they encountered it. The illusions that we will "get to it later," or that we're "only doing this for a brief time," or our various other distraction strategies keep us from fulfilling the relationships that present themselves to us in our world.

As I said in the beginning, it's only by taking all of this as a whole that my response to the chapter's question can be made sensible. All of what I have said above are fundamental aspects of what it is to be a human being; none of them can be excluded. By keeping all of this in mind, we are able to successfully coach people and work with them beyond the short-term fix or the clever technique.

As you read this you may have caught on to the fact that asking the question "What is a human being?" is equivalent to asking the question "Who am I?" In what ways are you open to what is being said here? In what ways are you open to life? By asking these questions, we can keep ourselves awake as coaches and can avoid the hindrances to coaching that were spoken about in the section "What Is Coaching?"

In applying what has been said in this chapter to Bob's situation, there are several preliminary points. First of all, he had to embrace a pragmatic

approach to his situation, which implied that he had to let go of his perfectionist tendencies that led to his dismissing others and denigrating himself. Second, he had to catch on to and live from the notion that the principles of relating were going to determine what was possible at his job. Third, by remembering his own mortality, Bob could bring some perspective to his work so that issues could take on their proper level of importance.

Of course, it is one thing to list these aspects and it is quite another matter to live from them in a moment-to-moment, day-to-day, year-to-year way. That's where coaching comes in and that is its job. The next section of the book presents some of the distinctions that Bob used in order to get to work on some of the insights he was having from our conversations about relationship. The topics are presented here in a more rigorous way than I did in speaking with Bob, so that you can adapt them to your own individual circumstances.

LANGUAGE, OBSERVATION, AND ASSESSMENT

Language

Given that some of the best philosophical minds of the twentieth century—Heidegger, Wittgenstein, Habermas, Gadamer, and Searle among others—have written extensively about language and have not produced a consensus among their readers, it may sound presumptuous for me to address the same topic. Nonetheless, language is an essential part of coaching and, in fact, it could be said that the essential job of the coach is to provide a new language for the client. Consequently, I will attempt here to provide enough background about what I mean when I say "language" to both make it easier for you to coach and to allow you to make greater sense of what follows.

Many people consider language to be a tool that they use in order to get things done. This seems to me to be too narrow an understanding of language. Isn't it language, existing before any of us, that provides what it is possible to do, what is worth doing, how we can observe whether we did something, and so on? So, along with Heidegger, I would say that language uses us, in the sense that language provides for us the horizon of possible actions, experiences, relationships, and meanings. Those of you who speak languages other than English know that each language provides all of these possibilities in a way that is unique to that language. By thinking about this for a while, you may be able to see the importance of language in coaching: if language provides the horizons described above, then the biggest new possibility that a coach can provide for a client is in language.

Many times when people think about language, they only consider public, verbal communication. Clearly this is only half of the story, since speaking without listening is not only nonsensical but also impossible, because even as speakers we are always listening. Many of the points that I'm making here may raise objections; however, if you will stop and study your own relationship with language for a while within the distinctions we've already made, no doubt you will observe what I have been speaking about.

Since this is not a book about the philosophy of language, I want to narrow the focus and make a few particular points about language and coaching. Language is an orientation to our common world. Watch how mothers interact with their infant children. They name many of the objects and people that the child is close to and, by nearly endless repetition and the maturation of the child's nervous system, eventually the child is oriented to the world that is made by the language the mother speaks. The same thing happens to us as adults when we visit a foreign country or take a job in an industry that is unfamiliar to us. We become oriented, that is, we become able to act effectively within that country or industry, when we learn the language particular to that place. In addition, language is what allows us to coordinate our actions with others. I don't know how it would be possible to meet someone for lunch at a particular place at a particular time unless we were able to make requests or promises. This is so pervasive in our everyday life that many times we forget that our competence in coordinating actions essentially has to do with our competence in speaking and listening.

The authors mentioned earlier do not even agree on a definition of language—many of them would claim that there is no possibility of a definition, or of defining any single word. What then are we talking about when we say "language"? Martin Heidegger (1971) said that the best he could do was point to a path that might be the way to language. Searle (1969) works hard to take the mystery out, but does he work deep enough to adequately address Heidegger? Many professional philosophers say no (Kockelmans, 1972). Others claim that his views are useless and irrelevant.

What can the nonprofessional philosopher make of all this and why should we care? Well, it seems to me that Wittgenstein (1953) got it right when he said that language exists as a type of game that exists and makes sense only in the context of the world created by speakers of the language. This seems self-evident to me. French speakers, for example, construct and inhabit a world that I cannot enter until I speak French. The worlds of science, computers, and mathematics are similarly constructed by speakers of particular languages. If you accept what I'm proposing here, then much can follow in terms of being a student of language as a way to comprehend and design our world. In terms of coaching, here are some questions that a student of language might ask: "What is revealed or concealed to my client in the language she speaks?" "What possibilities or experiences are unavailable to my client in the language world he lives in, and what can I do about that?" Coaches only *speak* to clients. Even when a coach is silently demonstrating an action, she is making distinctions that are only possible because of the shared language world of client and coach.

Imagine a piano teacher demonstrating an intricate fingering pattern in the air to an eager, experienced student. The student can observe the patterns and progressions and perhaps even hear the music, because she is a speaker of musical language. A nonspeaker of musical language might observe the same finger movements and see them as imaginary keys being struck on a typewriter, and try to figure out what words are being spelled, or as an unusually complicated way to dry nails wet with polish.

Upon reflection, it seems impossible to escape the conclusion that we observe in and only because of language. Provide new language, plus the chance by practice to have the language become part of us, and new observations, new actions, and a new world will inevitably follow. That's the importance of language to coaching.

Two other aspects of language are essential for coaching. First is that language allows us to design our world. Yes, it's a fact that each of us is born at a particular historical moment into a particular culture and family. At the same time it is possible for us to not only bring a different meaning to the circumstances into which we were born but also to bring about a different set of activities, relationships, and outcomes by our capacity to skillfully deal with language.

This is the key to dealing with a sense of powerlessness in both personal and political realms. For example, probably the best way to coach someone who is in a mood of resentment is to teach him how to make effective requests. A corollary is that, in language, we can establish a public identity that may be different from the one that accrues to us from historic circumstance. Probably the clearest examples of this are in the work of artists who, by being able to say something more cogently than their contemporaries, were able to influence the future course of their discipline even though historic circumstances did not give them a prestigious place in their society (e.g., Walt Whitman, Emily Dickinson, and James Joyce).

Observation

Language forms the basis for observation and it is, in fact, not possible to make any observations outside of language. If the purpose of coaching is to change behavior, then the coach's mission is to find what affects behavior in a way that will bring about the desired change. Figure 1.3 shows that behavior follows from the *structure of interpretation* of the client. This means that the way we see the world at a particular moment determines the actions we take. This is such an obvious point that many times it's invisible to us. We walk into a building that we recognize as a restaurant and we immediately do the series of routine actions that we consider to be consistent with being in a restaurant. We discern whether to seat ourselves or wait to be seated, we look for someone to give our food order to, and so on. We wouldn't take any of these actions if the same structure appeared to us to be a hardware store, ballet studio, gymnasium, or tennis court.

My point is that it's not only the physical surroundings that lead us to take the actions that we do, it's also the meaning that we bring to those surroundings. Even in the restaurant example, we would take different actions if we were employees of the restaurant or vendors selling supplies. The structure of interpretation as shown above then includes the commitments, projects, and relationships that make up the world of the observer, as well as the environment in which the observer finds himself.

To recapitulate an earlier point, a coach is able to alter the structure of interpretation of the client by providing new distinctions and practices that become permanently part of the client's structure of interpretation, for example, interns learning the symptoms for appendicitis, drivers learning to look left before driving through an intersection. Thus it is that the client, after being coached, takes new action because she is able to observe something that she was not able to observe before. Once this observation becomes part of the structure of interpretation of the client, the client is able to be independent of the coach and is able to respond to all similar situations in the future without need for the coach.

Another way of saying this is that a coach has to be able to make the client's own structure of interpretation explicit and accessible to the client, or at least that part of the structure that will allow for the client to make observations that will lead to the successful completion of the coaching program. To do this, the coach has to be able to observe the way that the client observes and be able to articulate this so that it can be observed by the client. This is what makes a coach distinct from a good performer only. This is also why coaches themselves don't have to be able to perform the action being observed.

A point that may be obvious already from this discussion, but that I want to point out anyway, is that observation is always according to *someone*, that is, it's not just a reporting of "what's really there." We find this out every day when we ask people the simple question, "What happened?" and hear different reports from people who are speaking about the same event, and even hear different reports from the same person about the same event when they're speaking about it at a different moment.

What makes one observation better than another, at least in terms of coaching, is that by observing it in a particular way, that is, in the particular way that we are presenting it as the coach, the client is freed to take action. Many times our coaching efforts fail when, instead, the client makes observations as a result of our coaching that lead to explanations that make action impossible. Sometimes, for example, in explaining the intricacies of a piece of Chopin music, the coach may so intimidate the would-be pianist that he never even attempts to play the piece, or never begins a practice that will enable him to play it in the future. Maybe the coach does this to impress the client with how much the coach knows, but this approach very often fails even though the coach was accurate, truthful, and comprehensive in her observation.

Assessment

While it is the case that observation is always according to someone, in coaching observations are always made within a tradition that provides distinctions and standards. It's at this point that observation can begin to be spoken about as assessment. In coaching, assessment must precede the formal coaching process, because the coach's providing of distinctions and practices must be suitable for the individual client. Although beginners must learn the basics, for example, how to play scales or how to shoot free throws, excellence in coaching always comes from an adaptation of standard procedures and practices to suit the individual client.

The initial, largest, and most challenging part of assessment is the coach's attempt to understand the structure of interpretation of the client. Sometimes this appears as such a gigantic project that people dismiss it as undoable, or use it as a reason not to start coaching at all. This is the wrong way to understand assessment in coaching, because it leads to no action. It's the same as the piano teacher explaining the extreme complexity of the Chopin piece. Instead of trying to recreate the whole world of a person on one's first outing as a coach, it's probably better to determine what part of the structure of interpretation of the client is relevant to the coaching effort and to focus on that. Being coached ourselves by experienced people and the use of relevant models is essential in these initial coaching endeavors. As the coach becomes more experienced, it is possible to understand the client in more and more dimensions, therefore leading to more sophisticated, subtle, and customized coaching programs. A chapter on assessment and assessment models follows (see Chapter 6).

The other aspect of assessment has to do with assessing the level of competence or, in some cases, the presence of a quality in a client. This, like all assessments, is based upon observation of the client either as the client goes through normal routines or in specially designed exercises that reveal levels of competence. A good example of this kind of exercise is when, during the first meeting with a tennis or golf coach, the coach asks to play a game of tennis or a round of golf with the new client.

Probably the most difficult part of assessment is the verification of its validity. How do we know that the assessment is more than just our own prejudices or projections on the client? The way to verify assessment is ultimately, of course, in the success of the coaching program itself, but before that there are some tests that the coach can apply (some of this is a summary of what's already been said):

- Is the assessment being made with distinctions that are part of a tradition?
- Is the assessment based upon observations that can be made by any competent observer, and is the coach able to cite particular instances of the observation?

- Can the coach accurately predict future action the client will take based upon the current assessment, or can the coach say what action the client is taking in other unobserved domains based upon the assessment?
- Does the assessment show life to the client in a way that the client wasn't able to see it before?
- Does the assessment allow both the client and the coach to synthesize many of the observations of the coach and to make sense of many of the actions of the client?
- Does the assessment free the client to take action—that is, does it do more than merely describe something?

By now, you probably understand why language, observation, and assessment are being addressed simultaneously. They are inseparable; none ever occurs without the others. Whenever we make an observation or even use a particular word, there is always some level of assessment as part of its meaning. The coach has to be very rigorous in the use of language; that is, he has to be precise, consistent, and grounded in the way he speaks and listens to the client. This is the essential competence in coaching and it is what will allow coaching to occur.

My coaching program with Bob had two main parts. Part one was our one-to-one conversations and the part two was the work that Bob did on his own. The latter work was obviously more important because that is what would continue after our coaching ended. In order to work with himself and realize the products of coaching, Bob had to become a more acute observer and a more grounded assessor, which meant he had to learn a language that would allow him to make new observations and assessments. Practically, it meant that I sent Bob out at the end of each of our sessions together with a self-observation exercise.

A self-observation exercise is a precisely defined set of observations that a client performs over a period of time. The point of the exercise is to free up the client to take up new action, provide grounded assessments for decision making, and provide some power in intervening with recurring patterns of behavior. Many examples of self-observations appear at the end of this book.

SUGGESTED READING

The listed books are challenging, so be patient as you read. After studying several of them you'll likely appreciate the topic of language and its relevance to coaching in a deeper way.

Gadamer, Hans-Georg. *Philosophical Hermeneutics*. Translated by David E. Linge, ed. Berkeley, CA: University of California Press, 1976.
A student of Heidegger explains, clarifies, and expands many themes of his teacher's work. Sheds much light on how we understand each other and our world.

Gergen, Kenneth J. *Realities and Relationships*. Cambridge, MA: Harvard University Press, 1994.
A gateway book to a powerful generative discourse—social constructionism. The astounding author shows the philosophical foundations, answers objections and demonstrates the amazing power of narrative. Strongest recommendation.

Heidegger, Martin. *On the Way to Language*. Translated by Peter D. Hertz. San Francisco: Harper & Row, 1971.
Heidegger's poetic and metaphysical essays on the nature of language. Very rigorous. Somehow opens the reader up to the possibility of what language is without defining or limitation. A book of wonder and mystery. Worth many readings.

Johnson, Mark, and George Lakoff. *Metaphors We Live By*. Chicago: University of Chicago Press, 1980.
Change the metaphor and change forever the worldview; for example, what if time weren't really money?

Kockelmans, Joseph J. *On Heidegger and Language*. Evanston, IL: Northwestern University Press, 1972.
A collection of essays exploring the impact of Heidegger's work on many aspects of contemporary thought. More accessible than Heidegger's own books.

Lakoff, George. *Women, Fire, and Dangerous Things*. Chicago: University of Chicago Press, 1987.
The way language provides what's possible for us to be, to feel, and to do.

–. *Moral Politics*. Chicago: University of Chicago Press, 2002.
Reveals through rigorous writing and though the linguistic cognitive foundations for U.S. ethics, politics, values, religion, and child rearing. Resolves paradoxes. Dispatches enigmas. Forever shifts the way one observes U.S. culture. Seminal.

Rosenberg, Ph. D., Marshall B. *Nonviolent Communication*. Encinitas, CA: PuddleDancer Press, 2003.
Miraculously blends realism, courage, and compassion into a fully developed method for conducting conversations that respects everyone involved without compromising authenticity or integrity. Shifts the reader with every chapter.

Scott, Susan. *Fierce Conversations*. New York: The Berkeley Publishing Group, 2002.
Encouraging, pragmatic structures for conducting essential conversations. Engaging, full of stories and examples.

Searle, John R. *Speech Acts*. Cambridge: Cambridge University Press, 1969.
A presentation (in a fairly dense philosophical style) of the basic moves possible in language.

Sieler, Alan. *Coaching to the Human Soul*. Blackburn, Victoria, Australia: Newfield Australia, 2003.
Not a religious or spiritual take on coaching but the first published version of speech act theory that Fernando Flores (a student of Searle and Maturana) brought to the world. Many references to the roots of the philosophy of language. Useful reference text.

Stone, Douglas, Bruce Patton and Sheila Heen. *Difficult Conversations*. New York: Penguin Books, 2000.
A thorough presentation of the obstacles that so often make conversations challenging. And a proved methodology for preparing ourselves and guiding the conversation to mutually satisfying conclusions.

3

The Flow of Coaching

Where do you start your work as a coach? This chapter suggests a particular flow that has proved useful over the years. As you read, recall particular times when you coached or were coached. How does the flow map onto your experience? Does it show you why the coaching succeeded or failed?

This chapter will serve as an overview of the whole coaching process—what I'm calling the *flow* of coaching (see Figure 3.1). The presentation is linear and our experiences, conversations, and lives are not. Consequently, the flow is usually not as simple or direct as is shown in the text. The stages are really buoys, which indicate for trained observers where they are on their journey through the bay, and can indicate to the coach how the work is progressing. The point of the chapter is to identify the indicators and provide a framework in which a coach can think and design.

As you being to work with this flow, it will make more and more sense to you and at some point you won't need to refer to it for guidance anymore. Instead, you will naturally move in your own particular way through the various stages of coaching.

Until then, here is a proven structure for you to use. Each stage is distinct; however, the boundaries between stages frequently merge so that it is difficult to determine when one ends and one starts. For learning purposes, though, it's useful to keep the stages separate and distinct and to speak about each of them individually. The remainder of the book will address each stage in its own chapter. The purpose here is to show you an overview of the flow and the interconnection between the stages. You can use the flow to design your actions and as a diagnostic tool when your coaching isn't working. When diagnosing, start with the stage you're on and work backwards, assessing whether you have successfully fulfilled the requirements of each stage. Keep working in this way until you have discovered the exact source of the problem. Correct it at the level at which it appears by providing what's missing or by revising what has already been done.

Some readers may feel that this is too much structure, that it will inhibit their spontaneity, slow the flow of their natural intuitive responses,

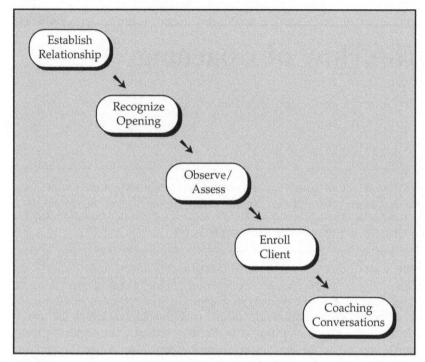

FIGURE 3.1   The Flow of Coaching

or that somehow the structure will become more important than either the interaction or the outcome. You will find in practice, I think, that none of this is the case. Doing coaching is like playing jazz: the coach, like a jazz player, must understand where to begin and where to end, and what a basic structure could be in the moment, while at the same time listening well to the music that the others are playing so as to blend with it and move the entire joint effort forward. Even while a jazz musician is improvising, she is always playing within a structure. That's why I say that coaching people is like playing jazz. By knowing the structure so well that it fades into the background, the coach has the freedom to creatively respond in the moment, while still being confident that the desired outcomes are being realized.

I will use the example of Bob, which I have referenced earlier, as illustrative of the different stages in the flow of coaching. First I'll present the theoretical basis for the stage and then I'll fold in the story of Bob.

STAGE ONE: RELATIONSHIP

By now you've seen this word appear again and again in the text, and its meaning here remains the same as earlier. Relationship remains the beginning point of coaching and its foundation. I keep bringing it up because this is the stage that more than any other is neglected, ignored, or considered to be unnecessary. Given that it's the foundation, it can cause the most problems when it is taken for granted. The basic ingredients for the relationship are mutual trust, respect, and freedom of expression. We will study each of these in turn in the chapter devoted to the coaching relationship.

Sometimes people believe that relationships are natural and either happen or don't happen, and that any interference in such a "natural" process is a manifestation of some neurotic need to control or be in charge. The type of relationship necessary for coaching is not one that's based upon "chemistry." It's more a matter of openness, communication, appreciation, fairness, and shared commitment. Frequently we'll find that we are in a position to coach someone who is not the person we would choose to be our best friend or our selection as a dinner companion. There may be no escape from the experience that we like some people more than others. This doesn't matter in coaching people, however, and it doesn't matter in building a successful coaching relationship.

Back to the story of Bob. My first task with Bob was to clarify my relationship with him. He wanted to know if I was an agent for the company, brought in to whip him into shape, or if I was working for him. The answer to this question would determine the amount of candor Bob brought to his program. My usual stance in such circumstances is to work for the individual client knowing that if I improve his competence, it will be of benefit to the company as well. Bob did his best to check on my sincerity by presenting potential scenarios in which the direction of my loyalty would be questioned. He asked, "What if I decided to leave the company or what if we found out that my boss really is making biased judgments about me? Or what happens when my boss asks you what is happening in the coaching, what do you do?" I told Bob that I would be giving progress reports to his boss that contained generic information and did not reveal any of the content of the program. I also assured him that when push came to shove, he was my client and I was working for his success, wherever that took him. I went on to tell Bob about other occasions when I had been in similar circumstances and that I followed the same principles then. This was enough to establish a working relationship that would deepen in time.

Some coaches already know their clients very well and the requisite relationship is already in place. At other times the relationship will have to be repaired before the coaching can commence. We will address both of these situations in the chapter on the coaching relationship.

STAGE TWO: OPENINGS

Coaching, like many other human activities, starts before the actual beginning of the official program. Coaching starts when either the client or the coach encounters an opening for coaching. It seems to me in our day-to-day world, in which we routinely and competently deal with mostly recurring situations, relationships, and conversations, there really isn't any opening for coaching. Imagine if someone offered to coach you in how you poured your cereal in the morning, how you opened your car door, or how you stood in the elevator on your way to the office. Most of us would think this was very strange or maybe part of a Monty Python movie.

An opening for coaching is necessary. Openings occur when the transparent fabric of our routine is disturbed—either by something breaking down, by an offer someone makes to us, or by a change in circumstance that requires a new skill from us. When one of these openings happens in a domain of life in which we are committed, then there is a chance for coaching. Usually it's the coach who, being experienced in such matters, recognizes these openings and steps forward with an offer to coach. On other occasions, the potential client may simply recognize a need for assistance and may ask for it without quite knowing what assistance she needs.

Beyond these orienting comments, it's up to you as the coach to discern when an opening for coaching has occurred. Sometimes the occurrence will be built into the time cycles of your activities, as in annual performance reviews, assessment of the progress of projects, or the beginning of a new budget period. You will know best when these recurring events happen. On other occasions, the opening is not presented by a recurring event but is instead associated with a particular circumstance. Examples include difficult problems, complaints from customers, equipment failure, a crisis within the enterprise, a new possibility in sales or marketing, a promotion, or the requirements of a new position.

The story with Bob is somewhat different from the other openings described because I wasn't on site to observe the course of day-to-day events. Managers or supervisors who double as coaches will have the chance to stay continually vigilant for openings so that their coaching can have the maximum leverage.

In Bob's case, my job was to figure out what the real opening for coaching was. Was Bob sincere in asking for coaching or was he merely going through the process because of his boss's instructions? How open was Bob to taking a look at his own actions, motivations, level of skill, blind spots? If he wasn't open, the coaching would go nowhere. In speaking with

Bob, I determined that there was a simultaneous phenomenon of his ambition meeting the genuine support of his management in the possibility of his promotability.

STAGE THREE: ASSESSMENT

Before coaching can begin, the coach must understand a lot more about the client than what is usually necessary in the day-to-day routine. While your friend who is a physician may give you offhand advice about what to do for a cold, when you go to that same friend's office you will undoubtedly receive a physical exam so that the particulars of your malady may be identified. Similarly, even when we know someone well, it's necessary for us to take time to do assessment before we begin to coach him or her.

What may not seem important under most normal circumstances becomes paramount when coaching begins. For example, our enjoyment of the person's company or the wisdom of her advice may be what we most appreciate about her, but this is usually not relevant in our coaching endeavors. So even though the coach may not feel completely comfortable when doing such an official assessment, it's a vital step.

The subject of assessment is threefold. First, the level of the client's competency is assessed. Second, the coach assesses the structure of interpretation of the client. Finally, the coach takes time to study the array of relationships, projects, and practices that make up the life of the client.

Perhaps it's readily apparent why these three kinds of assessment are necessary. In the chapter dedicated to assessment, I will discuss each in detail. For this section, however, I will simply explain their relevance. In order to know what to include in the coaching intervention, the coach must determine how competent the client is in the topic of the coaching. As you know, the way one works with a beginner is certainly different from the way one coaches an expert. So that the coach knows best how to present and conduct the coaching intervention, she must have an appreciation for the structure of interpretation of the client. That is, the coach must have a general sense of the way the client is in and makes sense of the world. Later, I will provide some models that will make this daunting task seem easier. Finally, the coach must understand what the client is already in the middle of, so that, whatever the form of the coaching intervention, it will be possible for the client to follow through on it with a minimum amount of interference from the rest of life.

The best way I know of doing an assessment when I am brought in from the outside to be a coach involves two parts. The first is to speak with the client and the people who work around him. The second is to observe the client in action. I do this by following the client around for a day or more so that I can begin to understand his world, the way he responds to varying circumstances, and I can have some insight into the environment in which all this takes place. I'll present the specifics about what I found out about Bob in the chapter on assessment.

STAGE FOUR: ENROLLMENT

Enrollment means making apparent in the coaching relationship the intended outcomes of the program, the client's commitment to the outcomes, and the coach's commitment to the same. Presuming enrollment, which is common, leads to many mistakes and misunderstandings. We'll study the potential mistakes in detail in the chapter on enrollment. In a general way, enrollment mistakes include presuming a level of commitment that the client doesn't in fact have, acting as if no commitment is necessary from the coach, and not stating in a mutually clear way what the intended outcomes are and what are the potential obstacles to their realization.

Enrollment goes beyond simply asking, "Well, are you up for this?" It's an active dialogue that takes into account the particulars of the circumstances, the vagaries of the future, and the limitations and strengths of both the client and coach. Openness, honesty, and completeness are vital in enrollment.

You can probably understand in the story of Bob how enrollment naturally flows from the recognition of a genuine opening for coaching. Bob was ambitious and the company had expressed some interest in promoting him, but the question remained, was he willing to do the necessary work? In our conversation I did my best to describe the challenges that would face Bob. He'd have to become familiar with, immersed in, and skillful with the politics of his organization. He would have to become familiar with how decisions were made in processes that would at first not make sense to his logical, analytical, accounting thinking. It was likely that he'd have to become more proficient at presenting his views in a way that coalesced support rather than stirred up resistance. We would be doing all this while also tending to his well-being, maintaining his integrity, and sustaining the fulfillment he had enjoyed in his career until the most recent circumstances.

In a way this enrollment conversation was the other side of the relationship conversation that had happened earlier. This time it was my role to question the depth and sincerity of Bob's commitment in the face of the "what if?" scenarios I presented. We talked through each one until we were both as confident as we could be that we could resolve each of them by pooling our mutual commitment and expertise. This description may make it sound as if the conversation went really smoothly or that the outcome was clear going in. Neither is the case. The conversation kept looping back on itself until at the end we both felt sure of where we were headed and of each other's partnership in getting there.

STAGE FIVE: COACHING ITSELF

Part of the coach's job is to determine the scope of the coaching project. Can it be accomplished in one conversation? Will it take a series of conversations? Is a more comprehensive program with assigned practices, milestones, and a communication structure necessary? As a coach you may have an idea about this even before you do some of the earlier stages. Stay open, though, to the fact that your initial conclusion may change as you understand the client and the circumstances in greater detail. I've already said what the outcomes of coaching are and have said in a preliminary way how it's done. I'll provide a lot more detail on these topics in the chapter on coaching itself. Here, I'd like to remind the coach that the task is to have the client observe something in such a way that competence improves. Even after all the work of the earlier stages, it's sometimes easy for a coach to slip into a more familiar role of being a teacher or a therapist, or a manager, and many times when we are under pressure, we will return to one of these roles. In fact, one of the reasons for having a structure is to help the coach stay in the role and not slip into territory that may be more comfortable, but not as immediately relevant to the task at hand.

In Bob's case, I concluded that our coaching ought to take place over a six-month period. During that period we would meet for six half-day meetings and speak on the phone each week. In between, I would assign self-observation exercises and new practices. My intention in all this was to leave Bob independent of me and in possession of the skills necessary for promotion.

SUGGESTED READING

This is a short list, because the flow of coaching doesn't appear in any other book. The texts listed here will give you a background for understanding systems and interdependence.

Bethanis, EdD, Susan J. *Leadership Chronicles of a Corporate Sage.* Chicago: Dearborn Trade Publishing, 2004.
  The author has invented an effective way to work with corporate leaders who are very busy, working in global organizations, and accountable for big results. A different method of coaching than the book advocates but originating from similar roots. Extremely pragmatic and humane.
Macy, Joanna. *World as Lover, World as Self.* Berkeley, CA: Parallax Press, 1991.
  This beautiful, moving book explores (with exercises, stories, and examples) the interconnectedness of all life, all phenomena. Terrific background for understanding any system.
Senge, Peter M. *The Fifth Discipline.* New York: Doubleday, 1990.
  This book is about creating learning organizations. It appears here because the fifth discipline of the title refers to systemic thinking, which is central to coaching. The book is well written and well organized, and it is full of real-life examples drawn from the author's years of experience. Fascinating and worthy of much study.

4

The Coaching Relationship

You don't have to have "chemistry" with your client. You don't have to be best friends or dinner companions, but you must have a workable relationship in order to fulfill your coaching work. Sometimes people attempt to hide behind roles—executive, parent, boss—and have the power or authority of the role replace the relationship. It won't work. Roles may provide the circumstances, but only the relationship can provide the foundation.

"To communicate is to enter the other, while watching ourselves carefully, to enter without usurping….To usurp the other is to annul him, to prevent him from returning the gift; it is the refusal to accept his discrete word; it is to violate his inner home without allowing him to enter ours; it is the arrogance of someone who believes himself to be an entirely fecundating force and refuses to receive. The univocal gift, without reciprocity…is not communication, but violation."

—M. F. Sciacca

In a sense, the coaching relationship is a strange topic to bring up because, as Medard Boss said earlier, we already and always have a relationship with everyone and everything we encounter, whether we are aware of it or not. Consequently, it's always the case that we do have a relationship with our potential client. The question remains, however, what is the nature of that relationship? Is it sturdy enough to sustain itself during the sometimes tumultuous events of coaching, and does it have the necessary qualities to allow the coaching to readily succeed?

I'm attempting in this chapter to bring into the foreground that which is usually in the background. I've indicated earlier my view that coaching is more a "be" than a "do," but usually this distinction is not very useful. I intend in this chapter to give more substance to the distinction, and thus set up a way to observe, correct, and develop what you're doing. When such a movement is made, a new background has to be put in place in order to frame the new foreground and give it meaning and a reference point.

The background for the kind of relationship that we will explicitly discuss is the shared commitment of the client and the coach. Both people have to, in some way, be committed to the same thing, however vague that may be in form. Otherwise there would be no impetus to explore, create, or maintain a relationship sufficient for coaching. As you read this, you may discover why some of your coaching efforts have failed. Could it be that you and your client did not share a commitment, or that you hoped that your commitment and enthusiasm would somehow bring your client along?

In my view, sometimes the commitment and enthusiasm of the coach do energize the coaching effort, especially in moments of uncertainty, but what makes such energizing possible is the already existent (although at the moment dormant) commitment of the client.

Of course, some people may now ask, "Well, what do you do if this shared commitment isn't present? Does that mean coaching can't happen?" My answer is yes. I do not mean that the coach is then powerless to take any action. What can occur is an inquiry into what the client *is* committed to, and sometimes a bridge can be built from that to the commitment of the coach, therefore leading to something genuinely shared. In any case, the shared commitment is the background for the coaching relationship.

The elements of the relationship are mutual trust, mutual respect, and mutual freedom of expression. Let's discuss each in turn after some general comments. None of the elements is independent of the others. What would it mean if we trusted someone who we didn't respect, for example, or if we felt free to express ourselves to someone who we didn't trust? Additionally, working on one element will strengthen the others. I'll address each element individually so that you can have a way of understanding what the dynamics are in any particular relationship. The modifier "mutual" indicates that the quality must go both ways, so that the client and coach trust each other, respect each other, and both feel free to express themselves.

MUTUAL TRUST

What do you mean when you say that you trust someone? How does trust come about? How is trust repaired? Do we have a say about whom we trust and whom we don't, or is it just a matter of instinctive, unconscious selection? Your answers to these questions are more important than anything I'll have to say on the topic because it's always going to be your experience that informs your coaching. And although I know that readers rarely do it, I invite you to take some time to consider your answers to the questions above before you continue with the text.

All of us enter into the world of coaching with our own personal history. For some of us, that means that we have met many people we have found to be trustworthy. We discovered that we could take action from what they said, rely on their sincerity, and feel secure that they would maintain confidences. Of course there are others of us who are on the other side of these examples.

We have encountered people who we have found untrustworthy. We've felt let down, betrayed, not supported, or lied to. Either set of experiences can leave us in either a strong position to coach or in one fraught with difficulties.

Since we can't change our background, the most important task becomes to understand where we are personally in our ability to authentically trust. A background full of trustful experiences may facilitate our trusting new people. But at the same time, a background of betrayed trust can leave us with an eagerness to leave the past behind us and find people worthy of our trust. The other side of the equation is equally symmetrical. People who have had many trustful experiences may miss the sometimes subtle cues that alert us to a betrayal of trust about to happen. A background of trust can lead us blindly to certain circumstances. It is probably obvious for someone who brings a background of untrusting relationships to coaching that there may be an additional vigilance required for the coach to be present in the current relationship and not reenacting one from the past. As I said in the beginning, and perhaps as these examples have made more clear, the essential step is that a coach become aware of her own background and how that could shape the current relationship with the client.

Whatever background we bring, at bottom it seems to me that trust is a gift that we can give to people. I say it this way because I've often heard that trust must be earned, but I've never heard a listing of the criteria for earning it. Yes, it makes sense to prudently observe someone in a variety of circumstances over a period of time before we determine that we are going to trust them. In the end, however, it's my contention that we trust people because we make up our mind to do it and not because the circumstances compel us to do so.

Trust is not a matter of accounting—adding up positives and negatives about a person, keeping a scrupulous log of virtues and vices, applying a formula that extends the calculation into the future, and then allowing the dynamics of the formula to determine whether we trust or not. To the contrary, usually we just find ourselves in the middle of trusting someone, or not, and we don't quite know why. We continue trusting until the person betrays us with sufficient severity that we withdraw our trust or we wait until he does something to "redeem himself." Coaching by its nature is less serendipitous than that. I'm proposing a middle ground between the accounting method of building trust and the mystery-shrouded method of somehow finding ourselves in the middle of trusting.

The first step in this middle ground is to determine what, in fact, we trust about the person. In what domain of life or activity do we trust this person? In coaching, it's rare that we have to trust the person in all aspects of life and through unbounded time. Once we have chosen what the pertinent domain is, then we can begin to assess two aspects of the person's behavior.

The first is asking if this person is sincere in what they say. Do they go into action to fulfill promises made? Do they tell the same version of events to different groups, or is the story recrafted to fit particular audiences? In sum on this point, I am saying we can assess a person as sincere when words and actions are consistent and when the person maintains consistency in speaking to different people.

The second element in assessing trust is a matter of evaluating competence. Has the person demonstrated a capacity for fulfilling what he said? Have you observed over a period of time that the person has successfully shown the competence in question? Thus we would not trust a seven-year-old child of whatever level of sincerity when he promised that he could perform a tonsillectomy on us when we complained of a sore throat. It's in the same sense that both these elements of assessment, sincerity and competence, come together when we are working to determine whether or not we trust.

What I've said here may sound like it's a sophisticated version of the accounting method of determining trust, and I can understand how it could appear that way. However, I'm attempting to make a distinction that trust does not have to be a universal judgment about a person. It's not whether we trust him or not; it's whether we trust him or not in a particular domain based upon our personal judgment of him given the above criteria. In other words, we're keeping the power of determination with us as the observer and assessor, and not in an automatic, rigid accounting procedure.

MUTUAL RESPECT

Like trust, many people say that respect has to be earned, but they never quite tell you what actions a person is required to take in order to earn this respect. It's probably also true that in most people's thinking, respect is not very distinct from agreeing with or liking. For example, when people say, "I respect her opinion," what are they really saying—that they agree with it, that they like it? And what do people mean when they say, "I respect him"?

The essence of respect is accepting a person for what they are and what they present themselves to be. Respect exists in a range from mild acceptance to total admiration. On the acceptance end of the spectrum, we decide that the values and the behavior of someone are within the wide range of what we find to be tolerable. We may not fully understand the person or her motivation, but we've found a way to accommodate her that minimizes conflict. On the admiration side, we fully endorse the values and behavior of the person and hold them up as a model for ourselves and others.

When I hear people say that they do not respect anyone, my guess is that they are saying that there is no one that they admire in all aspects of life. Very few people hold up to this high standard for respect, especially in these days when the private lives of public figures are put under the close scrutiny of the media. In coaching people, it's not necessary that you maintain this high-end standard of respect. What is required is that we respect clients in the domain of activity in which we will be coaching them, and within the day-to-day relationship that we personally have with them. It may be the case, for example, that we do not respect a client's political views, or how she spends her money or her time. This doesn't mean that we can't coach her in an area of life that doesn't include these topics.

Like trust, respect is not an accountant's printout of deposits someone has made into our private bank of acceptable behavior. When we are attempting to decide whether we respect someone or not, we can reflect on their past behavior and make up our mind whether we find it at least tolerable for us. If we don't, then it is the case that we don't respect them and they are not a candidate for our coaching. In such an instance, it's sometimes possible to speak with the potential client to find out more about what he or she was up to in the circumstances that we have been assessing. Such an investigation sometimes sheds a different light on what happened so that we can find a way to tolerate it.

In a way similar to our discussion about trust, the stance that a coach takes regarding respect necessitates close, fair examination of what has really happened. To do this the coach must be able to separate what happened from what he thought about or felt about what happened, that is to say, make distinct what occurred from his reaction to what occurred. Without the competence to make this separation, we will continually find ourselves coaching people who we "like" or "feel comfortable with," and we will find many reasons, stories, excuses, or justifications for not coaching the people we don't react to positively.

Our culture has some strange notions about first impressions and these can get us into trouble as coaches. For example, I often hear in the executive ranks that a potential executive has been ruled out for promotion because "We don't feel comfortable with her." Upon closer examination, the statement turns out to be a euphemistic way of saying, "I don't like her," which probably really means, "She is not enough like me."

It is obviously very difficult for a woman to be sufficiently like a man for him not to notice the difference. The glass ceiling has been held in place for decades through this mechanism, and to their detriment, some coaches have attempted to show women how they can be "just like one of the guys" and thus get ahead. But doesn't that stop anybody who has a genuinely fresh perspective from ever entering a leadership position? Doesn't it condemn organizations to making the same mistakes over and over again because the leaders share the same prejudices and blindness? How can we learn if we are not willing to listen to someone with whom we don't agree?

In the same way, coaches can put unnecessary distance between themselves and their clients when they don't pass the "sufficiently like me" test. As an alternative to disrespecting people like ourselves, I suggest we enter the relationship with curiosity and a willingness to have our way of seeing things undone. Otherwise, we will as coaches keep coaching people who are just like us, and work to make them more and more just like us. More on this in a later chapter when we take on the temptations that a new coach falls into.

Consequently, our respecting someone comes down to a judgment we make, and like any judgment, it's a choice. In order to make a prudent choice, we weigh the observed evidence and do our best to screen out our own prejudice in the light of the consequences that will follow from the choice. That is to say, ask yourself what your relationship will be like if you determine you respect this person compared to what your relationship will be like if you decide not to respect him. Which choice will further your shared commitment with this potential client?

I'm not arguing here that it's best to always come down on the side of respecting someone, but I'm trying to point out that our choice has consequences that ought to be part of our choice-making process. It's not a mistake or wrong when we make up our minds not to respect someone if we have taken the time to go through a procedure like the one described here. In fact, we can do so with a clear conscience as long as we stay open to the possibility that we can change our minds in the future based upon the different behavior of the potential client and/or our different understanding of it.

Our malleable ability to tolerate can be the leverage point for increasing our capacity to respect. Perhaps in reading this discussion, you've seen that many times the limitation on our respect for someone is not so much in what they're doing as it is in the imposition of our values on what they're doing. Our doing this is perhaps no more apparent than when we study other cultures or historical periods. In such a study, we often find that we feel repulsed by what we learn. A deeper reflection on our reaction, though, will often reveal to us that it is possible for us to accept what people did given the circumstances within which they lived, even though our immediate, automatic reaction is one of distaste or dislike.

MUTUAL FREEDOM OF EXPRESSION

Usually when people hear this phrase, they understand it to mean that people have the freedom to say whatever they want to say, in whatever way they want to say it, whenever they want to say it, to whomever they want to say it. Perhaps such an understanding is basic to the American psyche. Everyone, after all, has a right to his or her opinion. Reporters stop citizens in the street and ask them their views on complex economic and world issues because everyone ought to be given a voice. In talking to executives and managers, I've never met one who has said he is not open to everything anyone has to say to him at any time. Simultaneously, I've spoken to others in the same organization who say that they cannot talk about certain subjects with these executives, or that if they decide to, they have to work hard to find a special language to use so as not to upset them. How can we reconcile these contradictions?

As many management consultants and philosophers alike have reported, communication within organizations is shaped by many forces that seem beyond the power of the individual. Argyris (1990) and Habermas (Morgan, 1983), speaking from widely different domains, both address what is undiscussable. Argyris, working as a consultant in business, has devised a famous exercise for uncovering the undiscussable, for example, any speaking that would embarrass someone or that would reveal that such face-saving is occurring. He directs participants to draw a line down the middle of a page. In the right column they write what they said aloud. In the left column they write what they said privately to themselves. Over time, Argyris invites people to reveal their left columns and discuss what made the statements undiscussable. Eventually, it becomes possible for others to ask the same questions. At that point, the real basis of assessment and actions can be revealed. Usually, tremendous progress in group effectiveness follows. Habermas takes on the constraints to open communication in an astoundingly rigorous way. His books often are a daunting challenge for professional philosophers. The book cited above gives access to some of his more germane distinctions. In some, he proposes that true freedom of expression exists only when anyone in a conversation can challenge (without fear or negative repercussions) the truth, sincerity, intention, and appropriateness of any utterance. That's a high standard. How many of us have conversations in which all the listed criteria are met? How many of us conduct relationships in which all parties are willing to question and be questioned? How many of us are even willing to attempt such conversations and relationships? Coaching is a place to begin and a place to practice.

The forces shaping communication remain invisible to participants within a given culture or organization. Participants are unaware that they are, in fact, not speaking about certain topics and not bringing up certain ideas, or that they are inhibiting others from speaking to them. When an outsider attempts to broach these subjects, many excuses are immediately presented to justify the continuation of the moratorium on them. On other occasions people claim that, given how much complaining happens, it must be true that people are able to say everything they want to say. The assumption in such a conclusion is that complaining must be the most difficult kind of communicating to do, and if it occurs, then all the rest of the necessary conversations must also be happening. It doesn't take much observation of any relationship to see that that's not the case, but rather, in many instances, that complaining is the easiest, most habituated, most automatic way of talking. Because after all, among other things, it deflects responsibility away from the speaker who is complaining.

What can a coach do to ensure that freedom of expression exists in a coaching relationship, even when the dynamics described are in place? First, the coach can recognize that freedom of expression has to be constructed within an individual coaching relationship. It's not a given. The construction begins when the coach invites the client to speak openly, and simultaneously opens himself to receiving what the client has to say without argument or defense, responding instead with clarifying questions and assurances that the client has been heard. The construction continues as the coach reveals his own views, knowing that the degree of honesty and completeness in the communication will be determined by how much he embodies and models these qualities. It's not so much that the coach has to reveal his difficulties to the client; such an event may reverse the client/coach relationship, making the client into the coach and vice versa. It's more that the coach makes it abundantly clear that there is nothing that he is hiding or withholding, and he is available to speak on any subject that the client wishes to bring up that is relevant to the topic of the coaching.

Second, besides constructing a relationship within which a person can freely speak, for true freedom of expression to exist it's also necessary that the coach actually listen to what the client has to say. Listening in this sense is not merely the engagement of the ear and the auditory nerve, it's a full engagement of the attention, thought, and intention of the coach in the conversation. Given that there are hundreds of books and dozens of courses on listening, I'm not going to attempt to provide a program for improving listening skills here.

Suffice it to say that freedom of expression means that each member in the conversation is listening and considering what the other member is saying. How often have you been in a meeting where people talk one after another without taking into account what earlier speakers have said—where it seems as if what is said is triggering what is going to be said next, rather than triggering consideration of what's being said (some deeper reflection on the topic or an invitation to a more comprehensive dialogue)? Such speaking without listening quickly undermines or destroys freedom of expression, because people soon learn that what they're saying doesn't matter anyway—no one is really listening and no one is thinking about what they are saying. In such circumstances, speaking becomes a kind of release of internal pressure and is not a genuine connection or conversation with someone else. The coach can readily remedy this condition by actually considering what the client is saying. I'm not proposing that you try to make it look as if you are considering what the client is saying. Really do consider what they are saying. If you're not going to be open to what's being said, you can be assured that your partner in the conversation will not be open to what you are saying, even though they, like you, may have become expert in the appearance of communication. For coaching to work, the relationship must be genuine and not just look genuine. At the heart of this genuineness is communication as I am describing it here.

The final component in constructing freedom of expression is maintaining absolute confidentiality. Yes, this is difficult at times within organizations, but as you know, it doesn't take very much leaking of a particular conversation for it to get back to someone. When the client discovers that the conversation has been shared, great damage is done to the coaching relationship. Even though the client may continue in the program while pretending that nothing's really changed, the depth of the partnership that exists afterwards is usually not sufficient to bring about the products of coaching. To remedy this, be certain that you inform your client about whom you will share the coaching program with and in what detail. Keep your promise even if you feel that your client could never find out that you haven't, or if it seems expedient not to. If you don't, you will not only damage your current coaching program but also alter your public identity as a coach, which may negatively affect future programs with different clients.

By skillfully combining these three elements—openness, listening, and confidentiality—you will ensure freedom of expression in your coaching relationship.

As you've read through this chapter on the coaching relationship, you may have discovered that everything is in place with your potential clients. That's great news, because then you can move into the next stage of coaching. If, on the other hand, you've discovered otherwise, make sure that you attend to what's missing or inadequately present before you continue. Relationship is the foundation for coaching, and a solid one will see you through many mistakes you may make later in the program, while a shallow or shaky relationship will ensure the demise of your coaching efforts at the first hint of any misstep on your part.

Some readers may already be in a relationship with someone in which they now want to coach. If you are such a person, you may find that as you read the description of the coaching relationship, you discovered what's lacking and became discouraged. Here is some practical advice about what to do:

1. Begin by strengthening trust. You can strengthen the trust the client has for you by saying what you are going to do, doing exactly that, and then pointing back to the fact that you did what you said you would. For example, you can say, "I will enforce this policy with everyone in our department, the new hires and the experienced, the high performers and the low performers, no one will be left out." Then do what you said. After a period in which it has become obvious to everyone that you have done what you said, announce to your client that that is what happened. Over time and if you give no chance for counterexamples, your client will begin to trust you more.

   If your trust for the client is missing and you still want to find a way to coach, begin to find a small area in which you can trust them. Look, for example, to validate your primary conclusion of your client's trustworthiness in this arena.

2. In order to strengthen the respect clients have for us, we can begin to invite them into our decision-making process, showing them the degree of care,

openness, and analysis that goes into the major decisions we make. We can reveal to them that we can see different sides to the question, that we understand that no decision is perfect, and that often someone will be disappointed. As we do this, our clients will begin to appreciate more and more the steadiness and groundedness of our intention to do what is best.

Building respect for a client is a process similar to strengthening our trust in her. It is a matter of finding those topics and occasions when we do respect them, and then alerting ourselves to any circumstance that can corroborate what we have found.

3. We can strengthen freedom of expression in two ways: first, by demonstrating that we have changed our mind, our point of view, or our actions because of what someone has said to us; and second, by practicing saying things that are not readily spoken about in our environment. This will take a high degree of skill if we are going to avoid upsetting people, but at the same time, if we don't speak out, we are in a way colluding with what is happening. As coaches, we must be examples of what we are asking of our clients when our courage to speak up is lacking. We can only expect the same from our clients.

We can encourage freedom of expression in our clients by withholding our judgments, by looking for what's true or interesting in what they are saying, and by demonstrating willingness to learn from them.

My assumption in all this is that we are, as far as we can tell, working with the best of intentions to enhance the competence and fulfillment of our client. Also I am assuming that our potential client is not a criminal and is doing the best she can to bring about these same outcomes. I am not promoting naïveté, but I am proposing that there is a lot more we can do to repair and enhance relationships, and that we give up way too easily in many circumstances (see Figure 4.1).

With Bob, the relationship was pretty easy to form. From the strong recommendation of Nancy, he was predisposed to trusting and respecting me and what I brought to coaching. Besides that, we had an easy rapport and were comfortable in speaking about a wide range of topics.

- Mutual Respect
- Mutual Trust
- Mutual Freedom of Expression

FIGURE 4.1   Elements in a Coaching Relationship

That being said, there still was work to do in the relationship. Bob was in a habit of being in "performance mode." He would shape his reports to me according to what he imagined I wanted to hear. Like many of us, he had learned through his family and educational history how to please people and the benefits of doing that. For our coaching to have any genuine impact, Bob and I had to find a way of communicating that was beyond this habitual mode.

I'll tell you in a moment how Bob and I moved to more candid conversations, but I want to make a larger point about coaching first. We coaches are not immune to being flattered and although some of us don't like to admit it, many of us are still seeking the approval of others as a validation for ourselves. Consequently, when we meet clients who figure out what we want to hear and then tell us that, our desire for validation can readily lead us to a blindness concerning the real state of the coaching program. As coaches we must do our best to find places of support and appreciation outside of our client work. Otherwise, we are like dehydrated sponges seeking the water of approval when we are with our clients.

I caught on to Bob's communication style early on. I then began to ask the following questions to reveal more of what he had been observing and experiencing:

- Besides what you said, what else did you observe?
- What unexpressed concerns are you experiencing so far in our coaching?
- How would you make the same report you just gave me in your own diary where you wouldn't worry about what other people thought?
- Remember, Bob, that this coaching is for you, not for me. So is there something else that you might want to explore beyond what you already said?

By working through these and similar questions, Bob became more fully disclosing of his experience. It was important for me to be vigilant in all of our conversations and keep speaking with Bob until I felt that I had heard both the positive and negative sides of his experience. Over time I learned what Bob was most uncomfortable revealing and I would delicately ask him about these areas. After two or three sessions of doing this, Bob began with uncomfortable areas since he knew that I would be asking about them. Given that I didn't criticize Bob for anything he said, these uncomfortable areas over time became easy for him to talk about. At this point we had accomplished establishing freedom of expressing in our coaching relationship.

SUGGESTED READING

You won't find these books at your bookstore underneath the "relationships" sign; nonetheless, each reveals a unique understanding of relationship that is valuable in coaching.

Fiumara, Gemma Corradi. *The Other Side of Language.* Translated by Charles Lambert. New York: Routledge, 1990.

It's listening. The book is a detailed ontological exploration of the importance of this topic which is often neglected even in philosophical texts about language. Definitely not a self-help book.

McCarthy, Thomas. *The Critical Theory of Jurgen Habermas.* Cambridge: MIT Press, 1978.

Among other topics, Habermas writes about the societal forces that shape the way we communicate and what can happen in our relationships.

Unger, Roberto Mangabeira. *Passion.* New York: Macmillan, Inc., 1984.

A long essay that argues for the central role that created context plays in a life of meaning.

Winnicott, D. W. *Holding and Interpretation.* London: Hogarth Press, 1986; reprint, New York: Grove Press, 1986.

A classic text from an important therapist and theoretician. By closely following a course of therapy, the author demonstrates relating with dignity and respect.

5

Openings

In coaching, timing is everything. Knowing when to start may well determine if you get anywhere. Since most people aren't walking around soliciting coaching, it's the coach's job to determine when the correct moment occurs. Of course, we can only find an opening by knowing what it is and then looking for it. Here's a chance to begin both activities. The underlying principle of this chapter is from Heidegger. He claims in Being and Time *(1962) that the artifacts and routines of our everyday life are transparent to us until they break down. For example, we normally don't notice the flow of traffic until it jams, and we don't feel our shoes until the heel becomes loose, etc. Similarly, most people don't seek out and are not ready candidates for coaching until their everyday life is interrupted. Also see Flores and Winograd (1986) for a lucid explanation of breakdown.*

An opening for coaching is an occasion: an event that makes it more likely that the potential client will be approachable for coaching. Undoubtedly, there is a certain percentage of people who are always open to coaching, people who are open to ideas and input from everyone else nearly all the time. One category of such people may be folks who feel guilty all the time and are attempting to settle their feelings by going off in as many directions as people want them to go in. Other people don't seem particularly attached to any way of doing something and will readily change according to someone else's ideas. And then there are the rest of us.

HABITS

Many of us are not looking for coaching even though in many organizations the buzzwords of "continual improvement" and "international competition" seem to necessitate that we do. Maybe the best way of explaining why we aren't open to coaching is by attempting to explain why we're doing what we're doing now, and how we came to do it that way.

When I say we should explore why we are doing what we're doing, I don't mean it as a beginning of an inquiry of a theory of motivation. Instead, I mean it as an invitation to study the conditions present in every human being that can account for the consistency in our response to life. Coaches take on the task of intervening in this consistency of response which we usually call habit. Coaching, though, is not a matter of a client changing matters; instead the point is to build the client's ability to observe and select appropriate action. The difficulty in coaching adults is that we are already in the middle of habitual ways of acting, although with great effort we can sometimes suppress one action and start another. It is more problematic when we attempt to continuously undo our habits and freshly approach life. That's what I mean when I say that a client is self-correcting and self-generating.

In essence, coaches coach the nervous system. That may sound strange to some readers and obvious to others. By saying that, I am proposing that it's only by reeducating the nervous system that behaviors, responses, and reactions—as they occur in real time, not in reflection—change. We make the novel, be it a new behavior, process, or protocol, into the everyday and familiar by allowing it to migrate into the background of our consciousness. The migration occurs when we consciously take on new practices and persist with them. All of what it takes to bring about this reeducation, in alignment with the principles specified in Chapter 1, is what I'm calling coaching.

We learned to do everything that we do. All right, there are certain things we're doing that we didn't learn how to do, but these are mostly physiological and reflexive and are not the topic of coaching anyway. In the process of learning, we found a comfortable way for ourselves to accomplish a desired outcome. Usually we listened to other people, read instructions, or took a class, and then did our best to put into action what we heard or read. Over some period of experimentation, we sorted out what worked best for us in terms of our temperament, preferences, and ability. After this experimentation, we practiced what we decided to do again and again until we were able to do the task without having to stop and think about it. This period of practice has habituated us both mentally and physically.

A simple example of this is how you dress in the morning. Try sometime to reverse how you do it. Start at the top if you usually start at the bottom; start at your right side if you usually start on the left; and notice how you react as you do this. It's likely that you'll feel awkward, uncomfortable, and that you'll come to the conclusion that the way you were doing it before was better.

When I say we're habituated physically, I mean that both our nervous system and muscular system have become accustomed to a repeated action or response and have built structures such as opened neural pathways and strengthened particular muscles to facilitate the duplication of the behavior. When I say we've become mentally habituated to something, I mean that we have learned to perform the action without it having to take the forefront of our attention, or at least that it requires less attention than it did at the beginning.

Our nervous system has learned to readily recognize exceptions to the usual pattern, so that we can respond to the exception automatically. The next time you're in a diner, notice how the short-order cook is able to attend to many different dishes in preparation simultaneously. That's because she has learned to immediately notice and correct any anomalies and, in fact, she usually does so with such skill that we do not notice the correction being made. We perform the same level of sophisticated response when we are driving through city traffic and maneuver around pedestrians, potholes, and road hazards while continuing to think and plan for our day or talk on our mobile phones.

Clearly, our propensity for habituation has survival value and is the product of long evolution. Consequently, it has the momentum of any similar biological survival mechanism, for example, fight-or-flight response, and our reproductive urges. For this reason, it's highly unlikely that we can escape having to deal with habituation when coaching someone. This partially explains why simply telling people how to change rarely works, and why making a resolution ourselves to change has the same low degree of success.

In summary, people generally aren't open to being coached because they already have a habitual way of accomplishing something with all the resultant components of that process, both physical and mental.

As you may have gathered from my description of Bob, he was someone with a very strong will and had accomplished a lot through pure determination. He put himself through night school, completed his MBA, and acquired CPA credentials while holding down a job. The forcefulness of his will, though, was now becoming an impediment in his career. He had to learn to be more collaborative, more flexible, more entrepreneurial, and more open. He had to change his habit of applying his strong will as a way of prevailing and he couldn't use his strong will to change his habit. That's why Nancy saw that he needed some coaching. He needed a chance to develop new skills in a safe situation in which he could gradually let go of his old habits of success, which were now his biggest obstacles. Maybe from this brief description you can see why it is hard to undo our habits; we use our old habits to try and make new habits. It's rather like trying to wash off red paint with red paint.

SOCIAL IDENTITY

Besides the power of habits, a person's social identity presents an obstacle to coaching. Social identity has several parts. The first is how the person is known by people around her. That is to say that each of us has a particular reputation that determines the way people interact with us. Our preferences are known, our accomplishments are public, our prevailing mood is familiar, and our style of work and communication is expected. Given the prevailing nature of our social identity, people begin to interact with us in a way that makes it more likely that we will respond in the anticipated ways. When we don't produce the expected behavior, often the social environment will press back on us expressing surprise, questioning change, and perhaps voicing a negative judgment about the difference.

You might remember from Chapters 1 and 4 that I emphasized the importance of relationship in coaching. A social identity is a relationship with others that has become hardened through a repetition of behavior and bound by the inflexibility of expectation. The point of the coaching program for Bob really was for him to establish a social identity so that he could be promoted and have the opportunity to lead a large part of the organization.

In addition to the public factors of social identity, there also exists a private component made up of the story we tell about ourselves. We have a narrative, in other words, that we add to each day as life goes along, as we meet people, as we make decisions, as we take actions, and as we compare what's happening with what we want to have happen. In short, we give a meaning to life within the boundaries of our narrative.

So frequently do we repeat the story and so fervently do we believe it that, in many instances, we lose the distinction between what actually happened and how the event fit into our story. For many people, the story takes on a greater reality than the event itself. In a sense, we become a character in our own stories. Naturally, other people are also characters in our stories, and it's this automatic procedure of making people, including ourselves, into characters that I'm referring to as social identity. We then do our best to act the way we think the character should act, staying in role.

Of course, there's a symbiotic relationship between the roles that organizations and cultures provide for people and the roles that people take on in their private narratives. Each reinforces the other and, in most cases, cannot exist without the other. The structure of social identity as briefly described here has people believe that what they're doing is correct and is the best possible action, given the circumstances and their role in the circumstances.

When, as coaches, we attempt to question someone, frequently we encounter defensive routines that are consistent with the role that person has taken on. The point of such routines is to ensure the continuation of the public identity, since it has a structure that has proven successful in some way up to this point. Sometimes we forget that when we are asking a person to be coached, we are bringing into question her self-characterization and her public reputation, which are, as I said, woven together into a narrative and protected with stories, justifications, excuses, and so on.

Self-characterization and justifications are in most cases undiscussable. I don't mean to say that as coaches we ought not do such questioning, but rather that we ought to do it with awareness, keeping in mind the forces with which we are dealing.

For most of us, habituation and the power of social identity are in the background as unexamined elements in our commonsense coping with life. They allow us to function in a more or less conflict-free way in our daily dealings, and we don't question them until an event occurs that contradicts our story or frustrates our intentions. These types of contradictions or frustrations create the most obvious and powerful openings for coaching and, in many cases, they are the only openings, especially for people who are performing adequately in a stable environment.

OPENINGS

Sometimes coaching fails because the coach has not coordinated the beginning of the effort with an appropriate opening. So much for the constrains or challenges to beginning coaching. Let's spend some time looking at what are the powerful occasions in coaching. Probably the biggest opportunity coaches will have with their work is when the client is experiencing an interruption in her ability to fulfill a commitment. Who of us would not be open to the support of someone when we were somehow held back from accomplishing that which was very important for us? For example, imagine getting a flat tire on a snowy December Michigan night when the temperature is 25 degrees below zero. That would be bad enough, but what would it be like if you opened your trunk and to your dismay discovered that you did not know how to use the tools that were there to change your tire. Wouldn't you be very happy if someone arrived on the scene to coach you in how to use the tools? Perhaps you can see from these examples the importance of timing. If your tire-changing coach had arrived one half hour earlier and tried to flag you down so she could teach you how to change your tire, it is likely you would have ignored her as your car was humming along through the night. Similarly, if the coach had arrived too late, you might have already abandoned your car or succumbed to the elements.

Besides breakdowns there are other recurring events that leave clients more ready to receive coaching. Many of these are obvious ones that I am sure you already know about. They include performance reviews, the need for a new skill when someone takes on a new position, business needs such as requirements for higher quality and lower costs, and the client's request for coaching. The essential point is that the opening exists with the client, not simply with the coach.

A coach may feel as if it's now time to improve a person's performance or improve her competence in some way because of something the coach believes is important. On other occasions, coaching starts because the coach sees the client doing something that she doesn't like or isn't comfortable with. Although it may be necessary on some occasions to take action because of those criteria, it won't lead to the products of coaching. Even though such interventions in someone's behavior have been called coaching, in my view they are really behavior modification with all the accompanying techniques and coercive force of that approach. My proposal is that genuine coaching never happens unless there's a partnership. We'll discuss this at length in the chapter about enrollment. It's important to remember that long-term excellent performance cannot be foisted on someone by an external party, even with the best intentions or level of expertise. Unfortunately, Fournies (1978) proposes just such a course of action.

Sensitive clients, in fact, will immediately recognize what's occurring in such circumstances and will employ sophisticated avoidance and resistance procedures to ensure that their independence is maintained. Probably all of us have seen, or maybe even participated in, such charades. The charades occasionally degrade into full-scale power struggles reminiscent of encounters with 2H-year-old children or recalcitrant adolescents. The point is, you must have an opening for coaching before you start in order for the program to be successful.

There are occasions when a potential client is stopped in her intention to accomplish something, or when her social identity is challenged. In order to find such occasions, it's necessary to look for them. Stay alert for times when someone expresses to you her frustration, disappointment, or need for help in getting something important done.

At such moments, it's often an easy and appropriate time to offer your coaching, and you will probably find a willing recipient. I have already listed some other examples of events that can be openings for coaching. You will have to determine for yourself how open the person really is because, in the end, it's not going to be the event that leads to the potential client being open; it's the interpretation the potential client brings to the event and how it fits in with her narrative and her habitual reactions.

If you already have a solid relationship, you won't be putting much at risk if you offer coaching and it's turned aside. I recommend that you take a chance and offer, even when you're not entirely sure that your coaching will be welcomed. At the same time, be willing to hear someone tell you no, and make it easy for the person to say that to you. Making it easy means that you don't act surprised or disappointed when you are told, and that any subsequent conversation you have with the person never becomes argumentative, forceful, or coercive. It also means that you say explicitly in your invitation that you fully understand and will accept no as an answer.

Someone declining your invitation does not leave you helpless. You can discuss in detail why the person is declining. Be careful at this point to keep honoring the person's decision. You can do that by keeping your questioning in an interrogative tone rather than as a strategy for maneuvering the person into what you want them to do. You'll have to stay alert and honest in order to do this. Alert means paying attention to the way the potential client is reacting to what you're saying. Did she have a bad experience in the past? Does she feel it's hopeless? Does she feel as if no one could help her? Maybe she didn't regard your offer as sincere. Explore all these possibilities before you conclude that, at this point, there's no real opening for coaching.

It's also possible that when someone declines coaching, you are still accountable for the results of this person. What do you do then? I recommend that you use traditional management procedures at that point. For example, be sure there's clarity about outcomes and the consequences for not reaching those outcomes. Offer any support that you can in terms of training or advice and hold the person to what she committed to accomplish. Provide appropriate sanctions and rewards as necessary. I'm not going into detail with these techniques because traditional management literature is full of advice on these points. Besides that, they do not lead to the products of coaching, as I've said before, and consequently are not within the scope of this book.

Additional Openings for Coaching

Additional openings for coaching include

- Performance reviews
- Broken promises
- Need for new skills, such as new equipment or a promotion
- Requests for coaching
- Business needs, as in requirements for greater quality and lower cost
- Project milestones

Let's take a moment to apply these ideas in analyzing what happened in my coaching with Bob (see Figure 5.1). He was experiencing a breakdown, that is, his commitment to being promoted was being stopped by circumstances that he was unable to resolve. This left him very open to my interventions, and even though he did not contact me initially on his own, he was eager for what I could provide.

When to Coach

1. Performance assessment
2. Breakdowns
3. Broken promises
4. Request for coaching
5. Need for new skill
6. Business need, e.g., quality, lower cost

FIGURE 5.1 Openings for Coaching

SUGGESTED READING

These books provide many distinctions with which you can frame the opportunities for coaching you observe. By "frame," I mean a way of relating to a situation that provides sufficient clarity for action.

Bar-Levav, Reuven. *Thinking in the Shadow of Feelings*. New York: Simon & Schuster, 1988.
  A tract that warns readers about the danger of losing clarity of thought in the emotional stream of feelings.
Bellah, Robert M., Richard Madsen, William M. Sullivan, Ann Sweidler, and Steven M. Tipton. *Habits of the Heart*. Berkeley, CA: University of California Press, 1985.
  A classic sociological study of two forces that shape every U.S. resident: commitment and the pull toward individuality. Clear, precise, and powerful. Many useful examples.
Brown, Lyn Mikel, and Carol Gilligan. *Meeting at the Crossroads*. Cambridge, MA: Harvard University Press, 1992.
  Pinpoints the time when girls give up expressing their experience openly and begin to stifle their self-expression. Also proposes a new way to conduct longitudinal studies, which requires personal observation. Provides profound insights into the way U.S. culture shapes women's realities.
Drucker, Peter F. *The New Realities*. New York: Harper & Row, 1989.
  The author, a famous consultant and professor, outlines his views of contemporary cultural trends that influence the success of any enterprise. It's the gap between the competencies that an individual (or organization) has now and what competencies will be needed in the future (as described by Drucker) that can be the opening for coaching.
Hacker, Andrew. *Two Nations*. New York: Macmillan Publishing Company, 1992.
  Everyone living in the United States resides in a country divided by race. The author cuts through rhetoric and cites many statistics that reveal the pervasiveness of racism.
Johnson, Robert A. *He*. King of Prussia, PA: Religious Publishing Company, 1974; reprint, New York: Harper & Row, 1986.
  An exploration of male psychology through the retelling of the quest for the holy grail in Jungian terms.
Morgan, Gareth. *Images of Organization*. Beverly Hills, CA: Sage Publications, 1986.
  Uses nine metaphors to show how organizations form, grow, meet conflict, and eventually dissolve. Evenhanded. Solidly grounded experientially and academically. Full of useful charts and summaries. An invaluable reference for understanding organizations and the people within them.
Nehamas, Alexander. *Nietzsche: Life as Literature*. Cambridge, MA: Harvard University Press, 1985.
  By discussing the life and world of Nietzsche, the author makes a larger point about all our lives being stories full of plot and character with ourselves as the protagonists.
Reich, Robert B. *Tales of a New America*. New York: Random House, 1987.
  Reich's version of what's required for U.S. business to flourish in today's world. Gives us background for diagnosing current problems and predicting future ones.

6

Assessment Models

It's easy for us to be reductionists. We've been raised in the Newtonian version of the scientific method, wherein the universe is considered to be a huge mechanical clock, each part separate, discrete, and measurable. So we ask in nearly all situations, "What's the driving force?" Many of us work in U.S. businesses and are seemingly compelled to ask, "What's the bottom line?" We feel rushed, impatient. As you read the following chapter, however, see if you can be antireductionistic. Instead of boiling it all down to a facile, and therefore potentially more futile, formula, keep allowing your understanding to become more complex and therefore potentially more creative.

"I think I have seen the western mistake. You are very able to distinguish things, but you are unable to put all things together. Your scientific conceptions, therefore, all have holes in them and numerous incomplete principles are set forth. If you continue in this way, you will never be able to repair this."

—Hsia Po-Yan, Chinese Philosopher

Although no one would seriously mistake the map for the territory, very often people confuse assessment models with the person who is being assessed. It seems an obvious point that no assessment model, however sensitive or comprehensive, could ever fully capture or display the full range of a person's actions, feelings, thoughts, potential, and relationships. Nonetheless, whenever we're lazy we start to use models for labeling people.

I've been in so many corporate meetings where people, when identifying themselves, immediately tell the group their Myers-Briggs type so that the audience can know what to expect from them and how to shape their communication to them. In my view, the person might as well stand up and say, "I am an IBM-compatible computer. Do not expect me to be able to connect up with an Apple computer or a washing machine."

Of course, I'm familiar with the disclaimers that go with many assessment models which state that, in the best of circumstances, these models are only talking about tendencies or preferences. In real life, however, we often forget this and begin to exclusively expect the behavior from the person that the model predicts.

Our expectation does, in my view, influence the person's behavior and of course frames our observation of the person. Both these aspects lead to a self-fulfilling prophecy which, when coupled with laziness, leads us to endorse these models, promote these models, and believe in these models. If you think back to an earlier section of the book in which I talk about hindrances to coaching, you'll remember that one of the main hindrances to coaching was understanding people as collections of fixed properties with desire attached. The use of assessment models as I've described it so far is understanding people in this way. In other words, by using assessment models this way we are reinforcing our understanding of people as things, and this way of understanding makes any effective coaching impossible or nearly so.

Why then am I talking about assessment models, since they seem to be mere flypaper for observations? I claim that it's possible to use these models as a way of giving form and shape to our observations without limiting the person to the parameters of the model. This requires remembering at all times that an assessment model is a way of speaking about a person—it is not the person—and that our assessment is always up for reevaluation. In the light of subsequent observations or other insights we have about the person, we have to be unattached from our assessment model, and not argue for all the consequences of the model to be present all the time in the behavior, feelings, or outlook of the person assessed.

Even in the face of seemingly convincing statistical analysis verifying the validity of such models, I urge the coach to remember that human beings in every case will exist beyond the borders of whatever model is used to describe them; that a model is at best a well-focused snapshot; and that human beings are living, changing, adapting, and self-interpreting. A whole other way of keeping us awake is to imagine how it feels to be labeled by someone and then to have that person treat us as if that's all we are.

I guess if we didn't expect much from ourselves or didn't want to be counted on for much, it's possible that we would be comfortable with being labeled. But as soon as we get committed to accomplishing something big, or feel as if we have important ideas to express, or want to make a significant contribution, having been labeled will be an enormous obstacle. For example, you have probably heard about all of the studies that were done of elementary school children in which low-performance students were labeled as high-performance students. This label was given to the teachers who then took actions to bring about the validation of the label of high performance. So even though I understand that in business, for example, it's important to understand people quickly, I still argue for staying awake in our use of assessment models. That's because the Pygmalion effect is powerful and pervasive.

While reading this, some people will imagine that I'm saying that as long as we don't use a negative label it's okay. Permanently assessing someone as having positive qualities or attributes is just as denigrating to that person as the opposite, because it still assumes that the person is a thing which can be found out about, figured out, and predicted.

One example of this predilection in our behavior was permanently etched into my memory one day when I was waiting at a checkout line in a supermarket. I looked down and read the cover of *Life* magazine, which depicted a set of quintuplets at age one. Each child was labeled with a name that was meant to capture them, for example, the curious one, the charming one, the intelligent one, and so on. What happens to a child who grows up having been labeled at an early age?

Of course, it's not only others who label us—we do the same thing to ourselves, as if we could figure ourselves out once and for all and could stop having to learn about ourselves as we went through life. How many relationships, opportunities, and adventures have you neglected or ignored because you labeled yourself as a person who would not begin that relationship, opportunity, or adventure? How much can you set yourself free by releasing yourself from the various ways you've labeled yourself? Perhaps worst of all, we determine our own possibilities by the expectations that inevitably flow from self-assessment. Any action that follows such a declaration of identity can at best be a palliative or coping response, regardless of how expensive, energy-demanding, or emotionally stirring the activity may be.

What would happen if you became unattached to the labels you've given to the people around you, especially to those people you are coaching? In the following presentation of several assessment models, I urge you to keep all of this in mind and to remember at all times that I'm presenting a way of speaking about people that can lead to effectively coaching them.

None of these models captures a person; they only allow for a way of appreciating a person that facilitates a coaching intervention. As a coach, you'll know that you have not become attached to any particular assessment model when you still find your client mysterious and you still observe unexpected behavior. Finding your client mysterious, then, is an indication that you are doing effective coaching, staying awake as a coach, and not making your client into a thing, and is not an indication that something is missing in your assessment.

For example, when we go to visit a favorite masterpiece in a museum and are able to appreciate it in a new way each time we view it, it means that we are becoming more competent as a viewer of art. This is distinct from figuring out a painting and having our conclusion reinforced each time we look at it.

Probably nothing leads to the resignation we so often find in adults more than the notion that after a certain age, say around 35, we have turned out, we are done, we are the way we are. As I said earlier, it's probably the coach's most important task to undo this resignation and this is only possible when the coach has not fallen into it himself.

With all this as essential background, here are three assessment models you can use in your coaching programs. It's helpful to remind yourself at this point that as a coach you're working toward building a competence and not toward "The Truth." The validity of any assessment in coaching is based upon its usefulness—does it enable the client to take action, does the assessment synthesize and bring meaning to the coach's observations, and so on?

MODEL ONE: FIVE ELEMENTS MODEL

Immediate Concerns

This model (see Figure 6.1) draws strongly from the work of Fernando Flores as presented in his seminars, The Action Workshop and The Competitive Edge Sales Course. There are five areas of observation. The first area is immediate concerns. Immediate concerns are what the client has on his mind at the moment—what is the most pressing problem, either because of its current effects or its potential effects. None of us can listen very well when we have a huge immediate concern, and even when our concerns are small, they still shape how present we can be. Sometimes immediate concerns seem trivial to someone else. For example, a man's whole day can be determined by the fact that he has a hole in the back of his pants that no one must discover; or a long, leisurely drive in the country can be affected because we hear a strange noise in our car. Once we hear the sound, we stop seeing the scenery.

We can only find out a person's immediate concerns by asking. We can't legislate what someone's concerns ought to be. It's easy for us to project our immediate concerns onto someone else. What we're doing in this case is not being present for the other person because of our own immediate concerns. It will probably be a continual challenge for you as a coach to establish the borderline between you and your client. Are these your immediate concerns or your client's immediate concerns? Is this your mood or your client's mood? Is this going on with you or with your client? Part of the reason I'm presenting

Elements of Interpretation

- Immediate Concerns
- Commitments
- Future Possibilities
- Personal and Cultural History
- Mood

FIGURE 6.1   Five Elements Model

these models is so that you can begin to put some certainty on exactly where the border is.

Commitments

The second area is commitments. Anybody who we coach will be in the middle of dedicating his life to something or someone. Often, this something is not a specific goal or outcome, but rather a particular kind of experience or set of possibilities. It's easy for nose-to-the-grindstone types to say that such a person isn't really committed, but I say that it's always a case of discovering to what or to whom the person is committed, and it's never the case of whether or not he is committed.

Some of us try to figure out what a person is committed to by watching how he allocates his time, money, and other resources. But you'll find when you speak to people that many times they will tell you that their commitment lies elsewhere, and that what you've been observing is merely the actions they're taking in order to make something happen that you haven't observed yet. This can be the case, for example, with a salesperson who is working very hard and making lots of money, but who is doing it so that he can retire at age 40 and sail around the world.

On the other hand, it's often difficult for us to hear someone say she is committed to something for which she is taking no action, for example, a person who is very overweight saying she is committed to being thin. We may readily conclude that this person is committed to being fat given that the actions she has taken have led to this. I think that it's a mistake to argue back from the outcomes to determine what the person must have been committed to. This is because a person may be committed to something but be incompetent in bringing about the outcome. Also, by not honoring what people claim to be committed to we are taking over the role of defining what they are committed to, a role that we are neither authorized to do nor capable of fulfilling.

I think of commitment as if it were the engine of a car. It doesn't matter how powerful the engine is, or how well tuned up it is, or how much gasoline it is getting if it is not connected to the wheels by the transmission. The transmission is a metaphor for competence. This competence takes many forms: sometimes it is skill, as in learning how to fly a plane; sometimes it's a capacity to observe ourselves and not become defeated by negative emotions or self-assessments. The overweight person, in other words, may be very committed to losing weight but incompetent in bringing it about. Understanding someone in this way will allow us to keep looking for what is missing in his ability to fulfill his intention rather than dismissing him as not being strong enough to fulfill it.

It is American utilitarianism that, in my view, keeps people in the United States concluding that the reason for failure is usually the lack of will. How often have we said to people, "If you want it bad enough it will happen"?

We may have come to this conclusion from watching too many interviews with the winner of the Olympic marathon who says that he won because he really wanted it. We don't interview the person who comes in at 112th place and ask if he really wanted it as well. The tautological argument that the person who wins wanted it the most gets us nowhere because we can only know at the end that people "really" wanted it, and this is too late for coaching. Instead of freeing people to take action, this way of explaining things often leads them into the insoluble dilemma of trying to figure out how to want something more, or into berating themselves for not wanting it enough. It's like telling people whose cars lack transmissions to keep revving their engines if they really want to get somewhere.

Future Possibilities

Third is future possibilities; what is the person interested in bringing about in the future? As I said in an earlier chapter on language, because we are speakers of a language, we are always simultaneously existing in the past, the present, and the future. We are taking action now to fulfill something we initiated in the past in order to bring about a particular future outcome.

By discerning what future a person is attempting to generate, we can begin to make a different kind of sense of the actions she is taking presently, and perhaps we can even think backwards and begin to discern the origins of her actions.

Given that people are always projecting themselves into the future, any request or suggestion we make will be considered to be either a support or a detriment to bringing about this future. All this is done quickly and without conscious deliberation. A person would only be aware of liking a request or suggestion and being drawn to it or, on the other hand, finding it uncomfortable or distasteful in some way. That's because in our day-to-day consciousness we are not making decisions based upon weighing future consequences. It's more that we are coping with each situation, relationship, and conversation as it comes along in the light of what we set out to do in the past.

If you observe yourself for a few days you'll see that this is in fact the way you move through life. Of course, this is both good news and bad news. The good news is that we don't have to stop and weigh all the actions that we're taking in the light of future consequences. The bad news is that it's easy for us to become automatic in our responses and consequently to miss being present with what we are encountering.

This phenomenological way of describing our day-to-day life does away with the commonsense notions many of us have about motivation. The problem is that, in the middle of life, we forget what is supposed to be motivating us. How often have we remembered after we ate the chocolate cake that we are supposed to be, according to our doctor, on a diet? Or perhaps it's according to our wish to fit into our summer clothes. Somehow this "motivation" fades into the background in our day-to-day coping. One solution is to threaten others with such a dire outcome that they would not dare forget the consequences of noncompliance. And I suppose this could work as long as you are able to keep finding fresh ways to threaten people, because threats certainly do become stale when they are repeated again and again. Even if this kind of motivation were positive, that is, providing a reward instead of a punishment, the person being motivated would still be reliant on the continuation of the reward to support him in accomplishing what he set out to do. Such a scheme never leaves the person more competent, but rather leaves him searching forever for a lasting motivation which cannot exist.

It may be obvious that the important role of a coach is to be someone who can remind us of what we set out to do and can work with us to keep building a way of observing and acting that is consistent with our projects. It is the job of the coach to leave the client able to fulfill the future that the client intends. One of the first steps in bringing this about, of course, is to find out what future possibilities our client has in mind—thus its placement in our first assessment model.

Personal and Cultural History

Fourth is personal and cultural history, which I suppose is self-explanatory. It simply means that each of us has had a different history of interactions with people and circumstances, which has influenced subsequent ways we respond. All of this takes place within influences that are particular to individual cultures. Regardless of how hard we try, none of us born and raised in the United States will ever really understand what it is to be Japanese. And a Japanese person couldn't even tell us what it is to be Japanese in a way that would allow us to become Japanese ourselves. Perhaps it is through the artwork of a particular culture that we are most able to understand what it is like to be a member of that culture. Such a study will take us beyond clichés or stereotypes into the otherwise inexpressible core of a particular culture.

Mood

Fifth is mood, which we spoke about briefly in the section "What Is a Human Being?" In this model, which is based upon the work of Solomon (1983), I mean it in a slightly different way. I usually don't make any attempt to have my models be consistent with one another. If they were, it probably would be possible to collapse the models down into one and a coach would lose the power of assessing the client from various perspectives simultaneously. It seems to me that it is the job of a coach to understand the client in more and more ways rather than in fewer ways, even if fewer ways would be simpler for the coach.

Mood is the semipermanent emotional tone within which a person exists. It gives meaning to present circumstances, defines our engagement in them, and colors our view of the future as well. In this discussion, I will speak about three aspects of mood: the judgment that is the basis for the mood, the actions that are consistent with the judgment, and finally, how the mood maintains our self-esteem. In some cases the maintenance of self-esteem may seem strange, but we human beings are always attempting to find ways of making sense of what we encounter, giving ourselves a sense of power when circumstantially we have none, and maintaining our sense of dignity even when, outside of the internal logic of the mood, none of it makes sense.

Understanding a mood, then, is similar to understanding a person. The task is to understand the mood on its own terms and not fall into dictating what it ought to be or must be. I'll give some examples of moods that are quite prevalent in business and are difficult to deal with. Some readers may find these moods too negative. I'm not claiming that they are the only moods present in business, but they are present enough to be used as examples to illustrate how mood works.

I've divided this set of moods into two parts, the moods of people who feel as if they are superior to others and the moods of people who feel as if they are inferior to others. Of course, there is the paradox that people feel as if they are inferior because they are asserting their inferiority in order to feel superior. Some people have also told me in discussions about these moods that people who assume superior moods are really attempting to make up for an inner sense of inferiority. To keep things simple though, and to be able to present it in a book, I'm going to maintain the distinctions of superior and inferior in this discussion.

Superior Moods

Skepticism

The judgment is "I doubt." In healthy cases it ends there. In more pathological cases it becomes insatiable doubt. There has been a strong movement in philosophy called skepticism. David Hume is perhaps the strongest proponent of this view. Philosophers following him have never been fully able to successfully refute his contentions, so nowadays, most philosophers don't try. Perhaps nonphilosophical skeptics know in some way that there cannot be a final absolute answer to any question and that by continuing to ask they will keep their opponents off balance.

The behavior is to question. Skepticism maintains self-esteem by disguising itself as sophistication. I call it pseudosophistication. Skeptics take themselves as experienced, knowledgeable, or seasoned, and attempt to inform others of these qualities by the number of, and insightfulness of, their questions. Is there any reader who has not encountered a skeptic? If so, I would be surprised.

Here are some examples of professions, roles, historical figures, or famous people who stereotypically embody skepticism: newspaper reporters (at least starting out, later they move to cynicism), scientists, parents of teenage children, accountants reviewing expense reports, IRS auditors, purchasing agents, bartenders on Wall Street, police officers, and high school principals.

Cynicism

Cynicism is the judgment that no one and nothing is worthy of respect. Cynicism is harsher than skepticism in that cynics make judgments about the person, not just the information he is providing. The behavior of cynics is to insult, disparage, and put down everyone.

Cynics do not exclude themselves from their own judgment. You'll recognize cynics because they say things like, "Well, yes, he does look good on the outside, but we all know that on the inside he is out to crush everyone who gets in his way, just like all of us."

Cynics maintain self-esteem the same way skeptics do, that is, by taking their cynicism as sophistication. The capital of cynicism in the United States is Washington, D.C. Being close to the government and hearing the promises of administrations being made, Washingtonians see the promises unfulfilled time after time and conclude that none of these political types is worthy of respect.

Cynics are always looking for the secret motivation behind even the most laudable actions. No one is good enough for a cynic. Human foibles of any size are enough evidence for a cynic to convict anyone of being guilty of a crime, which necessitates the cynic's withdrawing of respect.

Here are some examples of cynics: older newspaper reporters, Mark Twain, Sinclair Lewis, William Faulkner, many political consultants (e.g., Lee Atwater), people involved in organized crime, strident promoters of laissez-faire capitalism, the character portrayed by Michael Douglas in *Wall Street*, many of the movies of Scorcese (e.g., *Goodfellows*), the editors of many supermarket tabloids, and anyone who attempts to make a living by exploiting the weaknesses of others. This includes some people in management as well as some of the more obvious examples like drug dealers and bookies.

Resignation

This is the judgment that "nothing new is possible for me." The behavior of resigned people is to withhold commitment and to stake out a small, controllable territory in which to become very comfortable. Many times resigned people can be initially deceiving, because their resignation is covered up by a thin veneer of optimism. The veneer falls away, though, when a resigned person is asked to take action that can result in an observable outcome measured by some degree of change. At this point the resigned person will find many ways to show why the change is not necessary and may, in fact, be harmful, or may find a more politically powerful ally to make sure the action won't occur. Of course, no one in an organization can say that he or she is resigned, so the maneuvering and withholding of support is done underground, but the consequences are nonetheless real.

Resignation maintains self-esteem by posing as pseudowisdom, that is, wisdom that sees justification only for everything to continue as it has. Resigned people think of themselves as having profound understanding based upon firsthand, long-term experience. They forget that it's often because of their own resignation that the change effort of others or even themselves is thwarted. Besides, changing is uncomfortable and uncertain. What has happened up until now is familiar, comfortable, predictable, and controllable. Any of you who has ever attempted to bring about change in an organization or a relationship probably has encountered some resignation. What to do about it, I don't know. I've given up. Just kidding.

Here are some examples of resignation: Chekhov, Kafka, many people involved in large bureaucratic organizations, postal workers, factory workers, and people who work for the federal government.

Inferior Moods

Frustration

Frustration is the judgment that "I must make something happen and I cannot make it happen." The commitment is one that I cannot walk away from and the circumstances make it impossible, as far as I can tell, to fulfill the commitment.

A physician working in an inner-city emergency room where people sometimes die while they're waiting for treatment is a good example of frustration. The physician cannot just walk away from the seemingly endless parade of wounded and drug-ridden bodies and, at the same time, she doesn't seem to have any power to provide quick and sufficient care for the hordes of people waiting, or any power to affect the system that keeps people cycling through the emergency room.

Dedicated workers in large corporations who are attempting to bring about major change often find themselves frustrated. In fact, I would say that much of the good work done in organizations is done by people who are frustrated. That's because the behavior characterized by frustration is to work very hard, and to complain about the hard work and the circumstances that make success seemingly impossible, but, like Sisyphus, to never give up. Frustrated people are not going to let the circumstances of the system beat them. They keep going, sometimes to burnout and beyond.

Here are some examples of frustration: Wile E. Coyote, the Oliver Sachs character in the movie *Awakenings*, the mayors of major U.S. cities, teachers in public school systems, and the coach of the Chicago Cubs.

Resentment

Resentment is the judgment that "something unfair has been done to me deliberately by someone else and I have no power to do anything about it." The judgment of powerlessness is what gives resentment its unique character, because someone in the same circumstances who judged that he has power would instead be in a mood of anger.

The behavior of resentful people is to put distance between themselves and the object of their resentment and then to begin to plot covert revenge—also known as sabotage. Angry people, on the other hand, seek a confrontation with the object of their anger and plan to get justice in a face-to-face encounter.

The sabotage of resentful people can be shown in many different ways, including many of the passive-aggressive behavior patterns that show up in business, for example, forgetting meetings, slowing work to a near crawl, misplacing files, and spreading negative gossip.

The emotional distance that is part of resentment is also easy to observe; often it takes the form of a precise, brittle politeness or a coldness that is reminiscent of stepping into the Arctic Ocean. Given that the resentful person does not seek to bridge the distance, many times the person being resented is at a loss to explain or understand the emotional distance. Often, attempting to uncover it only increases the distance, which can be readily covered up by denial and by projecting the distance-making activity onto the person being resented. Resentful people are avengers for justice. This is how the mood maintains self-esteem. Even if it takes a thousand years, the resenter will make sure that justice wins out.

Here are some examples of resentment: the daughters in Shakespeare's *King Lear* and Shylock in *The Merchant of Venice*.

Guilt

The all-American mood, guilt, is last in our listing. I call it the all-American mood because American culture is a particularly fertile environment for guilt. Guilt is the judgment that "I have done something to injure someone and I can never make up for it."

The behavior of guilty people has three parts. First is apologizing a lot. Guilty people will apologize about the intemperance of the weather, traffic jams, and the high prices in stores. Second, guilty people work really hard to try to make up for what they did, saying things like, "I feel so terrible about making an addition mistake on page 312 of the budget. This year I will give up my vacation, send my children to childcare, and set up a cot in the accounting office to make sure that I don't make any mistakes this time." Last of the actions of guilty people is emotionally punishing themselves. How much? As much as is possible this side of death, because death would preclude the possibility of further punishment.

In the United States, guilt takes on at least three different forms that I know of. There is guilt that has to do with relationships—"I gave up all of my life to send you to college and this is how you treat me. You never call or visit. What kind of a son are you anyway?" There is guilt that has to do with sex—it's a sin to think about it, it's a sin to plan it, it's a sin to do it, and it's a sin to remember doing it. There is guilt that has to do with work—"I'm so sorry, dear, that I have to leave you while you're giving birth to our first child, but there are some really important reports I have to get out of the office," and "Sorry to leave Thanksgiving dinner, but I really must check up on my voice mail."

Why would anyone take on this mood when it seems so painful? Well, first of all, guilt gives people a false sense of agency. Feeling bad about something that has happened gives a guilty person the sense that he or she could have done something about it. Thus, the secret service agent assigned to protect John Kennedy still feels guilty because he feels as if he could have been one second faster and saved the president's life. The examples above of people apologizing for weather, traffic, and prices are another variation on this theme of false agency.

Guilty people are also the most self-righteous people. "I know I did it, but at least I feel bad about it. There are lots of other jerks doing it and not even feeling bad about it." You can be assured then that the people who are acting the most self-righteous are simultaneously feeling the most guilty.

Here are some examples of guilt: Oedipus, Hawthorne's Hester Prynn and the minister in *The Scarlet Letter*, and St. Augustine.

MODEL TWO: DOMAINS OF COMPETENCE

This model (see Figure 6.2) is based upon the work of Habermas, although he might not recognize it. Its premise is that in order to accomplish anything of

FIGURE 6.2   Domains of Competence

substance, we must be minimally competent in each of the three domains depicted in the pyramid. Each of the domains requires a different kind of thinking and, consequently, different people will gravitate toward different domains.

I'll begin talking about these domains by first explaining the bottom one, *Self-Management*. Self-management occupies the foundation position for the pyramid because it is the basis for the others, but please do not think that because it is the most important it is the only domain in which we ought to become competent.

Self-management means that we follow through on what we said we would do, we arrive on time, we understand the standard practices of the organization for which we are working, we present ourselves and our ideas appropriately, and we don't allow any personal issues or concerns to impinge on what we said we would do.

The skill of self-management is based upon our ability to observe ourselves and the effects of our actions on the outcomes we intend and on the people with whom we relate.

Although they are often confused, self-management is distinct from self-justification, which is the story we tell ourselves and others when we don't accomplish what we said we would. In fact, people who are skillful in self-management can readily sense any iota of self-justification creeping into their thoughts or into their conversations and delete it forthwith.

Here's a list of the qualities and skills of self-management:

- *qualities*: vision, passion, integrity, trust, curiosity, daring
- *skills*: self-observation, self-knowledge, self-management, self-remembering, self-consistency

The middle third of the pyramid is labeled *Relationships with Others* and refers to our capacity to develop and maintain long-term, mutually satisfying relationships. Most readers probably understand that it's only through this capacity that we have any chance of being successful in any organization. It is not possible for any person, regardless of his capacity for work, to do everything, and it is always the case that any one person's thinking is limited.

The essence of successful relationships is openness and appreciation. By openness, I mean allowing ourselves to be influenced by the ideas, emotions, and world of a person with whom we are relating.

For those of us who are saying to ourselves that this excludes most of our relationships, I wonder what these relationships are like. Are we positioning ourselves as heroes in the relationship, as the ones who have all the wisdom, as total givers and providers? If we are relating in this way, it's very easy to slip into a mood of arrogance so that we are no longer really relating at all, but only proclaiming our own notions and building our own empire. You've probably noticed people around you doing this and, even if they are in positions of apparently irresistible power, they are generating an environment of resentment around themselves that makes their work more difficult than it has to be and less effective than it could be.

Appreciation means that we understand the validity of other people's worldviews and take it on as our task to see to it that there is a forum for the expression of those worldviews, if only in our own relationship with those people. Appreciation means that we are not trying to bring the other person around to our way of seeing it, or letting him in on how it really is according to us, or trying to get him to do what we want him to do.

For example, those of you who have children can clearly see that children under age seven live in their own world which is only tangentially connected to the adult world in which most of the readers of this book live. When we attempt to take apart our child's world with the norms, logic, and customs of the adult world, we are in fact damaging our relationship with that child. We don't have to worry; life will soon enough present its constraints to our child. There's no need to do it preemptively, even if that was done to us by our parents.

Dealing with the world of relationships means that in order to be successful we have to learn about emotions as well. Emotions are what bind us together. Attempting to have even the most professional relationships without emotion is like attempting to build a brick edifice without the use of any cement. It may stay for a while, but it will not hold up under pressure or when any significant force is applied to it.

Whenever we try to step out of the world of openness, appreciation, and emotion in our relationships with people, and attempt to speak with the language of one of the other domains of competence, we are ensuring the demise of the relationship. A sure sign that we are doing this is when we attempt to be right in an argument rather than trying to understand.

Here's a list of qualities and skills of relationships with others:

- *qualities*: empathy, reliability, openness, optimism, faith
- *skills*: listening (teamwork, real concerns), speaking (possibilities, inspiration), setting standards (developing others), learning, innovating

The third layer of the pyramid is called *Facts and Events* and refers to our capacity to understand mechanisms, processes, statistics, systems, and models. This is the layer with both the most experts within it and the most fear attached to it. There are many of us who don't want to enter this domain at all and wish the experts would just handle it all for us.

The problem is that if we don't have a rudimentary understanding of the domain, we can't understand the decisions being made on our behalf and we will have a difficult time in our attempts to improve the systems and organizations of which we are a part.

On the other hand, some people of high technical expertise attempt to ignore the other two domains of competence. Sometimes this works if the expertise is vital and present in only a few individuals. The expertise, however, may become less valued and, given that this expert has not developed relationships successfully or managed himself very well, there will be very little chance of him finding a place within the organization at that time.

Here's a list of the qualities and skills of facts and events:

- *qualities*: rigor, objectivity, persistence, creativity, focus
- *skills*: analyzing (inhibiting factors, sources), predicting (long- and short-term effects), simplifying (Occam's razor), building models, organize/prioritize/release

Sometimes strength in one domain is used to try to cover up a weakness in another domain. For example, some people try to have relationships or justify not having them by insisting that other people maintain the same values and standards as they themselves have. This is an attempt to have relationships work by using one's capacity within the self-management domain.

We probably all have met people who are charming and politically sensitive who acquire positions of authority and prestige because of their ability to succeed in the relationship domain. Such people will try to avoid making specific promises because they are weak in self-management and will call on others to take care of any technical situation that arises in the domain of facts and events. But can these people deal with the sometimes harsh facts and events that present themselves? And can they sit down and do the long, tough, sometimes boring work required to really learn something of value?

By attempting to steer the world from within only one of the domains, we will minimize our chance of success and will make what was once our strength into a blindness that many times leads to dismal failure.

MODEL THREE: COMPONENTS OF SATISFACTION AND EFFECTIVENESS

In a way, this is the simplest model (see Figure 6.3). It is a listing of the competencies necessary to be both satisfied and effective. They are specific to the area in which we are working so that intelligence, for example, in fixing a car engine is not the same as intelligence in playing the violin or baking a soufflé.

The so-called intelligence quotient test that many of us took as children measured very specific types of intelligence that have to do with, it seems to me, success in a very narrow band of activities. I wonder how someone whose intelligence was in choreographing beautiful ballets would do on a standard I.Q. test?

You can use my definitions of these competencies when observing coaching clients, when assessing where breakdowns are occurring or are likely to occur for a specific person, or when determining what the subject of a coaching program could be.

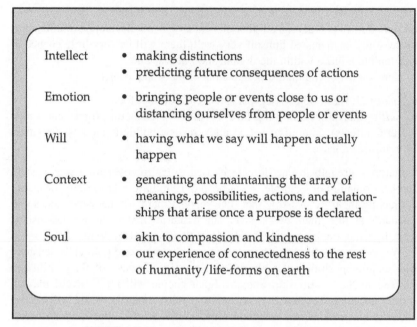

Intellect	• making distinctions
	• predicting future consequences of actions
Emotion	• bringing people or events close to us or distancing ourselves from people or events
Will	• having what we say will happen actually happen
Context	• generating and maintaining the array of meanings, possibilities, actions, and relationships that arise once a purpose is declared
Soul	• akin to compassion and kindness
	• our experience of connectedness to the rest of humanity/life-forms on earth

FIGURE 6.3   Components of Satisfaction and Effectiveness

Intellect

By intellect, I mean the capacity to make distinctions and predict the future consequences of actions. That is to say, someone can see that if one course of action is taken today, six months from now such-and-such an outcome will occur. This description attempts to include both people who build logical step-by-step processes leading to conclusions and people who make intuitive leaps that can also turn out to be accurate. I'm also attempting to describe intellect in the most general way without trying to describe the various processes that go into the capacity. For example, knowing many distinctions is a product of learning, and predicting future consequences of action has a lot to do with understanding the interconnectedness of systems. In any case, regardless of the origin, someone who is strong in intellect will have the two capacities mentioned.

Emotion

Emotion here means something very different from our usual understanding of the term. In this model, emotion means the capacity to bring people and events close to us when appropriate and to distance ourselves from people and events when appropriate. It's this telescoping ability that I'm referring to as competence in emotion. Some people have what I call fixed emotional distance. That is, they may hold everything very close to themselves, thus diminishing any sense of perspective, or they may view even the most intimate experiences of life from a great emotional distance and are not touched by birth, death, or love. In business, sometimes it seems as if the latter emotional distance is the one that is most fitting. It leads, however, to a draining of interest in any topic, the inability to inspire anyone else, and in the end, a weakening of resolve.

Will

By will, I mean the capacity to make what we intend to happen actually happen. People of extraordinary will, of course, can have their will seemingly exist in other people and sometimes even at a great distance. Founders of the world's great religions are the epitome of this. None of them is on earth now and yet millions of people are still following through on what each one intended to have happen.

Context

Context is the ability to build and maintain context. Yes, I know this is tauto-logical, but let me tell you what I mean by context. I mean the array of meanings, relationships, actions, and possibilities that arise once a purpose is declared. Purpose is our dedication to the fulfillment of people and causes beyond our own survival and comfort and the survival and comfort of our families.

For example, once I say that my purpose is to improve education for children in my city, I immediately have a different meaning for my own education—backward and forward in time—a different relationship with students, parents, teachers, administrators, and a whole long list of potential actions and new possibilities that I can address.

Our capacity to design a purpose and then bring our own life into alignment with it is what I mean by context. In my definition, context is never a given; it is generated by individual people. And because of that it is often a missing component in people's lives. In fact, many of us never even speak about what our purpose could be and instead work only on coping with day-to-day situations. This lack of context, moreover, becomes readily apparent in moments of crisis when we don't have any criteria by which to make decisions or when we are in an ethical dilemma and don't know what to do. It becomes most ines-capable as we near or face our own death.

Soul

Soul is the last competency listed in this model. First of all, I don't presume to precisely define what I mean by soul, but it's something like kindness, generosity, compassion, and connectedness to the rest of humanity. I'm trying to point to that quality in people who have what we call great souls.

This element is the one least likely to show up in performance reviews and, at the same time, it's the one we find most inspiring, powerful, and admirable.

In business, it's been the case up until now that people have been able to get by because they have had strong intellect and strong will—the same qualities, by the way, that have long been developed by the military. Living life stressing only these two elements has big consequences—one of them being that the game, which is all-consuming while being played, immediately becomes pointless as soon as we step away from it. Many workers experience this during long vacations or shortly after retiring. Also, stressing will and intellect presupposes a fixed emotional distance which leads to much separation between such a person and family, friends, and colleagues. See the movie *The Man in the Grey Flannel Suit* for a graphic example of this. Developing our capacity in all five of these elements will make us more able to do our work and will also give us a greater sense of fulfillment while doing it.

USING THESE MODELS

It seems common sense to me that we find something only when we are looking for it. For example, we don't notice how many red Hondas we've passed on a particular day's drive unless we are setting out to count them. It's not that our intent to observe brings the cars into existence, it is rather experientially the case that the cars aren't there for us until we intentionally direct our attention toward them.

The point of having presented these assessment models is to allow the reader to make observations with them in mind. When we begin to observe differently, new horizons of possibility begin to arise. In terms of coaching, this means that we discover new, powerful explanations for behavior and, more importantly, new openings for coaching interventions. I have often seen coaches dumbfounded because the models of observation they were using could not adequately account for the behavior they were observing, or made it seem impossible for any intervention to occur. For example, some coaches will say, "Well, there's nothing I can do until he gets himself motivated," or "Nothing can be done; she just doesn't have it." Almost always I have observed in these situations that the coach only understood the client as some kind of extension of the coach, which means that unless the client saw things and did things the same way the coach did, the client remained an impenetrable enigma. In such cases, I recommend that coaches employ another model, speak with a third party, or at least recognize the limitation of their own interpretation and not insist that their own understanding is complete, and consequently there must be something wrong with the client. You can imagine your own frustration if you visited a physician who could not adequately diagnose and prescribe for an ailment you suffered from and instead wrote you off as an insoluble case, a hypochondriac, or a malingerer. None of these conclusions would assist you in becoming healthy. I am sure we would hope that a physician who found himself in this situation would do additional research, call in someone with greater expertise, or interview us at greater length in order to find additional clues to the resolution of our ailment.

In a similar way, as coaches we must not let initial confusion or frustration prevent us from coming to a complete enough understanding of our client for coaching to begin. Here are some practical ways you can go about using the models presented to understand your clients.

Principles of Observation

1. Observe your client in a variety of situations, if possible. This will give you the chance to begin to notice behavioral and speech patterns. If our observations are limited to a narrow band of activity or to a single event, we won't be able to assess the degree of flexibility in our client's response.
2. Prepare yourself for observation by reviewing the assessment models and resist the temptation to make conclusions based on memory rather than on real-time observations.
3. Ask questions of your client in order to reveal more of her structural interpretation but not to verify the assessments you've made. For example, if you've observed a negative mood in your client, I urge you not to ask a question such as, "Don't you think your mood is cynical?" because that question will almost invariably lead to a defensive response from your client. Instead ask a question that could clarify whether or not the judgment you assume your client is making is the actual judgment she made. For example, with the client who you are assuming is cynical, you could ask, "It seems to me that you are not going to let those folks we just met with pull the wool over your eyes. Is that right?" If the client answers yes, that gives you more data with which you can verify your preliminary assessment, that some degree of cynicism is likely present.
4. Evaluate the validity of your assessment by using it to explain the behavior you've observed. Predict future actions, provide an opening for your coaching intervention, while simultaneously maintaining a dignified, respectful relationship with the client.
5. Always keep your assessments open for reevaluation and keep reminding yourself that there's much about your client that will continue to remain mysterious. The mysterious unknown and perhaps unknowable aspects of your client are what allow for change, improvement, and even transformation.

APPLICATIONS OF THE MODELS TO OUR CASE

To further clarify my explanation of these models, I will apply them to the case study we have been following.

Model One: Five Elements Model

Immediate Concerns

Bob's immediate concerns were different at each of our meetings. Sometimes he was experiencing the pressure of deadlines. Sometimes he was distracted by the preparation he needed to do for a big presentation. At other times, his immediate concern was whether he could get home in time to watch his son play Little League baseball. We ought never assume that we know what someone's immediate concerns are, but rather we should ask.

Commitments

Bob was committed to his wife, his two children, and their safety and well-being. He was also committed to the success of his team at work and the overall success of the company. He also was committed to his exercise program and his participation in his church.

Future Possibilities

The possibility that Bob saw most clearly was that he be promoted to an executive level so that he could enjoy the security and financial rewards of that position. He also was dedicated to the possibility of his children having the opportunity to attend college, travel, and be launched into the adult world. He saw his life beyond his work career as retirement in a warm-weather environment where he would have access to many outdoor activities.

Personal and Cultural History

Bob grew up in southern California, went to UCLA, and got his degree in accounting. He had been married for 15 years and had an 11-year-old son and a 7-year-old daughter.

Mood

For the most part, Bob found himself in the mood of frustration. He really wanted to be promoted but he couldn't figure out how to make that happen and he wasn't willing to give up.

Model Two: Domains of Competence

Self-Management

This was a very strong suit for Bob. He was clear about where he wanted to go and was disciplined in his approach. He was reliable, did quality work, and could be counted on to be a steady influence during crisis. He was organized and prepared himself well for meetings.

Relationships with Others

From everything I have said so far you can probably tell that this is where Bob needed the most development. He had to expand his ability to understand the varying concerns of the people around him. He had to find ways to communicate in a convincing way to people above him in the organization and he had to learn to become more competent in dealing with the political forces at play within his organization.

Facts and Events

By any standard Bob was an expert in his field. He had graduated at the top of his class and kept current by reading appropriate journal articles, speaking with others in his field, and occasionally attending seminars. He could quickly read through financial statements and determine the soundness of what was presented and what additional research had to be done. In everything that I could find out, no one had ever complained about the accuracy of his final reports.

Model Three: Components of Satisfaction and Effectiveness

Intellect

Bob had a strong intellect in accounting but had weaker intellectual capacity in relationships. He was not very sensitive to nuances of meaning, subtle emotional cues, or to the unspoken threads of meaning lying just beneath what was being said.

Emotion

Bob was very good at keeping an objective distance when conducting his financial research and writing his financial reports. However, he did not show a similar objectivity in assessing his own performance in relationships at work. In this realm he was more easily offended, was often off balance, and sometimes had difficulty in recovering after a real or imagined insult.

Will

Bob had a very strong will. He continuously demonstrated great determination in what was important to him. As I said earlier, he put himself
through school and got his advanced degrees and certifications while
maintaining a full-time job.

Context

Bob had never, previous to our coaching, had a serious conversation about
context. The closest approximation was some unfocused ideas about his
purpose in life which he had picked up from church and from reading
some inspirational biographies.

Soul

Kindness and compassion were very important to Bob and on many
occasions he wouldn't take actions when he felt they violated these two
values. Intellectually he understood his connection to everyone else but this
was not real for him as a feeling or an experience.

SUGGESTED READING

The more profoundly and systematically we understand someone, the more
effective and lasting our coaching can be. The listed texts propose many
different models. All are helpful—none alone is the answer.

Brown, Daniel P., Jack Engler, and Ken Wilber. *Transformations of Consciousness*. Boston:
    Shambhala Publications, 1986.
    *A compilation of essays in transpersonal psychology, a discipline dedicated to unifying
    Western and Eastern (hemispheres, not New York and San Francisco) traditions of human
    healing and transformation. Especially helpful are the three chapters by Wilber outlining his
    model for the stages of individual human transformation. His model includes the essential
    issues for each stage and helpful interventions for each. Provides a coach with many ways to
    understand the pain and possibilities of particular clients who may be quite different from him
    or herself.*
Dinnerstein, Dorothy. *The Mermaid and the Minotaur*. New York: Harper & Row, 1976.
    *The author delves deeply into how the roles assigned to women and men in our culture lead to
    profound suffering. Challenging. Often irresistible in its argumentation.*
Dreyfus, Hubert L., and Stuart E. Dreyfus. *Mind over Machine*. New York: Macmillan, Inc., 1986.
    *A book about the limits of computers that sheds light on how people learn. Especially useful
    distinctions regarding the stages of competence.*
Durrell, Lawrence. *Justine*. Vol. 1 of *The Alexandria Quartet*. New York: E. P. Dutton, 1957.
    *A sensuous series of four books telling the same tale from four perspectives. An unforgettable
    experience of the seduction and pervasiveness of interpretation. Wonderfully written. A novel,
    not an explanation.*

—. *Balthazar.* Vol. 2 of *The Alexandria Quartet.* New York: E. P. Dutton, 1958.

—. *Mount Olive.* Vol. 3 of *The Alexandria Quartet.* New York: E. P. Dutton, 1958.

—. *Clea.* Vol. 4 of *The Alexandria Quartet.* New York: E. P. Dutton, 1960.

Eliot, George. *Middlemarch.* New York: The New American Library, 1964.

The author shows her brilliant understanding of human life by creating many unforgettable characters. An incredibly moving story of loyalty and integrity.

Erikson, Erik H. *Childhood and Society.* New York: W. W. Norton & Company, 1950; reprint, 1985.

How does a culture ensure that children will be prepared to fill the roles of adults? Erikson addresses that question and presents many insights into the forces underlying behavior, including a well-known listing of stages of psychological growth. Fascinating and useful.

—. *The Life Cycle Completed.* New York: W. W. Norton & Company, 1985.

A pithy summary of Erikson's life work. Captures in two charts his decades of research and experience in how a human life unfolds, develops pathologies, evolves, and completes. Brilliant and elegant.

Goffman, Erving. *The Presentation of Self in Everyday Life.* New York: Anchor Books/Doubleday, 1959.

The way you observe will be altered by reading this sociological tract, which studies signs and artifacts for the notions of self that underlie them.

Goleman, Daniel. *Destructive Emotions: A Scientific Dialogue with the Dalai Lama.* New York: Bantam Books, 2003.

Presentation of a comprehensive dialogue on the topic between important researchers and teachers from the Eastern and Western traditions. Cogent. Insightful. Worthy of thorough study.

—. *Emotional Intelligence.* New York: Bantam Books, 1995.

A book of colossal importance. Makes the case for bringing the study of emotions into the workplace and into our schools. Clearly written. Well grounded. Vital for all coaches to read.

Harré, Rom. *Personal Being.* Cambridge, MA: Harvard University Press, 1984.

A learned text that proposes understanding people as the intersection of many conversations, some public, some private. A starting place for appreciating the way language individually shapes human beings.

Heidegger, Martin. *The Basic Problems of Phenomenology.* Translated by Albert Hofstadter. Bloomington, IN: Indiana University Press, 1982.

Probably the problems won't seem basic to you, but Heidegger forms his text as a response to the founding issues of Western philosophy (he calls them the basic problems). A closer and more expansive presentation of the ideas in Being and Time.

Keen, Sam. *The Passionate Life.* San Francisco: Harper & Row, 1983.

The author proposes understanding life as a series of roles/stages that form around our relationship to love and eros. Very accessible and liberating.

Keleman, Stanley. *Emotional Anatomy.* Berkeley, CA: Center Press, 1985.

The author proposes that with education, an observer can comprehend the emotional life of an individual by studying his body. Full of dramatic illustrations. Important competence for any coach. (See also Kurtz and Prestera, The Body Reveals.*)*

Kroeger, Otto, and Janet M. Thuesen. *Type Talk.* New York: Dell Publishing, 1988.

A popular introduction to the nearly ubiquitous (in business) Myers-Briggs method for understanding individual preferences and tendencies.

Kurtz, Ron, and Hector Prestera. *The Body Reveals.* New York: Harper & Row, 1976.

A handbook full of examples and illustrations that argues that an observer can determine the core issues of someone by assessing his body with a particular set of distinctions. A vital text for any coach who doesn't want to be fooled by what people say about themselves. (See also Keleman, Emotional Anatomy.*)*

Miller, Alice. *The Drama of the Gifted Child.* Translated by Hildegarde and Hunter Hannum. New York: Farrar, Straus, Giroux, 1983. (Originally published as *Prisoners of Childhood.* Frankfurt am Main, Germany: Suhrkamp Verlag, 1979.)

The author, noted in the field of childhood development and trauma, explains the roots of narcissism and depression, perhaps the two most prevalent emotional disorders in U.S. culture today. A small gem.

—. *For Your Own Good.* Translated by Ruth Ward. New York: Basic Books, Inc./HarperCollins, 1992.

Violence is taught. Young children (and their bodies) are the students, misguided adults are the teachers. The subtitle says it all: "Hidden Cruelty in Child-Rearing and the Roots of Violence." Disturbing and convincing.

Schutz, Alfred, and Thomas Luckmann. *The Structures of the Life-World.* Evanston, IL: Northwestern University Press, 1973.

A rigorous, phenomenological examination of the origin and continuation of the structure of everyday experience. Closely argued. Written for a professional (philosophical) audience.

Solomon, Robert C. *The Passions.* Notre Dame, IN: University of Notre Dame Press, 1983.

The author claims that emotions are judgments that we make, not mysterious forces that overtake us. Provides an extensive background for understanding his assertions and an encyclopedic listing of emotions from A to Z. The last section presents many common self-defense mechanisms. Belongs on (or near) the desk of every working coach.

Wilber, Ken. *The Atman Project.* Wheaton, IL: Quest, 1980.

A detailed survey of the stages of psychological and spiritual growth. Cross-references Western psychological and psychoanalytical models with Eastern spiritual traditions. Comprehensive and exhaustive. Huge bibliography.

—. *No Boundary.* Boston: Shambhala Publications, 1979.

A short, elegant text that quickly gets to the nub of human suffering and proposes many practical ways to deal with it. Lucid and friendly.

7

How Things Really Get Done

Things move in the human world when someone speaks. Our attention and energy become focused as we respond to requests we hear and possibilities we see. The entire social world of humanity is brought forth, sustained, and forwarded by conversations. Coaching itself is a blending of different types of conversations. Upon examination, it becomes clear that a huge number of coaching topics that clients bring us are resolvable by their entering into conversations that would resolve conflict, build alliances, and open up opportunities. This chapter crystallizes the last 50 years of study of the kind of speaking that moves things forward. Learning how all of these works is an essential skill for coaches and for anyone else who lives or works with people; obviously, that means all of us.

One of the amazing blindnesses of us humans is that we consider ourselves to be part of the mechanical world. Many of us really do believe that we are "driven" to do things, or that pressure is what brings about results in organizations. No amount of studying relationships, teams, or corporations in terms of mechanical effects will bring about any true lasting power. This chapter is about the competency that—when mastered—leaves us able to accomplish much more than ever before in a wide variety of circumstances.

SPEECH ACT THEORY

Here is a little background from where this way of working comes. In the 1950s, at Cambridge University, John Austin came to a simple and profound discovery. He saw that words, which up until then had been thought to be describers of the world, could function in another way as well. Words could perform, that is, they could make something happen by being spoken. For example, when we promise, we are not describing something but making it happen.

From this initial insight, much work has been done by Jürgen Habermas, Charles Taylor, John Searle, Fernando Flores, Chauncey Bell, Julio Olalla, Alan Sieler, and many others. The list of "speech acts"—ways of speaking that make something happen—now include promises, requests, offers, assertions, assessments, and declarations. These combine into conversations that explore possibilities, build relationships, and coordinate action: all the activities that are necessary for a business to succeed or for an individual to reach her goals. The more precise, fluent, and rigorous a speaker can be in employing these distinctions, the more she will be able to forge lasting accomplishments.

Principles of Communicative Action

Let's begin our study with some principles underlying the theory of communicative action.

- **Whenever someone speaks, she is bringing forth a type of commitment.**
  Here commitment means something that the speaker is willing to stand behind, be known for, and provide grounding for, as necessary.
- **The speech acts always occur in a particular language and community.**
  Any community shares a background of common custom and practice that provides the context in which the speaking makes sense. Outsiders never will be able to appreciate fully the nuances of what is being said, and a dictionary will only lead them in circles. For example, the words "beg" and "beseech" will look nearly identical when researched in the dictionary, but have a very different effect when employed within a community of people who speak English.
- **The speaking always reveals the speaker.**
  Her cares, concerns, commitments, and world are revealed every time she opens her mouth and says something. The selection of topics, the understanding of what is necessary to bring about outcomes, the network of supportive people involved, as well as personal history and mood of the speaker, always come forward in conversation. We cannot hide behind words. Even someone who imagines that she is reporting "objective facts" is in fact, in every case, selecting a subset of "facts" that she feels are relevant. The selection alone reveals her world of concern.
- **Speaking is not mechanical**
  It is never a matter of putting together a series of words to make a particular outcome occur. The same words spoken with a different emphasis, with different timing, to a different audience will bring about different outcomes. We all know this and are careful when we ask for something that is important for us to get. For example, pay attention when your children ask for the chance to stay over at a friend's house. They do it when you are in a good mood or showing particular affection towards them. In other words, to be effective, speakers must take into account the way they are being listened to.

This becomes a problem when, for example, we are preparing a presentation and don't know our audience. What questions or worries or historical background will they bring to what we are saying? When we don't know this, it makes it more likely that our presentation won't quite fit into what the audience is listening for.

You know this from your own experience. Have you ever walked into a meeting of biochemists and listened to what they are talking about? If you are not a scientist yourself, it may not have made sense, and what could have been most dumbfounding was the passion with which things that were incomprehensible to you were said.

Remember this the next time you get excited about something. It is not exciting in and of itself; it is the world that you are in and your own concerns that make it exciting. This might be quite clear in the moment when you are reading it but it is very different in the middle of a conversation or a meeting. As coaches, it is essential that we never dismiss something that is important to the client, even if we can't feel it ourselves.

• **Speaking and listening always arise simultaneously**.
  One cannot exist without the other. If we study our experience closely, we can notice that when we are speaking, we are listening; and when we are listening, we are speaking to ourselves. (We are editorializing, making judgments, and coming to conclusions about what people are saying at the same time that we are listening to them.) Because these two phenomena cannot be separated, it is vital that speakers become very good listeners so that they can, in the midst of a conversation, shift the form, emphasis and content of what they are saying. As listeners, it is very important that we begin to make note of what we are adding to what's been said to us. The quieter and the more impressionable we can be, the more we can receive and appreciate what is being said.

Moves in a Conversation

Although words and phrases appear in conversations, in order to study them it's important at first to take them out of that context and look at them, as it were, anatomically. It is the way a medical student would study a leg: as if it didn't have a hip attached and a knee attached. It is a good place to start but it is only a step along the way.

Each speech act has a different function. We will study each one in some detail. They are: *requests*, *promises*, *offers*, *assertions*, *assessments*, and *declarations*. All of these speech acts warrant years of study but here we will only be giving the barest of outlines that will still be sufficient for coaches to begin working with them. The bibliography at the end of the chapter can guide you to further study. After studying speech acts individually, we will show them in their more natural setting of conversations.

REQUESTS

Let's start by studying a request. Like all the conversational moves, a request is an utterance, which means it is a public event. Something only counts as a request if it is interpreted as such by a listener. Requests can be made verbally, in writing, electronically, through all kinds of body signals. However, wanting something fiercely in my own thinking doesn't make it a request until it enters a world shared by at least two people: me and someone else.

As with all the speech acts we'll study, a request is a type of commitment. A requester is committed to a very specific outcome being accomplished within a certain time. When we hear someone making sounds that could potentially be a request but without sufficient commitment, we don't take it seriously. You might see this at a public place like an airport when parents are asking their children to quiet down and the children go forth blithely with their activity. The same thing happens in meetings when someone asks us for a report, but we consider their request to be something they are doing pro forma and we don't ever take action on it.

Elements of a Request

With a background commitment in place, the following elements must arrive in the interpretation of the listener for the utterance to be considered a valid request.

1. **Speaker:**
   This perhaps seems obvious, but a request has to have a committed person who is making it, someone whom we can identify and bring our clarifying questions to. Too often managers hide behind sentences like, "Management requires you to arrive at meetings 10 minutes before the posted time." As a reader of this announcement, we don't know who is saying this, what the context is, what the importance of this request is in comparison to others that have been made, and so on. As you've noticed, this leads to quite a bit of mischief in the workplace and elsewhere.
2. **Listener:**
   Requests happen within a relationship. The minimum condition for this relationship is that the speaker and the listener speak a common language, or at least can somehow make sense of what each other is saying. An utterance (as I've already said) becomes a request *when it is interpreted as such by a listener.* A shout in Croatian made into a crowd in Tokyo probably won't be heard as a request even if the speaker formed it into one.

   I'm not making an esoteric point. How often in business does the marketing department make a request to the research department in a language that is not common to both, resulting in huge waste? At home, how frequently do parents imagine they've made a clear request to their teenage son, who hears it as whining or complaining by the adult?

We have not made a powerful request until we have a listener who has been moved to action by what we've said. Our own clarity is nice but alone is woefully inadequate to coordinate action.

3. **Future Action:**
   Requests can only be about the future. It makes no sense for me to say, "I invite you to have lunch with me yesterday." That point is obvious. What often gets missed is that a request has to be actionable; that is to say, the listener must be able to do something to fulfill what is being asked. Requests such as "Have this make sense to me," or "Do something to make me happy," really are not actionable requests, because there is not something that one can do to bring about clarity or happiness in someone else. Yes, we might be able to do something that moves the situation in that direction, but the fulfillment of the request will be an action taken by the requester, who will understand something or feel happy.

   You might be able to see from this point how much frustration occurs when a listener has taken away a request from the conversation and sees no action that can be taken to fulfill it. Some organizations and families insist that any request made from a boss or parent must somehow be filled by the subordinate or child, as if a position of authority gives the power to make someone else understand what to do, even in the case when the requester doesn't know what it is.

4. **Conditions for Satisfaction:**
   Embedded in every request is a promise that the requester makes that if the specified conditions are met, she will be satisfied. We alienate people when we refuse to be satisfied though our requests are fulfilled. Our dissatisfaction will shift our public identity and, after a while, people will avoid being in a conversation with us in which they may be asked to fulfill such a request. A lot of emotional turmoil within companies and families is around the unwillingness of requesters to be satisfied.

   Unfortunately, in our current culture, dissatisfaction is sometimes seen as a sign of sophistication or an unwillingness to compromise on high standards. Nonetheless, emotional/relational damage is done when we thwart the intention of others to satisfy what we are asking. Check this out for yourself the next time you ask your young child to bring you some water and they bring it to you in a less than pristine manner. How do you respond? What effect does your response have on the relationship? This same dynamic happens many times every day in the world of work. The mood of organizations is, for the most part, shaped by the willingness of superiors to be satisfied.

   Making a powerful request also requires us to clear about what we are asking for. It is one thing to have a conversation in which we are exploring possibilities, in which I might say, "Well, put a few things together, try it out, come back next week, and tell me what you have found out." It is quite another to say, "By this time next week, bring me a product that I will be really happy with." Being in a position of authority does not negate our job to make sure that the conditions of satisfaction in our request are discernable by the listener.

5. **Time:**
   In each request, the speaker specifies the time by which the request is to be fulfilled. Technically, time is a subset of the conditions of satisfaction but it so often gets left out that it is worthy of its elementary status. Time is usually best said as a date and time. Within certain contexts, either "right away" or "as soon as possible" might be sensible time requests; but in our complex day-to-day dealings, it is best to say precisely when we are asking for something to be accomplished so that the listener can give the request its proper response.

6. **Shared Background of Obviousness:**
   People in shared language communities share a huge background of obvious, "everybody knows" common sense that forms the background for all requests. It is impossible to specify every single tiny bit of a request (even though some government contracts attempt to do this). For example, when we ask a friend to bring us some water, we don't specify drinking water in a clean drinking glass. We would be shocked if they brought us muddy water in a teaspoon.

   The background of obviousness then is so huge and its knowledge so embedded in our everyday practices that it could never be fully articulated. Consequently, we have to understand the world of the listener sufficiently before we make a request. Perhaps you've made funny mistakes in ordering food in a country with a culture quite different from yours and you were surprised by what you were brought. I've seen many chagrined Americans sitting in cafés in Paris when they see what is brought to them after they've ordered "regular" coffee.

7. **Assumed Competence:**
   As a requester, we are assuming that the person to whom we are addressing our request is competent to fulfill it. We don't ask our three-year-old children to drive us to the airport or a new intern to do a heart transplant operation. Sometimes of course we don't know someone's competence until we make a request and notice its effect. The listener might become afraid or anxious or uneasy because she feels inadequate to fulfill it. Sometimes this discomfort is brought about by the listener's own self-doubt. Frequently, though, it is because we've asked someone to do something beyond her current capacity. Becoming more forceful at such moments is not helpful. You can yell as much as you want at someone who doesn't know how to do something. That does not suddenly build their skill, and emotional pressure can easily lead to big mistakes when people take on something way beyond their ability.

8. **Sincerity:**
   Even though we're not aware of it, whenever someone asks us to do something, we evaluate how serious the speaker is; especially when we are busy or jammed, we listen to determine how important the request is to the speaker. We're very unlikely to take something on if it seems trivial or procedural to the requester.

   This situation comes up a lot in organizations when someone who is not committed to an activity passes along its component actions to others. Even if the form of the request is in every other way perfect, if the speaker is not personally committed to the outcome, the listener will likely detect that and hold back her own full commitment. This little bit of insight may shed light on when you ask for something to be done and it doesn't get accomplished. After a while of being with someone, we can readily discern his level of commitment to what he is saying. A speaker who is merely going through the motions will find himself disappointed when the intended results are not achieved.

   This point around sincerity brings into relief an aspect of speaking that we rarely study. Even though many people think so, language is not a free-standing tool that we use to describe reality. Rather, in every case, language is the way we humans bring forth a shared world so that we can together coordinate actions and build the world together. Attempting to hide behind the meaning of words or construction of sentences will not be sufficient to camouflage the speaker. What we are up to is revealed every time we speak.

9. **Something Missing:**
   This refers to the obvious point that a request is always about something that is not currently present. We don't ask people to stand up if they are already standing. There is additional background to this element of the request. The something missing must be some type of activity or outcome that the speaker can bring forward. It's nonsensical to ask someone to have the sun come up earlier or for the tides to change their rhythm.

   Being able to specify precisely what's missing facilitates the listener in determining if she has the ability to fulfill the request, given her current level of skill and the other activities she is engaged in. Frequently, people in authority make very vague requests, such as, "Make sure that the deal turns out in a way that everyone involved is happy 10 years from now." When this kind of directive is given from someone of sufficient authority to someone who feels as if he must fulfill it, the exact "something" that must be provided for the request to be fulfilled remains unknown to everyone involved. As a consequence, many false starts will be attempted, timelines might be missed, and undoubtedly much waste of time, money, and other resources will occur.

10. **Token:**

   Token is a word taken from computer theory, and it means a method for the conveyance of the request. Verbal, written, electronic, somatic: all can be methods for making requests. This element reminds us that there has to be a phenomenon in the public shared world that can be pointed to as the conveyer of the request. Claiming that "you should have known" or "I should not have had to ask" are not helpful and probably point to the inadequate action that the speaker took or neglected to take.

   Yes, there are times when events are so frequently recurrent and so standardized that making a request around them is merely troublesome. But at the beginning of relationships or when an activity has special important or unique conditions, then it is important to make sure that we give a complete form to our request.

Intention someone has when they make it	For the specified results to be accomplished by someone else taking action
Implicit commitment speaker makes	First, to make the request comprehensible to the listener; second, to be satisfied when the results are achieved
Essential elements	Speaker Listener Future Action Conditions for Satisfaction Time Shared Background of Obviousness Assumed Competence Sincerity Something Missing Token
Examples	▪ "I ask that you have the report completed and sent to me on email by 5 PM on Friday." ▪ "I suggest that you redo the plan that you sent me so that the work can be accomplished by the 15th." ▪ "I invite you to go out to dinner with me on Friday night."

FIGURE 7.1   Summary of a request.

PROMISES

A promise is a speech act or an utterance in which the speaker commits himself to take actions as specified in a request. The elements of a promise are exactly the same as those of a request. The only difference is that in a promise, it is the speaker who goes into action to fulfill the request. A promise is not giving in to a request or going along with it, but it's a genuine, personal commitment to the actualization of the intention in the request. Roles, procedures, chains of command cannot make promises. Only individuals can. Bringing clarity to this point undoes much of the mischief and excuses around agreeing to do something and then not doing it. Of course, there has to be room in a request for the listener to say no. Otherwise, the situation is one of force or compliance and not of commitment. We will study this point more when we put these elements into an entire conversation.

Intention someone has when they make it	To address the mutual concerns shared with requestors; to address the concerns we share with other people
Implicit commitment speaker makes	To take all the necessary action, even if initially unknown, to fulfill the specified conditions
Essential elements	Speaker Listener Future Action Conditions for Satisfaction Time Shared Background of Obviousness Assumed Competence Sincerity Something Missing Token
Examples	▪ "I promise that I will keep the spending on the project within the allotted budget." ▪ "I assure you that the software will be ready to install by Monday morning at 9 a.m." ▪ "I will meet you at noon in the conference room to continue our conversation."

FIGURE 7.2   Summary of a promise.

OFFERS

Offers are speech acts that we use nearly every day. They blend promises and requests together. A simple example is when we make a business proposal. In it, we promise to take certain actions and bring about particular outcomes (this is the promise part) in exchange for monetary compensation that we specify (this is the request element).

Offers are important in coaching in several aspects. First, as coaches, it is important to be able to articulate what our offer is. In order to attract clients and build a business, we have to articulate what it is that we are promising to bring to the coaching engagement. Making these promises in generic or clichéd language does not show clients the unique experience and value they'll receive from working with us.

The area of offer is fertile because many coaches (in fact, many people) have extraordinary difficulty in saying in their own voice what they are providing—and, on the other hand, usually have even more challenge in formulating how much they will charge for their services. As you can no doubt readily see, issues of self-knowledge, clarity, knowledge of client interests, and issues of self-worth all play into the coach's ability to create their offer.

Working with offers is also important for our clients for many of the reasons stated above. Although many of our clients will not be entrepreneurs who must find a way to market themselves, they might instead be managers looking to be promoted, or single folks looking for relationships, and so on. The same constraints as mentioned above also appear here when people design their offer.

Beside the internal issues I listed above, knowing the interests of the person to whom we are making the offer is fundamental. This is not a simple matter of asking what people want. It's more a matter of feeling and observing into the world and matching breakdowns in people's lives with potential resolutions. The most famous offerings in the recent commercial space are equipment such as iPods, cell phones, GPS units, laptops, and Blackberries. Nobody at Apple Inc. went around and asked people if they had a need for carrying 15,000 songs with them wherever they went. The offer came more from a question like, if you were able to "X," would that be worth spending "Y" amount of money?

Fresh offers, in other words, open up new territory in which people can take action, connect to the world in a different way, and even establish a new identify for themselves. This last point becomes most clear in the offers of social networks where we can be known by different people, and even known differently with people we've had friendships with for a long time.

Perhaps you can tell from reading this that working with clients around offers resolves many, many coaching situations. Expanding on an example already given, when a client intends to be promoted, it is very powerful for her to put together in writing the offer that she is making. For example, what value, innovation, commitment, skills, resilience is she bringing to the current and future situation the enterprise will be in? How does this list fit with what the organization is looking for and values, and how does it open up thinking to what will be unfolding in the future? Employees are seen as extremely valuable when they are looking ahead to what difficulties and opportunities the organization will be having in the years ahead. When a client includes this in her offer, she seems to be extraordinarily desirable as a team member.

With that as background, it is often easier for the client to ask for compensation that is a meeting point between what they are bringing and what the organization is receiving. Instead of the amount of compensation being made up out of whole cloth, it has a sound basis in the whole package of skills, commitment, and thinking that the client had articulated.

A similar process can be initiated in any area where clients want something in the world that requires the cooperation and involvement of others. It is at this intersection of mutual needs and commitments that making skillful offers is most germane.

Intention someone has when they make it	To build or strengthen a partnership of mutual benefit
Implicit commitment speaker makes	To fulfill the promises made and to be satisfied with what is provided by others in the conversation, in compensation for the promised being fulfilled
Essential elements	All of the elements of a request and a promise
Examples	<ul><li>"I offer to paint the outside of your house the color you picked by Sunday night for $1,500."</li><li>"I will find a new VP of Operations for you by May 1st for a fee of $25,000."</li><li>"I'm glad to drop you off on the way to work if you can pick up the groceries for me on the way home."</li></ul>

FIGURE 7.3   Summary of an offer.

ASSERTIONS

Assertions do what most people think language itself does. Assertions are big pointers, bringing our attention to particular aspects of the world. In everyday parlance, assertions are called "facts." Today is Thursday; the temperature is 65 °F; we are in San Francisco. All are examples of assertions.

Assertions, though, do not escape being connected to individual people. As Humberto Maturana famously said, "Everything said is said by someone." This means that every time we make an assertion, we are making a personal commitment to provide the underpinnings for it. Assertions are embedded in the common world of practice and it's here that the grounding occurs. When I say, "Today is Thursday," I'm relying upon the English language and its grammar, as well as the historic practice of weeks and days. (Any assertion only makes sense within a particular community. "Today is Thursday," makes sense to contemporary English speakers, but it certainly wouldn't to people living in medieval Japan.) Assertions, then, are never freestanding and self-evident. They require an historically shaped context to be sensible.

Maturana's statement also points to that an individual person is behind every statement. The speaker is stating that something is the case and that if asked, he can provide good grounding, sensible reasons for making it. Historically this is what distinguished the front page of the newspaper from the editorial page. The front page had assertions that could be verified if questioned, and the editorial page showed the point of view of the writers who relied upon their own power of persuasion to make their case. Of course, in the last decade, this distinction in newspapers has been muddled so that it is very hard to tell these days what is fact, assertion, or opinion.

In the world of coaching, it is essential for coaches to be able to make assertions. We have to be able to make statements based upon observations that we've made so that our clients can see and deal with the grounding of what we say. Telling our client that she is an ineffective leader and then going on to say why—with a coherent listing of observations—can be a powerful coaching moment. If we don't have the grounding, however, we are left with our opinion only, which means the client will not have a chance to observe what it is to be an effective leader and will have to lean on us to tell how she is doing.

Making assertions is also a central activity in business. Being able to cite numbers, statistics, and research findings gives our speaking enormous, influential power. Reflect back upon when you've heard presentations that have had solid evidence beneath them as distinct from when you heard opinions, speculations, and hope. Which one made it more likely that you would take action?

This is not the time or place to get into epistemological discussions as to what constitutes truth or even what can be counted on as fact. It is sufficient for our purposes that a statement that holds up in a community of practice counts as a fact. A number that is accepted by a group of experienced, ethical accountants is an example of what I'm saying, as is the result of a medical test shown to an experienced faculty at a teaching hospital. Outside of these groups, so-called facts would be unintelligible. That doesn't mean that they don't count as true, but that the truth claim is always made by a person who is a competent speaker within a particular community.

Intention someone has when they make it	To accurately describe a phenomenon
Implicit commitment speaker makes	To provide any necessary factors or elements underlying the description, including the reasoning behind combining them to come to this description
Essential elements	Words in a shared vocabulary that point to conditions surrounding particular object, person, event, or circumstance
Examples	■ "The rock you brought in weighs 27 kilos and is comprised of 30% silicon, 60% iron, and 10% lead." ■ "The stock price closed in Tokyo today at $32.00." ■ "Your blood pressure is 125 over 75."

FIGURE 7.4   Summary of an assertion.

ASSESSMENTS

Like assertions, assessments are quite easy to describe and can be sticky in application. They are exactly what you would take them to be: a judgment of a particular state of affairs based upon criteria that are shared within a given community. Assessments are distinct from assertions because the judgment includes the desirability of the situation. For example, saying "it's a beautiful day" is an assessment, while the statement "it is 68 °F with clear skies" is an assertion.

You can probably see the difficulties people get into with assessments. Here are some of them:

We shrink them to only being an expression of my individual preferences. This means that instead of adopting criteria that are shared, I use only my own. So, if I assess that the book I am reading is a good one because it is heavy enough to hold down papers on my desk, almost no one else would embrace this assessment as sensible.

Like all speech acts, an assessment is a phenomena occurring in a shared public conversation. Consequently, in order to be understood and accepted, it must be stated in a way that fits the practices of the community. This is a tricky point: the public at large might think that a given guitar player is fantastic; but within the cadre of professional guitar players, she may be seen as flashy but derivative, not really bringing anything new to the field and, in fact, merely being fast.

Especially in the States, people feel that one assessment is as good as any other. We have call-in shows and news programs replete with email messages from people who are only saying whether they agree or whether they like what has happened. These speakers almost never have training to distinguish what makes something of high quality or not. Instead, they say whether they like it. Especially in the face of something new, our untutored view of something almost never says anything more than a statement about ourselves.

For example, when people go to a modern or contemporary art museum without having educated themselves about the artist, the work, or the history of art, they often spend their time making derisive comments or exclaiming, "Well, I could do that" (or "My kid can do better than that"). These comments are totally understandable, but in no way they are powerful assessments. Powerful assessments are those that carry the day in a decision-making process, or open up a new field of human activity, or bring a new appreciation to the world.

Let me attempt to make this point more clear. When almost any of us visit the Louvre, we would readily appreciate European painting from the fourteenth century to the nineteenth century. Without study, we would not know that many of the paintings that we call beautiful were severely criticized when they were first brought into public view. The work of Rembrandt, El Greco, Velázquez, Manet, and Monet are examples of this phenomenon.

Each time a new art was brought to the world, art critics and the public had to learn new criteria for assessing it. The appreciation came easier for those people who were conversant with the history of art and the problems artists were attempting to solve. Absent this background knowledge, it is as if people were coming into the middle of a conversation and hearing a few words and trying to make sense of what was being said in that brief snippet.

A work by Jackson Pollack is one of my favorite examples of what I'm trying to say here. If you've seen his paintings reproduced in books, they may appear as a bunch of random spills onto canvas. If you study his work in more depth, you will find out that he not only found a new way of doing painting; but also for the first time created works that are beautiful—go see them in person to verify what I'm saying here—without any inside or outside, any lines between parts of the canvas. Pollack solved an impossible conundrum: how to do painting without making any lines. On that level alone, his work is masterful; but as I've said, it is also amazingly captivating and beautiful when viewed personally.

To make an assessment, then, we must learn how to make observations based upon the vocabulary of the given discipline. Unless we do this, we have only an uninformed opinion, which is fine in conversations with our family or friends; but in coaching, in the world of business, or in other places where the sharpness of assessment is vital, our words will be worse than useless and in fact may be harmful.

I've been speaking about grounding, which means that the speaker has made a commitment to provide the criteria that he has used to come to his assessment. What we call "an expert" is someone who is well informed in the evaluation criteria in a given field of activity. This is a commonplace occurrence. All broadcast sporting events have an expert who on the spot can say whether something was a good dive, a good throw, or a good shot. Their speaking is based upon being able to observe with the shared criteria of the activity. This is very different from asking someone, say, in the stands of the Olympic diving competition what she thought of a given performance.

The world of experts though can also be troublesome. Frequently, their assessments can be insulated from the real world of concerns of other human beings. No doubt you've noticed this in listening to political pundits talk through the week's issues in Washington, D.C. You may have found yourself wondering, what does this have to do with me or anyone I know?

The same can happen when experts in any field start speaking to each other. The distinctions that they make may have no practical consequence in our life or even in helping shape our appreciation for an activity. It's important for coaches to keep this in mind when making assessments, so that the purpose of the coaching endeavor is always kept in mind and assessments are not made for their own sake.

As coaches, then, we must learn to make assessments that have grounding. To do this, we have to learn the vocabulary of a given field of endeavor and how it is used. None of us have enough breadth of knowledge and experience to be able to make grounded assessments in all fields of human endeavor. We may be able to make an assessment about how a meeting or conversation went but not about the efficacy of a business strategy, the clarity of computer code, or the long-term consequences of a chess move. Practically speaking, this means that all coaches have a limited range of topics they can work with.

Coaching can be a great aid as clients begin at an activity, when they themselves are learning to make assessments. For example, when someone is entering a new work relationship at a new company and perhaps in a new field of business, she probably won't be able to assess how well she is doing on the job, but we as coaches can, if we have the wherewithal I've been describing to observe and assess.

A last point about assessments: one of the most powerful questions coaches can ask is the equivalent of, "What is the grounding for the assessment?" This is a somewhat awkward and technical way of speaking. In the same spirit of this question, coaches often ask, "How do you know that?" (which to me seems to be a much broader question about the possibility of knowing than inquiring into the basis upon which the client is coming to an assessment about an activity). Grounding our assessments keeps us from jumping to conclusions, acting from fearful/neurotic patterns, or acting from prejudice. Coaching requires us to be calm, present, and able to distinguish an historically based reaction from an observation and assessment we are making in the current moment. These two phenomena feel different, and it is essential as coaches to be able to tell which is which.

Intention someone has when they make it	To provide an opinion or judgment on a given topic
Implicit commitment speaker makes	If asked to provide grounding, to reveal what was considered in coming to this opinion or judgment.
Essential elements	Using widely accepted practices and language in a given domain
Examples	▪ "After examining the statue, it is my opinion that it is a genuine Rodin." ▪ "I've looked through the financials for this company and it is my opinion that it is worth purchasing their stock." ▪ "I visited the school, met with some teachers, students, and parents; and I think the school would be good for our children."

FIGURE 7.5   Summary of an assessment.

DECLARATIONS

The final speech act we'll study is declarations. When someone makes a declaration, she is committing herself to the possibility of something happening, then taking action to shape her life and circumstances to make its realization more possible. Declarations are very powerful because they open up whole fields of new possible action. The United States, for example, was brought into existence with The Declaration of Independence. John Kennedy's declaration that people would be on the moon by the end of the decade and Nelson Mandela's declaration that black and white people could live together peacefully in South Africa are other examples of world-changing declarations.

Declarations carve out possibilities that must then be filled in with action. If Jefferson or Kennedy or Mandela merely spoke and never took action consistent with their declarations, their words would have had no impact. At the same time, actions that do not follow from a declaration are random and reactive and unfocused. (Have you ever wandered into a messy garage or attic and just started looking through things, glancing at things, moving stuff around, and then looked up and noticed that two or three hours have gone by and nothing has really happened? That is what life is like when we are living outside of declarations we've made.) The genuine work of a coaching program begins when a coach and client both declare the outcomes that they are dedicated to accomplish.

Declarations form the boundaries of what we think/feel is possible for us. We generally do not stray from outside these boundaries, although life may force us from time to time. Clients tell us these declared boundaries when they say, "I am not the kind of person who ..." or "I'm the kind of person who ..." Notice that these phrases are cloaked as assertions or assessments when in fact they are declarations—committed statements about what is possible—that have no evidentiary basis, but gain their validity exclusively from the authority of the speaker.

No one else can declare possibilities for me (although, parents, life partners, and bosses are always trying). Each person alone is the authorized speaker to bring into existence the possibilities within which she will live and to which she will dedicate her life. A huge portion of coaching's power comes from clients intentionally making declarations, a deliberate stepping out from reacting to life, from one incident to another. Living without a declaration is truly being a cork in the stream, having no say whatever about how our life will go.

Contrary to what some people claim, we do not have the power to declare reality. (Check this out for yourself at the racetrack this week.) We do, however, have the wherewithal to say what we care about, what we will commit to, and what we will stay true to in the face of any and all difficulties. Human meaning seems to me to flow from our personal allegiance to our declarations, more than from any type of success. Getting what we want can often be a matter of propitious circumstance (the particular flight we pick may be the one that leaves before the storm arrives) and consequently have no real connection to us. I learned this by watching beautiful movie stars who did nothing to be beautiful, and therefore felt no connection to or meaning from the public's adulation and their monetary success.

When we live aligned with what we've declared to be central to us, though, our life is imbued with meaning in each breath, each activity, each conversation, and each relationship. (Winning the lottery may seem like it would be fantastic, but numerous studies have shown that it very rarely makes a qualitative difference in the lives of winners.) Who we make ourselves into determines our sense of meaning, value, and belonging; and who we become is a matter of the declarations we make and live into.

Declarations are the speech act that frees us from historic circumstance and the limitations of the past. In a bold way, they claim the future by remembering that it is still unwritten. We, as I already said, cannot change the laws of gravity, or how tall we are, or how long it takes to boil water from our declarations, but we can radically shape who we are by skillfully employing them. Our declarations must feel and be true possibilities for us in order to have any power to shape us and our activities. Have you ever tried to declare your love for someone when you didn't feel its truthfulness in your heart, body, and mind?

Notice what happens in your body when you make a declaration. Our body will tell us every time if we are serious in a declaration we are making and whether we are genuinely committed to it. Any reluctance, resistance, holding back or second-guessing will be revealed in our somatic impressions if we pay attention to them. You know this already. When someone makes a declaration to you, you can immediately tell whether it is nonsense, wishful thinking, or hot air. Maybe you didn't realize that your body was telling you this, but pay attention next time and see what you discover.

Intention someone has when they make it	To open up, close, or alter a possibility
Implicit commitment speaker makes	To take action consistent with what was said
Essential elements	An authorized speaker; the specifics about what possibility is being opened, closed or altered; and in what precise way
Examples	▪ "I declare myself a candidate in the upcoming Presidential election." ▪ "I commit to spend 20% of our revenue to explore what new products could be offered to the European marketplace." ▪ "I've decided to dedicate my life to being a physician."

FIGURE 7.6   Summary of a declaration.

A declaration then becomes rooted when we make it undivided from any parts of ourselves. When we work through any divisions in our self or in our commitment (and then, if necessary, within our speaking) we will truly bring forward a new possibility for us.

Now that we've studied speech acts anatomically, let's put them together into conversations, a natural place in which they occur.

CONVERSATION FOR RELATIONSHIP

The background for all conversations is relationship. Being able to communicate to someone means that a minimum threshold of relationship exists. For example, because we speak or read the same language, we understand that when someone looks in our direction and speaks that he is saying something to us. Maybe when you've been in a place that feels very foreign, you feel the lack of the relationship I'm talking about. But even in a country where we don't speak the language or know the customs, there is enough shared relationship in our humanity that we would do our best to help someone who tugged on our sleeve and pleaded for something even if we couldn't understand for what.

Besides this baseline of relatedness, in the world of commerce, education, friendship, and coaching, it is necessary for us to more intentionally bring forward a working relationship. We all know this, but I'm bringing it out here so that we can study it just a little bit and so that we remember when something is amiss, one of the first places to look is the current condition of the relationship.

My view is that relationships can't be forced. We might be on the same team and have to work together, but that doesn't mean that we have much of a relationship. People must freely enter the mutuality of relationship of their own volition. We do so, for example, when we meet someone who shares interests, concerns, or commitments with us. It is an easy matter for parents standing at the school bus stop to enter into conversation with the other parents because both people have so many obvious interests, commitments, and concerns in common.

These different elements of relationship provide different possible levels of relationship. Shared interests facilitate our being acquaintances and friendly participants in an activity. We readily enter into this when attending a sporting event or a concert. When we discover mutual concerns with another, we enter into a deeper relationship where we reveal more of ourselves and are open to hear more from our conversational partner. Shared commitment is the basis for genuine partnership because here we are willing to move through ambiguity, misunderstanding, and friction in the interactions in order to fulfill the commitment we share.

As coaches, we are presenting ourselves as people who are committed to the commitments of our clients. Such openness provides a strong foundation in working through the inevitable difficulties that occur during a coaching engagement. Any less depth in the relationship than this, in my view, is insufficient for bringing about any substantial outcomes. If we find that we can't commit ourselves to what the client is up to, it is best that we step out of working with our client and refer them to someone else.

It is a commonplace event in our contemporary world that clients live without much relational support. Yes, it is true that people have many social network friends or work friends or hang-out friends (all people that share interests, or maybe even concerns), but what is frequently missing are people who share commitments. Practically this means that clients often don't have anyone to call on when dealing with difficulties, confusing choices, or emotional turmoil.

An entire coaching program can be built around building the competencies for skillfully conducting a conversation for relationship. The elements could include:

- staying present and attentive to our conversational partner, which means—in practice—returning ourselves from self-conscious inner worries, or self-criticism, or wild speculations about what might happen next in the conversation;
- listening for mutual interests, concerns and commitments;
- participating equally in speaking and listening as the conversation unfolds so that neither partner dominates; and
- refraining from making judgments about what our conversational partner says and, instead, expressing respectful curiosity for whatever is brought up.

The conversation concludes with any future planning that feels appropriate given the level of mutuality that was uncovered in the conversation. Sometimes that might mean, "Well, let's go see that art exhibit" or "Let's get together on Tuesday and talk more about this"; or, on the other hand, "It was really interesting to talk to you—goodbye."

CONVERSATION FOR POSSIBILITIES

Conversations that explore possibilities have a bit more form. I mean something a bit different than brainstorming, although it could fairly be said to be in this genre. A conversation for possibility assumes a background of relationship. We engage in this way with someone that we already know shares interests, concerns, or commitments with us (we don't stop people on the street and ask, "What should I buy for my wife's anniversary present?").

With this relational background, the conversation starts when someone brings up a topic and asks a question, such as: What could be done about this? What's possible here? How could we address this? In a conversation for possibilities, the conversation flows pretty normally and naturally; what determines its efficacy is the acuity of the participants listening for a new possibility. "New" means outside the pre-existing solutions, categories, or conclusions that were present before the speaking and listening began.

Real possibilities begin to unfold when everyone involved suspends criticism and refrains from any version of "yes, but." There is no pressure for getting anything done other than a shared commitment to find any possibilities that arise. Following someone's idea out a few steps beyond what has already been articulated frequently opens up something new, as well as going the opposite way in the conversation by revealing what assumptions and views led to the possibility being proposed.

Being open to associations that occur while in the middle of a conversation can be very helpful as long as we don't get too unfocused. An unrestrained conversation for possibility can quickly, if misdirected, stray so far afield that nothing useful is collected at the end. For example, someone could go around exploring possibilities for where to go on vacation. A misdirected conversation could go like this:

Person 1: Have you ever gone to Greece?
Person 2: Oh, remember "Grease"? Didn't that star John Travolta? Wasn't he also in "Saturday Night Fever"?
Person 1: Oh, yeah, "Fever": great song. Didn't Peggy Lee sing that song?
Person 2: She always reminded me of Miss Piggy, who was infatuated with Kermit. Frogs are so interesting. They grow up from tadpoles so quickly.
Person 1: Life does seem to go by so quickly. I wonder why that is. Maybe it's just the effects of relativity like Einstein spoke about.
Person 2: Speaking of which, there is an Einstein's Bagel Shop on the corner. Let's go get some.

Maybe you've been in this type of conversation yourself. It's a matter of skill and delicacy to keep the conversation directed without too much constraint. Keeping the intention of coming away with possibilities that can be decided about by the end of the conversation will keep us from straying, as in the conversation above.

A successful conversation ends by the participants deciding to explore the possibilities further, move them right now into action, or declaring that none of the possibilities are of sufficient interest to warrant further engagement.

CONVERSATION FOR ACTION

Please notice that conversations for action sequentially follow those for relationship and possibility. Neglecting those earlier steps will have us engage in a conversation that will not be grounded upon sufficient mutual commitment and/ or not enough exploration of possible directions of action. Many, many, many conversations for action fall apart because people attempt to conduct them based upon roles or power. Parents, teachers, bosses frequently fall into this mistake. Readers are undoubtedly familiar with all the research around people being more committed to action if they have been included in the exploration preceding it.

The next time you're in a conversation for action that doesn't seem to be going anywhere, be it with a family member or work team, please consider whether enough depth of relationship is in place and enough possibilities have been explored to give a foundation for the current conversation to go forward. Don't be fooled by someone insisting that we be more and more specific in our request, when the truth of the matter is that we are speaking to someone who does not share our commitment and does not have any interest in the topic. Be careful not to substitute force or cleverness for relationship as the conversation for action unfolds.

The conversation itself is displayed in the diagram below. The first quadrant is preparation, which includes the two earlier conversations that we've already studied. Once complete, the preparatory stage leads to the performer making an offer, which, as you'll recall, is a combination of a request and a promise; or by someone (we are calling this person the receiver) making a straightforward request.

What follows in the next quadrant is any necessary negotiations so that both parties are clear about what's being asked for and what will be delivered at the end. In this stage, elements of the request or offer may have to be modified. The timing, quality, or quantity of what is being discussed may be altered and, for this to be a real conversation, there has to be mutual acceptance of these changes. Honesty, candor, and completeness are essential qualities to bring to this part of the conversation. Neglecting any of these will lead to immense waste as someone goes into action to fulfill something that is later changed or modified because something was withheld, spun, or misrepresented in the negotiation stage. Also, please remember that any request or offer can be declined, simply by saying "no."

In the performance stage, everything that is necessary for the conditions specified in the request or offer to be completed in the allotted time is initiated. Undoubtedly this will include unanticipated breakdowns, delays, and complications. Sometimes this means renegotiating timing or another part of the request/offer. The essential activity is ongoing conversations so that everyone involved can adapt to what's changed and coordinate her/his other activities accordingly.

Careful attention here will assure that, at the end, everyone is as satisfied as possible and that no serious damage has been done to the relationship. Giving the ongoing nature of personal and business relationships, these last two factors are vitally important.

The last quadrant is a conversation in which the involved people say that what is delivered is satisfactory. It is not up to the performer alone to decide this. It really is a conversation back and forth until both people willingly say that they are complete with what happened. Customer loyalty, personal credibility, feelings of mutual support, and partnership: all are based upon this final stage of the conversation.

For coaches, this third conversation—conversation for action—is one that can be explored, studied, and practiced with great benefit. We all know people

The loop representation for a "Conversation for Action" was derived from work originally copyrighted by Action Technologies and Business Design Associates and is used with permission.

FIGURE 7.7   Conversation for action.

who can generate ideas but have difficulty executing them. The conversation, as displayed and discussed here, lays out the necessary actions in a way that can be mastered. It is not beyond most people's ability to become proficient in conversations for action. Also, please note that the coaching engagement is an example of the action cycle: both coach and client enter into it with a commitment to produce particular outcomes within a particular timeframe.

Correcting and communicating along the way is essential, as is a conversation for completion at the end. This chapter is meant to lay out in a preliminary and cursory fashion the essential elements and conversations that bring forth and coordinate our shared human world. Every adult has to have a minimum competence in all three in order to function in the twenty-first century, yet nowhere in our educational system is this a topic of study.

Perhaps you have already made the step in seeing that a large number of coaching issues that clients bring are addressable and resolvable by the client becoming skillful in speaking and listening. Too often, in my view, coaches work in an inefficient and wasteful fashion; for example, working to build up someone's self-esteem when what is more germane is working with a client to be able to make a full request.

Working for conversational competence is a powerful place for coaches to engage because we do not have to enter into the historic psychology of our client, but can instead focus our coaching on the client's current skills and what it takes to build them. Perhaps surprising to some people, building these conversational competences will shift the client's experience of himself as well as the public identity he has in the world. Besides that, our success is forwarded or limited by our ability to speak and listen. Even the most brilliant inventor at some point has to ask for investors, and even the most innovative artist has to present her work.

As is typical with a successful manager, Bob was highly skilled in conducting conversations for action. He could readily understand and probe as necessary into what was being asked of him. He always had a very good sense of the current workload of his team and their capacity to take on something new. He didn't overcommit because he did not want to sully the reputation of his group or disappoint the people making the requests.

The step into the executive ranks required Bob to think and act and speak beyond the current situation of the facts and figures. He had to learn to look out over a longer horizon of time beyond what was predictable or extendable from the present circumstance. He had to learn to ask, "What if...?" Or, "How about...?" Or, "If this could happen, what might be possible?" For quite a while, Bob kept wanting to pull the conversations back into what could be done right now. These habits of thought and action were deeply embedded in his self-image and public identity.

Over and again, I kept pointing this out to him and inviting him to engage in conversations for possibilities: at first, with people where there would be little consequence, but then—as he got more confident—with people whose opinion could shape his future. The exercise he took on about building a network of support was the indispensable first step for being able to conduct a conversation for possibility.

As you might recall, these conversations only happen with people with whom we share interests, concerns, and commitments, and at first, none of these people existed in his world. Once this network was established, it was far easier for Bob to have these conversations regularly and learn both by observing others and by practicing himself. Bob became more at ease taking a risk of saying something that he did not have the data to support. He learned to clearly designate when he was speaking speculatively and when he was making promises or assertions. The simple matter of knowing that there were these distinct ways of speaking—that brought about different results and that let him be known in a new way within his organization—freed up Bob's actions tremendously.

SUGGESTED READING

The information presented in this chapter has been gathered through attending classes and lectures. The actual creators of the work as presented have not written books on the topic. Nonetheless, here are some books that can provide a firm foundation for the material presented and examples of its application. Many of the books cited at the end of Chapter Two have their place here as well. I've only repeated once, giving it a different emphasis in the context of this chapter.

Budd, Matthew, and Larry Rothstein. *You Are What You Say*. New York: Crown Publishers, 2000.
    While the author was on the faculty of Harvard Medical School and was a practicing physician in Cambridge, he studied extensively with Fernando Flores. He took what he learned about language and brought it to his patients. The book has many stories of symptoms being relieved and well-being restored by shifting conversations. The author includes many useful checklists and generously makes available the practical things he's learned along the way. Accessible, exciting, and inspiring.
Sieler, Alan. *Coaching to the Human Soul*, Volume 1. Blackburn, Victoria, Australia: Newfield Australia, 2003.
    This book provides the philosophical grounding for the speech acts theory presented in this chapter. The author is a practicing coach in Asia and Australia. His volume is ripe with useful examples and the writing itself is clear.

8

Enrollment

Probably more coaching programs flounder here than anywhere else—maybe because enrollment demands that we be human; no role or force will fulfill the stage. Manipulation or misrepresentation is quickly shown up. For many potential coaches, managers, teachers, and parents, the idea of stepping out of their accustomed roles and positioning themselves as human beings equal to their potential clients is uncomfortable and disconcerting. Thus, they easily slide out of coaching and into some other mode of interacting—managing or teaching, probably. Of course, justification accompanies the slide. Some potential coaches justify themselves by saying "the client was resistent" or "the timing wasn't right." If you find yourself as a coach in this situation, use your discomfort as an indicator that you are on the right path and not as a sign that you must change what you're doing.

Until now, the coach has been doing most of the work solo. In the next stage, enrollment, the coach/client partnership becomes explicit and the work shared. In enrollment, both the client and the coach make explicit what they are committed to accomplishing in the coaching program. The commitment of one member is not sufficient.

The second job in enrollment is to frankly discuss potential hindrances to achieving the outcomes. At this point, the coach can refer to the assessments she made. For example, perhaps the client is already very busy and the additional work of the coaching program would be difficult to fit in. Maybe the client has a boss, a friend, or a family member who would not be supportive of the coaching program. Maybe the outcomes are only contingently or temporarily important, leading to the likelihood that the client will abandon them. There can be many other hindrances, and without confronting them directly, honestly, and as completely as possible, the most sincere-sounding commitment will turn out to be hollow, shallow, and groundless.

Dealing with the hindrances so forthrightly may call into question what the outcomes of the program should be, and it's perfectly fine to go back and change the outcomes in light of what is discussed around hindrances. The discussions about hindrances and outcomes may also bring into question the commitment of the client to the coach and it is often necessary to reclarify this during the conversation.

These three topics—outcomes, mutual commitment, and hindrances—form the scaffolding for the conversation; other subjects will naturally present themselves. The coach can answer questions about other people who have successfully achieved the kinds of outcomes being discussed. The coach can also build confidence in the program's outcome by strengthening his credibility with the client. Credibility is built by citing past successes with similar coaching endeavors and in other ways connecting the outcomes to the coach's experience.

Additionally, the coach can provide logistical information, for example, how long an activity might take, how much a piece of equipment might cost to buy, or where a particular book might be purchased. As you may be able to tell by now, the enrollment conversation swirls around all these conversations and subjects.

As a coach, you'll know this process is complete when both you and the client know exactly what the outcomes are and what the commitment of each is to the program, and when both have a general idea about what it will take to achieve the outcomes.

Another way to look at this is that enrollment happens in the area where the commitments of the coach overlap with the commitments of the client (see Figure 8.1).

As a coach, you'll only be interested in doing the necessary work if, by doing it, you'll be able to further something important to you, and the client has essentially the same point of view in terms of engaging in activities that further her commitment. A key point in enrollment then is understanding yourself and your client.

In order to make yourself credible as a coach and to avoid any hint of skepticism or cynicism on the part of the client, it's usually necessary to make explicit your commitment to doing the coaching. You'll find that the client more readily trusts you when it's apparent that the program is in each party's mutual interest. As you no doubt have noticed, many times people—especially in business—are suspicious of altruistic motives, and when we attempt to present coaching as such, we may engender suspicion. At the same time, it's

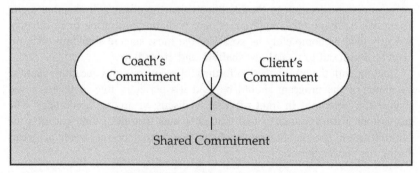

FIGURE 8.1   Where Coaching Happens

necessary to make the program attractive to the client. As I've said earlier, the real point of the program is to have the client be more able to take action on what she is already committed to, and not simply to fulfill the requirements of the coach. By taking both sides of the situation into account, you'll find it possible to balance the situation so that both the client and the coach are able to fully commit to the program.

The enrollment conversation itself requires that the coach listen very intently both to what the client is saying and to what the client is keeping silent about. The mood of the conversation is one of openness, forthrightness, and realistic viewing of possibilities. Be careful not to sugarcoat the program so that it seems as if it consists solely of fulfilling obviously wonderful outcomes. If you do that, you will find that your client becomes immediately discouraged at the first hint of difficulty. At the same time, do not let yourself be argued into diminishing what's possible by the statements of the client, who may be discouraged from earlier attempts to improve.

You've done a good job of describing the outcomes of the program when they are attractive to both parties and it is not obvious that they would occur anyway, without coaching intervention. Additionally, the outcomes must be stated in sufficient clarity that both parties will be able to recognize them as occurring or not and also be able to discern what progress has been made toward them. Spend as much time as it takes to come to such mutual understanding.

As much as possible, avoid generally descriptive words such as successful completion or outstanding performance. Such terms are so open to individual interpretation that it's frequently unclear whether they've been achieved or not, or whether progress is being made toward them. It's not that all outcomes must be reduced to a number or statistic, but they must be observable, and not exist solely within the private assessment of the coach or client.

When I said above that it's important to listen to what the client is not saying, I was referring to the sometimes subtle concerns clients may have. During the coaching conversation the client may be trying to appease the coach, or thinking of all the reasons she would give for failure, or recalling discouraging incidents from the past. Unless the coach is intently observing and listening to the client, these aspects of the conversation will not be revealed and dealt with and, as a consequence, the enrollment will be shallow.

The notion of commitment, which is essential in enrollment, is not universally understood in the same way. As the coach, then, I recommend that you work in the conversation to uncover what level of commitment the client is bringing. Commitment is not a matter of all or nothing; in other words, it's not a matter of "doing whatever it takes." We don't have many commitments like that in our lives and it doesn't mean that someone isn't committed when she doesn't act that way.

A commitment that seemed very important to us when we made it seems less important in the face of other commitments we make later, or in the face of unanticipated breakdowns or requests for help from people who are dear to us. The commitment the person makes in coaching has to fit into the whole array of commitments she is already in the middle of fulfilling. Many of us do not understand this array of commitments. That is to say, if we wrote down what we are committed to, we would discover contradictions, out-of-date commitments, or more obligations than we could fulfill. It's simplistic to reduce this to a matter of asking someone to make coaching a high priority, because in many instances we are not in charge of prioritizing our actions, and we often forget what is supposed to be our higher priority when we are in the day-to-day continuous swirl of events.

I'm not trying to make the job sound more complex or impossible, but rather to give you grounds upon which to appreciate the kind of commitment the client brings. Perhaps by asking the following questions you can appreciate the way coaching fits into your client's array of commitments:

1. What could interrupt this coaching program for you?
2. How does coaching fit into what you're already doing?
3. How will you respond when the program seems to be going too slowly, or gets boring, or repetitious, or even seems pointless?

The other side of the conversation is what commitment you're bringing as a coach. I recommend that you ask yourself these questions to clarify your commitment as a coach. What are you willing to work through to have the program succeed? What are you willing to give up? What will discourage you? How many times can the client break a promise before you abandon your commitment? What are you willing to change about how you work with people in order to make the coaching program succeed? Are you willing to be, at times, more committed than the client is?

Yet another way of thinking about enrollment is that it's an invitation the coach is making to the client. Invitations are very interesting requests because they also imply a promise. First, from the request end of the invitation, there is room for the invitee, in this case the client, to say yes or no, and to modify aspects of the invitation.

Consider, for example, inviting someone to your home for a party. The invitee can say yes or no without a negative consequence, tell you about what time she'll arrive, can ask if she can bring someone else, and so on. The implicit promise made in an invitation is that, if accepted, the invitor will do what is necessary to make it worthwhile. Naturally, we invite people when we want them to say yes. The same is true in coaching. We initiate it when we really want the person to accept. Haven't you been able to tell when someone is inviting you just because she is feeling obligated? Your clients will be able to tell the same thing about your invitations to be coached. They'll be listening for your sincerity in fulfilling the implicit promise. They'll be listening for the depth of your commitment, and whether or not you feel as if the program will succeed. I recommend that you address these questions within yourself before you attempt to do enrollment with your client.

All of this may seem like a dry academic exercise, but if enrollment stays merely cognitive, it's unlikely that it will be sufficiently powerful to propel the coaching forward. As Gurdjieff and others have postulated, the human will is not directly tied to the human intellect. Emotion fits between the two. You've probably observed this when you've seen that people know what to do and yet don't do it. People who continue to smoke cigarettes or engage in other self-destructive behavior are clear examples of what I'm speaking about.

I'm recommending that you speak in a way that touches the emotions of your client when you're doing enrollment, because emotions directly affect the will. All great coaches, in sports for example, have always known this and have spoken directly and sometimes exclusively to the emotions.

I'm not saying that your client has to cry or be moved to profound joy, but work to find a way to have your client experience an affective connection to the coaching. Naturally this will be easier or harder to accomplish according to the particular client, but it's almost always possible to find a way to stir some feeling about the subject. The more profound the change you are going after, the more profound the emotional force necessary to accomplish it. For example, if you are just coaching to improve a pedestrian skill like designing a filing system, you don't need much emotional connection to the project. On the other hand, if you're working with a client to alter the direction of her life, you'll find it important to tap into her emotions.

You'll be able to tell when you have made contact with the client's emotions in several ways. First, some clients will tell you that they are moved by something that is happening in the conversation or will somehow demonstrate their feeling. Second, you will feel a deeper connection with your client in a way that feels spontaneous and natural. Third, you will notice that you are starting to have stronger feelings on the topic yourself. To sum it up, here's a checklist for enrollment:

1. Say what *could* happen in the coaching effort.
2. Declare your commitment to the client and the possible outcomes.
3. Invite the client's commitment.
4. Confront potential hindrances.
5. Continue through steps one through four until both parties feel complete.

Here is a summary of how enrollment went with Bob. You'll see the purpose and outcomes I proposed and he accepted. I wrote them after our first conversation and after much thought. I found that the clarity and precision of such statements brought a powerful direction to coaching and enormously enhanced my credibility with the client. Additionally, when the purpose and outcome statements accurately capture the intention of the client, they provide enormous credibility for the coach, who is seen as someone who understands, appreciates, and supports the client in a profound way.

The main obstacle in the enrollment conversation with Bob was getting him to see what it would take from him to accomplish the outcomes. At first he thought it was a matter of learning to dress differently or reading a few books on leadership. The real changes, though, had to be in his comprehension of the executive world, an increased competence to deal with complex issues, and an understanding of the ebb and flow of political forces. Bob could build on some of his skills, but he would also have to develop new ones, and most challenging of all, he would have to abandon some long-term habits.

It was my job to keep presenting the path to Bob and do that in a way that was simultaneously attractive and realistic. It was as if I were enrolling him to enter training to run a marathon. Yes, there would be benefits in his health and self-confidence, but it would also require long hours of training, physical discomfort, and new skills in dealing with unexpected emotions. If an enroller only emphasizes one aspect of the program, either the benefits or the requirements, the coaching will soon fall apart. That is because someone who doesn't remember the point of the work will likely soon abandon it, and someone who is initially prepared to deal with the obstacles will probably abandon the work at the first hint of difficulty.

I learned all this through years of trying out many different methods, so I continued to speak to Bob until we had thoroughly discussed the range of experiences he would encounter during the coaching program. Throughout our talk I kept assuring him that I was confident in his ability to do it and in my competence in coaching him through the whole process. He had many questions, mostly in the form of "What if...?" Some I answered, some I postponed until the scenario he was concerned about actually occurred. Our conversation lasted about one and one-half hours, and at the end we both agreed to the purpose and outcomes presented below:

Purpose

- You will make a greater impact on people so that your career at your company continues to progress.

Outcomes

- You will have a better understanding of how people perceive you.
- You will have a strategy for dealing with each of your important work relationships.
- You will be seen as decisive and effective, and considered to be a strong candidate for executive-level positions.

SUGGESTED READING

The four books in this list don't directly discuss enrollment; however, each addresses in distinctive and pertinent ways the conditions in which enrollment occurs.

Havens, Leston. *Making Contact*. Cambridge: Cambridge University Press, 1986.
  An original, practical presentation of how to use language to create, conduct, and complete therapeutic partnerships.
Johnson, Vernon E. *Intervention*. Minneapolis, MN: Johnson Institute Books, 1986.
  Presents a powerful methodology for working with very recalcitrant clients. The principles are adaptable to other coaching structures.
Lavine, T. Z. *From Socrates to Sartre: The Philosophic Quest*. New York: Bantam Books, Inc., 1984.
  Every client lives within one or more of the discourses discussed in this clear, precise survey of the Western philosophical tradition.
Tannen, Deborah. *You Just Don't Understand*. New York: Ballantine Books, 1990.
  A study (with many verbatim examples of relevant studies, citations, and acute analysis) of the differences between the communication styles of men and women. This book is very useful in untangling seemingly insoluble relational and communicative issues. A great aid in designing and conducting coaching interventions.

9

Coaching Conversations

In this chapter you'll read about three levels of coaching interventions, from a single conversation to complex, multisession programs. The proposed structures have been tested over time and are meant to be used as a way to keep practicing and improving as a coach. How can you use them in your coaching efforts?

"He has to see on his own behalf and in his own way the relations between means and methods employed and results achieved. Nobody else can see for him, and he can't see just by being 'told,' although the right kind of telling may guide his seeing and thus help him to see what he needs to see."

—John Dewey

As was said earlier, probably the only activity you will do as a coach is speak to your client. Sometimes you may demonstrate, at other moments you'll be listening, but the form your coaching mostly will take is speaking with your client. That's why the earlier section on language has been included. So what do you say to your client? The most abstract way to answer the question is to respond that you say to your client something that will allow him to make a new observation. A more everyday way of answering is that you will speak with your client so that he will be able to see something or understand something or appreciate something that he couldn't before. But the job of a coach is beyond this way of speaking because the test of coaching will be in the action that the client takes, not only in the observation he can make. So another part of the answer is that the coach speaks in a way that frees the client to take action.

Sometimes the first speaking the coach does at this stage is to point out what the client is currently embedded in. The coach might, for example, say that the complaints that have been received about the client from a major account are probably the result of a misunderstanding about what it is to provide customer service combined with a severe shortage of time. The coach could go on and describe in detail obstacles, both personal and situational, that bind the client into his current behavior. On many occasions, the clarity that this conversation provides will be sufficient to liberate the client from the current situation and leave him open to try something new.

Naturally all of these conversations can only happen if all of the earlier steps in the flow have been attended to. Otherwise, the coach will not be able to speak in a way that makes sense to this particular client or be able to cite specifically what the current reality is. Additionally, if there's not a strong relationship in place, the client will not be open to hearing what's said, some of which might be bad news.

TYPES OF CONVERSATION

Having made these preliminary remarks, let's move to three different types of conversation the coach could have with the client:

- Type One: the single conversation aimed at building or sharpening a competence
- Type Two: a more complex conversation held over several sessions
- Type Three: a profound and longer conversation intended to bring about fundamental change

Given the scope of this book, we'll spend most of our time studying Type One and Type Two conversations. Because Type Three is more profound, it will bring about deeper change, and readers of an introductory text such as this may be reluctant to enter into such issues with clients. Besides that, in most business situations there is not very much of an opening for engaging in Type Three conversations.

Type One

Here are some examples of situations that probably can be resolved in a single conversation. What will make these conversations coaching is that at the end the client will be more competent. You may already be having these conversations and not calling them coaching, but if it fits the criterion of leaving the client more competent, it is a coaching conversation, regardless of its simplicity or complexity.

- Intervening in aimless complaining
- Responding to a request about how to do something
- Clarifying standards for performance and presentation
- Addressing the lack of phone etiquette in an otherwise cordial person
- Discontinuing the repetition of a simple mistake

Type Two

Type Two conversations are more complex and are usually held over several sessions. Here are some examples of situations that probably require more than one coaching conversation with a client to resolve.

- The client is not being open to the input of others.
- The client is not organized.

- The client is overcommitting himself.
- The client is acting timid and unassertive.
- The client must be trained to install and maintain a complex piece of equipment.

Type Three

Type Three is a longer and more profound conversation intended to bring about fundamental change. Following are some examples of situations that would require this type of conversation.

- Discovering one's life purpose
- Beginning or ending a primary relationship
- Making long-term financial commitments
- Career change
- Raising children

TYPE ONE: SINGLE CONVERSATIONS

Even a single coaching conversation must have a large background if the products of coaching—long-term excellent performance, self-correction, and self-generation—are to be produced. Don't let the short duration of time that you invest in the conversation lead you to neglect preparation. That is to say, only when the relationship is in place, you've done some assessment, and you have observed an opening for coaching are you in the position to approach your client to resolve a simple issue in a single conversation.

Outline and Example

You're a sales manager for a group that sells accounting software. About ten salespeople work for you in a fast-paced informal environment. Each salesperson works in a cubicle and you have an office with no door, so it is easy for you to overhear what is happening on the phones. On this particular morning you hear Frank being rude to the point of being obnoxious with one of your largest potential customers. You immediately decide that you must do something about it because you might lose the business, Frank may be doing this with other customers, and other salespeople have overheard Frank and may think that his behavior is acceptable. Here's how such a conversation might go:

1 Enrollment

- Ask the client for permission to coach.
- Say in general what the outcomes could be.

Coach: Frank, I just overheard your conversation with the Bank of Tokyo and it sounded to me as if it didn't go well. I'm wondering if you are open to discussing it with me, so that together we can discover a way that a conversation like that could go better in the future.

Client: To say it didn't go well is a bit of an understatement. But you know how those people can be. Pointed in their questions and guarded in their answers, and I can't figure out what to do. What can I tell you? I got, shall we say, annoyed?

2 Clarifying Intention

Ask the client:

- "What were you attempting to accomplish?"
- "Did it happen?"
- "How could you tell?"

You may think that asking "Why?" or "Why not?" is a more simple way of speaking here, but asking that will usually trigger justification and defensiveness, and what you're after is giving the client room to step back and observe rather than dig in and generate excuses.

Coach: So, what were you trying to get done in that call? And were you able to get that done?

Client: Well, I was trying to find out if they were interested in being able to network their northern California branches together so that they could take advantage of one database located in San Francisco. And I can tell you for sure that didn't happen. What happened instead was that I had to answer ten technical questions to help them solve problems that they already had and deal with five objections about how expensive our products are.

3 Revealing Thought Process

Ask the client:

- "How did you decide what to do?"
- "How did you analyze the situation?"
- "What were you feeling at the time?"

The idea here is to allow both you and the client to understand as exactly as possible how the action came about. In other words, you are working to reveal the structure of interpretation that led to what the client did. As a coach, it is important throughout all of this to remain calm and open, and to avoid reacting even if you disagree with what the client is saying, or if you find yourself judging the client as stupid or inept. Your judgments won't help the situation.

Coach: Okay, Frank, once you got in the middle of that, how did you figure out what to do? What was going on for you? How were you strategizing on your feet, as it were?

Client: Uh, let's see…I figured that if I could answer a few questions then they would think I was a good guy and they would open up to me. And then I thought that if I started to sound a little put off by their insistence, that they would stop asking questions and start answering my questions. I was putting them a little bit into my debt so that I could get what I wanted. And as the conversation went on and on, I got more and more frustrated because it seemed like they were willing to take everything I said and not give anything back. That's probably what you heard in my voice.

4 Invitation to See in a New Way

Given what the client stated as the intended outcome in step two above, you now have a chance to offer a new way of seeing the situation that can lead to more effective action. Here is where many people stop doing coaching and fall into solving problems or telling clients what to do. You will stay out of these temptations if you trust that the client will take the more effective action as soon as he can see it. You will keep coaching if you remain dedicated to providing the distinction and not recommending an action. A simple example is inviting the client who views incoming telephone calls as an interruption to instead view the caller as a customer for whom work is being done and as someone who funds his employment. A simple shift like that can completely reorient the way your client interacts to an interrupting phone call. The new way of interacting leads naturally to our next point.

Coach: You're right, the annoyance was obvious. So let's take a few moments and try and look at the situation in a different way. Probably the most important thing to understand in your relationship with the Bank of Tokyo is patience, patience, patience. I have discovered over the years that big institutions take a long time to make decisions and really have to trust the vendor before they invest.

My recommendation to you is that you understand the conversation with a huge bank as a long-term project which may take a year or more to develop, rather than a short-term project which you can close in one conversation or two. What I'm saying is to consider yourself a tree farmer when you are working with institutions, instead of a flower grower who is looking for growth and change every single day.

You can count on me to support you in nurturing these long-term relationships and not pressuring you to come to closure quickly. Is what I'm saying making sense to you?

Client: Yeah, as you talk I'm seeing that a lot of what was going on for me was impatience. They seemed so interested in their last phone call that I thought they really were ready to sign. You know how it is, even though

I've been in this racket for a year and even though it's not a deal until we have a contract and a check, I was already imagining driving the new car that I was going to get from this huge commission. So yeah, yeah, yeah, I'll be more patient and I do appreciate your not being on my case about spending time talking to these folks, or taking them out to lunch, or answering their questions, or whatever it is going to take.

5 New Actions and Offering Support

Stay with steps one through four until you feel confident that each has been accomplished. Then ask your client what new action he will take given the new way the situation is being observed. You can do this by asking, "Now that you are seeing the situation in this new way, what action will you take?" and "How will you be able to correct yourself in the future so that your actions are consistent with your new observation?" Additionally, you can be sure that you will strengthen your partnership with your client if you ask him in what ways you can support him and then take the action that is requested.

Coach: That's great, Frank, and you've already listed some new actions that you can take. Is there any way I can support you beyond what you've already said?

Client: I don't think so except maybe I could talk to you after my calls with the bank, and you could give me your best feedback about how it's going. Maybe you could even come with me on one of the tours they're going to give us of their main branch next week.

Coach: I'd be glad to do both of those with you. Let me know when it's scheduled and I'll clear my calendar.

The example follows the outline pretty closely, so I won't take any more time to make the connections which you can probably make just as well yourself. What made the conversation with Frank work was that he could observe how he was being in the phone conversation and see the same situation in a different way. It's the "seeing it in a new way" that is coaching. It's what will bring about the products of coaching and leave Frank competent in the future.

TYPE TWO: SEVERAL CONVERSATIONS

As you will recall, Type Two situations require several conversations (see Figure 9.1). I'll follow the same process as I did with Type One.

Conversation Number One

Background

During the first conversation, you formally establish the coaching relationship, which means that you request commitment from your client and promise your commitment. Authentic commitment can only happen after you've honestly

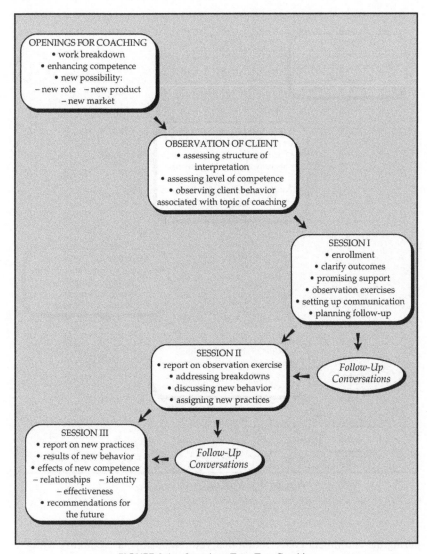

FIGURE 9.1   Overview: Type Two Coaching

confronted potential interruptions to the program's success. The conversation usually begins with a discussion of the opening for coaching that you have observed (see Figure 9.2). Be enrolling and encouraging during this conversation. Remember that your client may be unaware of what you're speaking about. Be prepared to cite examples, to use metaphors, and to describe your observation in different ways.

Once your client expresses some openness or interest, move to a conversation in which you formally establish the coaching relationship. It is important

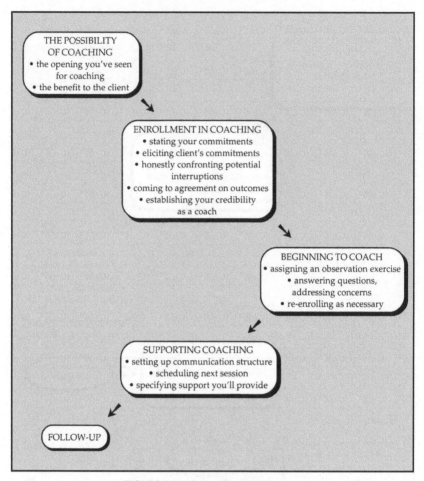

FIGURE 9.2   Conversation #1 Overview

during the enrollment conversation that you establish your credibility with the client. For this to occur, you must be competent to conduct the program, respectful of your client, and skillful in dealing with concerns, questions, or objections your client expresses.

Speak next about ways in which your client can observe what you are talking about. Before you can do this, you must sufficiently understand your client's way of observing. Use one of the assessment models to determine this. It is perfectly fine for the client not to completely understand what you're talking about.

The self-observation exercise that you assign during this conversation will allow your client to come up with his own data. The point is that your client will increase the opening for coaching. Since the point of coaching is to alter the client's structure of interpretation, it is more important initially to work on observation than on action.

At this juncture, you may have to reenroll your client in the program. Don't be alarmed. This often occurs, and a review of the conversation up to that point will likely remind your client of the program's benefits, your support, and your confidence in the client's success.

Beware any premature impulse you have to move your client into action. You are working toward a major change. Keep focused on the long term. The time you put into the coaching effort will more than pay for itself in the end. Acting this way requires discipline from the coach, which is why it's important for the coach to continually observe himself (see Chapter 11 on the two tracks of coaching).

End the first conversation by determining specific times and ways of communicating. Specify how available to your client you will make yourself for support. Last of all, schedule the date for Conversation Number Two—usually it's two to three weeks later.

After all those words, here is a preparation list and a summary outline with an example conversation:

Preparation

- Prepare yourself by using an assessment model to better understand your client (see the Assessment Exercise at the end of this chapter and also Chapter 6).
- Write out a self-observation exercise to give to your client during the session (see the Self-Observation Exercise at the end of this chapter and also Appendix A).
- List three intended outcomes that could be achieved in the coaching program. Modify them as necessary so that they're suitable for both client and coach.
- Consider what questions, concerns, or objections your potential client may have and be prepared to address them.

Outline

Introduction

- What openings for coaching have you seen?
- Is the client open to being coached?
- What could happen for the client?

Coach: Susan, I noticed during your presentation in our staff meeting on Tuesday that there were some awkward moments for you. I know I might be putting my foot in my mouth here, but during the question-and-answer period it seemed to me that there were times when you didn't know what to say or, to be more exact, you really weren't very open to what the questioner was saying. It seemed as if you had already come to your conclusions and that was that. Now I might be off base here, but that's how it seemed to me and as I thought back I remembered some other times when I saw the same kind of interactions between you and other people on our team. So, what do you think, Susan? Do you know what I'm talking about?

Client: What can I say when I'm being, even if it's in a nice way, accused of not being open? What can I say? I guess I'm open to what you're saying.

Coach: Well, Susan, that's really all it'll take for us to work together on this—you're open to finding out if what I'm saying holds up or not. It's my view that some of the recurring problems we have discussed happened partly because of the situation we're talking about today. So I feel that if we could work on this and support you in being a little bit more open in how you listen to folks, your work would go faster and be interrupted less.

Client: Well, you know me. I really am interested in getting this stuff out the door and if something I'm doing is getting in the way, I'm willing to find out about it even if it's not really comfortable. So, how do you think we could do it?

Enrollment

- What you'll provide
- What you ask of the client
- Possible interruptions and hindrances
- Agreement about outcomes (coach and client write these down)

Coach: Before we get into that, Susan, I really want you to know that I fully support you in your position and that, in general, I think you're doing an excellent job. And you can also count on me to support you all the way through this improvement effort that we are talking about today. I'll carve out time in my calendar so that we can talk about it, and I'll be patient with you as you are learning and discovering and changing.

Client: Well that's good, because the last thing I need is more pressure to get better at this quick while I'm still trying to meet those deadlines at the end of the month.

Coach: Yeah, I know what you mean and I think it's possible for us to work on both at the same time since we both are willing to do it and we see that it's important. The main hindrance I see is time constraints, which I'm sure we can work out between us.

Client: Okay, well, if we're going to talk about roadblocks, let me be up front with you and say that I'm not really sure there is a basis for what you said. I don't want this to look like I'm just going through the motions, so can you explain again what you are talking about?

Exercise

- Give observation exercise
- Answer questions/address concerns

Coach: My idea is that instead of telling you what I see, I'll let you discover it for yourself. This is what I mean—for, say, the next two weeks, whenever you are doing a presentation or answering technical questions for somebody, watch yourself very closely. Pay special attention to your mood. I mean how open you feel to the other people in the conversation. Notice if you feel put upon, or pressed, or threatened in any way. Also notice what you say at the end of each of these situations. Take a few moments after the conversation to jot down what you've noticed. And then you and I can get together, say, in ten days and go over what you've discovered, and we'll see if there is any basis for what I'm speaking about.

Client: Listen, boss, I can save you a lot of time. I don't know what you're getting at, but I don't ever feel threatened or pushed or whatever you said.

Coach: Instead of coming to a conclusion now, let's take some time and do this observation experiment and see what we come up with. What I'm asking you to do is keep an open mind and be honest with yourself, and not to go by the conclusion you have already made.

Support

- How you will communicate
- How available you are
- Schedule the next session

Client: It's only because I really trust you that I am willing to go along with it. But I am willing to along with it, so when I get back to my desk I'll call up your calendar on my screen and schedule some time at the end of next week and we'll go from there.

Coach: Sounds good to me and if you have any questions in the meantime, please call me or send an e-mail message.

Sometimes it doesn't flow so logically or smoothly, but you could probably tell in this example that it was the strength of the relationship that made it work. The next conversation would happen about ten days later.

Conversation Number Two

Background

During this conversation, the learning from the observation exercise is put into action. By beginning a new practice that you assign, your client will become more competent.

Usually, the conversation begins with a report from the client on what's happening in the coaching program (see Figure 9.3). This conversation is, in a way, a continuation of the follow-up you've had between sessions. You'll have more time now to address any concerns, questions, or breakdowns in more depth.

Build on what your client reports. Flesh out the observations. Find out together in what ways observation, action, and outcomes are connected. Use what your client reports to strengthen enrollment in the program, review the outcomes to see what progress is being made, and assess the efficacy of your work together. Keep listening to synthesize and to understand your client better.

Next, discuss what new behavior your client could initiate that would bring about the outcomes. See how much your client can suggest given what was observed. Speak about what competence is necessary to successfully perform the behavior. This conversation naturally flows to a talk about new practices.

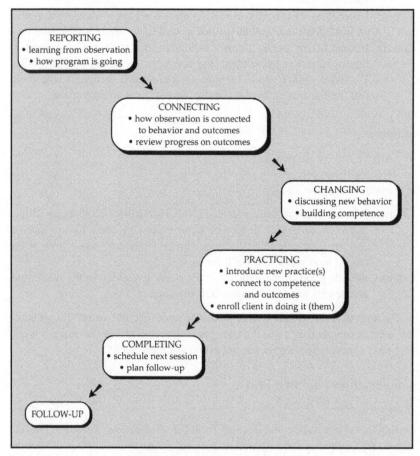

FIGURE 9.3   Conversation #2 Overview

Introduce the new practice(s) that you designed. Tie the practice(s) to developing competence that will allow the client to achieve the outcomes. Enroll the client in doing the practice(s).

The conversation ends by scheduling the next conversation (three to four weeks later) and planning the follow-up. Your client may require more support during this phase, because initiating a new practice frequently precipitates questions, breakdowns, and changes in behavior.

Preparation

- What do you intend to accomplish in this session?
- What is your assessment of how the coaching program is going? Are there any corrections to make?
- What questions or concerns is your client likely to have during this session, especially regarding the new practices? How will you address these?
- What questions do you have for your client?
- Design a practice for your client (see the Practice Exercise at the end of this chapter and also Appendix B).

Outline

Introduction and Connections

- Report from observation exercise
- Determine how program is going
- Show how what the client has observed affects behavior and outcomes
- Acknowledge all positive results
- Review outcomes for program

Coach: Susan, although I have a pretty good idea from some of the brief conversations we've had, I'd like you to, if you would, summarize what you've learned from observing yourself in the way that we spoke about last time we met.

Client: Well, I saw that there was probably more to what you had seen than I was willing to admit before. And I'm not exactly happy with it now but I think you're right—I have to relax a bit more and not be so anxious when people start pressing in on me. Otherwise, it starts to look like I don't know what I'm doing or I'm trying to hide something.

Coach: That was exactly the point of having you observe—so that you could come to your own conclusions based upon direct observation. I caution you about something—it's likely that you've been doing this for a while and it has become a habitual response, and so it won't change by just wishing that it were different. It's going to take a concentrated, sustained effort that's very focused.

Client: Why am I getting the distinct idea that you have something in mind?

Changes and New Practice

- Talk about initiating new behavior: moving toward outcomes, building upon results so far
- What competence the new behavior will take
- Introduce new practice
- Integrate practice into program
- Answer questions and concerns
- Enroll client in doing practice

Coach: Funny you should mention that. Here is my idea. It's that you start a new way of preparing for your presentations and a new way of conducting yourself during them.

Besides the usual thorough research you do, look through the list of people who are attending the meeting and ask yourself what questions, objections, or concerns they are likely to bring up, and then answer them in your own way before you go into the meeting.

Second, while you're conducting your presentation or are in a technical conversation with somebody, keep observing the way you did before. When you begin to detect the earliest sign of closing down, ask yourself one of two questions. The first one is, "What is threatening me?" Second is, "Is there any real reason to feel threatened?" By asking yourself these two questions, you will undoubtedly find that you're not being threatened.

Sometimes people may make points at your expense or have some political agenda going on, and sometimes people really don't know what they are talking about and they're just swinging away. The questions will remind you of all of that and return you to the presentation you have prepared.

On the rare occasions when the questions don't bring this about, say this to the person who you feel is threatening you: "I'm unclear about what you're attempting to accomplish with your remarks. Can you please take a moment to explain it to me, so that I may be more responsive to you?" While your question is being answered, you can regroup and, by listening to the response, get a better idea about what the person is up to.

Support

- Schedule next time to speak
- Schedule next session

Client: Okay, I'll try it. What I think I'll do is write those questions on the top of each page of my notes so that I can refer to them if needed. I especially like your third point about how I can speak to somebody who is starting to sound offensive in a way that doesn't sound defensive, but does move the conversation forward.

Coach: That's the idea. So why don't you try this out for the next month or so and then we'll meet and see how it went?

Client: Okay, boss, you got it.

Conversation Number Three

Background

The challenge now is to complete the program leaving enough structure and competence in place so that your client remains self-correcting and self-generating (see Figure 9.4). Several pitfalls may appear during this part of the program.

Pitfall #1: Client, in spite of observed outcomes, is convinced that no change has happened or that it was circumstantial or that it won't last. Remedy: Your client has demonstrated some competence. Continual practice will ensure continual improvement. Remind your client of the distinctions between outcomes/competence and negative assessment/mood.

Pitfall #2: Client feels/thinks/concludes that it's only by your continuing to coach that competence will remain or outcomes will continue to happen. Remedy: Review what has happened with your client. The client made the commitment, did the work, made the changes, and consequently, brought about the outcomes.

Pitfall #3: Your client says nothing has happened. Competence has not improved. No progress has been made on the outcomes. There's an edge of disappointment/despair/resignation, or maybe cynicism/skepticism, and maybe some accusation/antagonism directed at you. Remedy: Stay open. There's no need to defend. Examine what has happened—in every case something has improved, so it's a matter of the speed of the improvement, not its existence. Advise your client to be patient. Add additional observation exercises, practices, or sessions as necessary. In extreme cases, take what you've both learned in the program and begin again at Conversation One. Be sure to redo all of the steps, especially your assessment of the client.

If there are no pitfalls, or after you have worked through them, acknowledge progress in all parts of the client's life, and show the client his new competence and the outcomes of it in all domains.

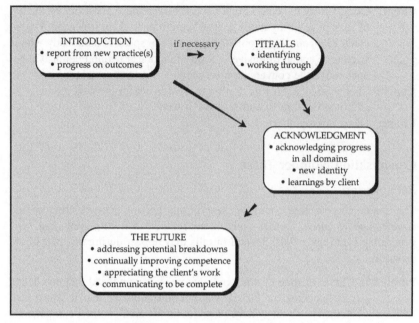

FIGURE 9.4   Conversation #3 Overview

Speak about the new ways that people can trust and rely upon your client. In other words, talk about the new identity the client has begun to establish. Discuss what new possibilities this opens up for your client.

Preparation

- Read over your notes from the follow-up conversation(s)
- Review the outcomes for the program
- Have many examples of your client's new competencies
- Answer/address the questions in the summary outline

Outline

The example cited does not address all of the points listed in the outline. That's because the coach and the client have an ongoing relationship in which these topics will eventually get discussed. In situations where there is not as much day-to-day contact, it probably makes more sense to address the topics of "Acknowledging Progress" in all domains and "The Future" in more detail.

Introduction

- Report results of new practice
- Progress on outcomes
- What openings? What breakdowns?

Pitfalls (if necessary)

- Identification
- Staying open to what client says
- Reminding client of outcomes
- Leaving client self-correcting and self-generating
- Adding observation exercises, practices, or sessions as necessary
- Beginning program again if required

Acknowledging Progress

- In all domains, not only coaching topics
- New possibilities for client
  - new relationships?
  - new identity?
  - new conversations?
- New learnings
  - about self?
  - about others?
  - about work?
  - about becoming competent?

The Future

- Addressing potential breakdowns
  - what to look for
  - actions to take
- Continuing to improve
  - in what?
  - new practices?

Example of Conversation Number Three

The conversation might go something like this. No pitfalls are encountered, but I suggest you prepare for them.

Coach: Well, from reading your e-mail messages, it sounds as if the ideas we came up with are working pretty well for you.

Client: That's right. I can't say that it's gone perfectly. There have been a few times when I feel like I have blown it, but there is probably a 75 or 80 percent improvement. The one guy I still can't figure out is Kevin Brown—you know, that new college kid in marketing? He seems to make himself into a human bulldozer whenever I start talking. And I have said the equivalent of "shut up" to him on several occasions in the last month.

Coach: Here is my advice. Take him out to lunch and find out what his story is. Find out if it's just his style and that's how he is with everyone, or if there is some way you've offended him or what. Perhaps you can set up a kind of signal you can give each other when it looks as if either one of you is going to get into it, and then you can handle it outside of the meeting.

Client: Well I'm willing to try that and maybe if that doesn't work, you can give it a try talking to him.

Coach: I'm willing to do that if we have to but I don't think it's going to be necessary. My guess is that you'll be able to handle it just fine.

Client: I appreciate your confidence in me and I do feel more able to keep myself out of trouble these days. Do you have any ideas about how I could keep getting better at this or do you feel like, you know, I'm as good as I'm going to get?

Coach: Well, maybe the next step you could take is to ask yourself questions like, "What question am I not answering that makes this questioner keep pressing in on me?" or, "What is it about the way that I'm speaking that is stirring up the response I'm getting?" My point is that you can start to hear yourself from other people's points of view while you're in the middle of speaking. That way you can correct yourself in the middle.

Client: Well, what you've said so far is really good, so I'm willing to go with these other suggestions as soon as I feel more able to handle what I've already started.

Summary

By now you may have forgotten where all of this began, which is with the premise of coaching. The principle of coaching is to provide language and practice that alter the structure of interpretation of the client. The coach in the examples above did that. From time to time the coach did more than that and gave specific instructions about specific activities. Perhaps these actions could even be considered coaching because the intent was to leave the client competent and not merely to solve the problem.

TYPE THREE

Type One and Type Two conversations will probably cover any conversations you have at work. The coaching situation with Bob is a good illustration of a Type Three conversation, so I will reference that work in the outline below.

Type Three conversation may be what you employ in coaching people outside of the work environment or with people with whom you have a profound relationship. The design elements are more intricate and probably will require more thinking on your part. But this additional work will more than justify itself in the depth and longevity of the changes brought about.

Some questions to address while designing the conversation are:

1 How will you specifically recognize the fulfillment of the coaching program? List observable phenomena.

Observable phenomena are changes that both the client and the coach can observe and agree on. Examples are speaking up more in meetings, initiating new programs, completing projects on time. Being clear in your thinking, feeling better about yourself, and having more certainty are not phenomena that can be observed by both the coach and client and therefore are best not listed as outcomes for the program.

In Bob's case, the program would be complete when:

A. He was promoted.
B. He was competent to deal successfully with the political environment at work.
C. He was able to take the necessary steps to continue on his upward career path.
D. He was able to do all of this while still attending to his commitments outside of work, including his family and his own well-being.

2 What distinctions must the client incorporate in order to fulfill the outcome as specified?

To address this you'll have to think in a new way. Instead of trying to figure out what new actions the client must take, ask yourself what the client must be able to observe in order to take this new action. For example, the client must be able to observe when he is interrupting a conversation, when he is continuing to put off taking action, or when he has stopped listening. The word *incorporate* is used in its literal sense, that is, that distinctions must become part of the body of the client. These distinctions become incorporated when they become part of a practice that is repeated again and again.

The important distinctions for Bob were:

A. That he listened from the point of view of a leader in the organization and not just a manager in the accounting department.
B. That he could detect levels of meaning and not obvious intentions in the speaking of others at work.

C. That he could detect who was trustworthy.
D. That he could observe when his communication was having the intended effect.
E. That he could observe as soon as his life began to go out of balance.

3 What distinctions (e.g., belief, fear, negative assessment) must the client abandon?

Perhaps this point is already clear, but with adult learners the greatest difficulty is in letting go of what is hindering learning. As coaches we often make the mistake of only pointing out new distinctions, new practices, and new actions and forget that there may be ways of observing and acting that are in the way. Clearly, it will take a period of observation to come to some understanding about what these distinctions are for a particular client.

From your reading of my case study with Bob, you probably could fill in this category yourself. Nonetheless, here are the distinctions I felt he must abandon:

A. Being obsessed with factual truth rather than the interpretation of events that was being acted upon at the job.
B. His strongly felt opinion that merely doing good work would lead to the recognition he wanted.
C. That office politics were below him and that he could ignore them.
D. That everyone should of course know about his good intentions and appreciate him for them.

4 What life-world structures (habits, relationships, practices, etc.) maintain the hindering distinctions?

In order to bring about the outcomes of the program, the client will have to undo structures that are getting in the way. For example, a client who is working on being able to listen better may have to give up the habit of working on his computer during conference calls, or flipping through his messages when a colleague is having a conversation with him. These are small examples, but I'm sure you can get the point.

For Bob to make progress he had to give up these life-world structures that had supported him up until now:

A. Micromanaging his department and personally verifying every number on every report they published.
B. Complaining about decisions upper management made instead of looking at the forces that shaped the decisions.

C. **Keeping quiet during meetings and letting his reports speak for themselves.**

5 What exercise(s)/practice(s) can you assign that will allow your client to observe these distinctions and structures?

This is designing a breakdown. Assign an observation exercise to your client, the point being for him to find out for himself the importance of the program.

Following are some of the self-observation exercises I asked Bob to engage in during our six-month program:

Focus: Gaining Strength—Initiating

- Invent, by declaration, an internal separation in yourself. Divide yourself into two persons, one who acts/reacts in life and one who observes and is passive in life.
- Using the following questions, begin to observe yourself in life. Observe quietly, passively. Observe your internal states as well as what you show the world.
- At the end of each day, scan through your day and note what happened and how you reacted. You may want to write notes so you can begin to notice patterns.

1. What actions, conversations, or relationships did you initiate?
2. What other actions, conversations, or relationships were there that you wanted to initiate but didn't? How are you justifying that?
3. What actions, conversations, or relationships will you initiate next? How can you ensure that what you initiate will be effective/satisfying?
4. What are you learning about yourself and initiating? How and when will you take what you're learning into action?

Focus: Gaining Strength—Making Decisions

- Invent, by declaration, an internal separation in yourself. Divide yourself into two persons, one who acts/reacts in life and one who observes and is passive in life.
- Using the following questions, begin to observe yourself in life. Observe quietly, passively. Observe your internal states as well as what you show the world.
- At the end of each day, scan through your day and note what happened and how you reacted. You may want to write notes so you can begin to notice patterns.

This exercise has two parts. Please attend to both parts each day.

Part I
1. What important decisions did you make?
2. How did you make those decisions?

3. Was there any conflict around your decisions? How did you deal with the conflict?
4. How do you feel about the decisions you made today? What are you learning about yourself and your decisions? How and when will you take your learning into action?

Part II
1. What decisions did you avoid making? What justifications, excuses, or stories did you employ in your avoidance?
2. When will you make the decisions?
3. What decisions will you make tomorrow? Write them down.

Use Part I and Part II of this exercise to support you in making decisions.

Focus: Gaining Strength—Making Requests
- Invent, by declaration, an internal separation in yourself. Divide yourself into two persons, one who acts/reacts in life and one who observes and is passive in life.
- Using the following questions, begin to observe yourself in life. Observe quietly, passively. Observe your internal states as well as what you show the world.
- At the end of each day, scan through your day and note what happened and how you reacted. You may want to write notes so you can begin to notice patterns.

This exercise has two parts. Please attend to both parts each day.

Part I
1. What requests did you make?
2. How successful were your requests (i.e., did what you requested happen)?
3. What made your requests successful?
4. How do you feel about your requests? What are you learning about yourself and requesting? When and how will you take what you're learning into action?

Part II
1. What requests did you avoid making? How are you justifying that?
2. When will you make the requests?
3. What requests will you make tomorrow? Write them down. What can you do to increase the likelihood that your requests will succeed?

Use Part I and Part II of this exercise to support you in making successful requests.

Focus: Gaining Strength—Pushing Back
- Invent, by declaration, an internal separation in yourself. Divide yourself into two persons, one who acts/reacts in life and one who observes and is passive in life.

- Using the following questions, begin to observe yourself in life. Observe quietly, passively. Observe your internal states as well as what you show the world.
- At the end of each day, scan through your day and note what happened and how you reacted. You may want to write notes so you can begin to notice patterns.

Pushing back means declining a request, publicly questioning someone else's assumptions, stating what you'd prefer instead of what's being offered, refusing to be characterized or pigeonholed, avoiding being manipulated—all done with as much respect, tact, and skill as possible.

1. In what ways did you push back in relationships, conversations, meetings?
2. What happened from your pushing back? How did you feel? Did it produce any conflict? How did you respond to the conflict?
3. Did you feel like pushing back and not do it? How are you justifying that? What were the consequences of not pushing back, especially in terms of your emotions, mood, energy?
4. What are you learning about yourself and pushing back? How and when will you take your learning into action?

Focus: What Are My Resources?
This assignment is slightly different. It's an inventory you complete by both observation and research.

1. What are your greatest strengths professionally and personally?
2. Who is part of your network of support? What specific support does each person provide?
3. What does it take for you to live the way you do? Specifically address the question in terms of:
   - monthly expenses (include yearly items such as property taxes, etc. by dividing them by 12)
   - hours dedicated to job (include travel), work at home, your spouse/lover, your children, meal preparation, cleaning, maintenance of home, clothes, car, etc.
   - emotional energy
   - hours devoted to self-care
   - any other costs, physical, mental, or monetary
4. What resources do you have to address all the costs listed in #3 above?
5. What are you learning in this exercise? Does your costs/resources analysis require any changes on your part? What new actions will you take from what you're discovering?

Focus: What Do I Want for the Future?
This assignment is slightly different. It's an inventory you complete by both observation and research. Please answer the following questions this week. For each time frame listed, please answer the questions below.

Time Frame
6 months
1 year
2 years
5 years
10 years
20 years

Questions
1. What do you want to be doing?
2. Whom do you want in your life? In what capacity?
3. What resources do you want to have?
4. What experiences do you want to be having?
5. In what ways do you want to be growing/learning?
6. In what other way could you describe your life?

Focus: Accomplishments at Work
- Invent, by declaration, an internal separation in yourself. Divide yourself into two persons, one who acts/reacts in life and one who observes and is passive in life.
- Using the following questions, begin to observe yourself in life. Observe quietly, passively. Observe your internal states as well as what you show the world.
- At the end of each day, scan through your day and note what happened and how you reacted. You may want to write notes so you can begin to notice patterns.

1. What did you actually accomplish at work today?
2. What will this accomplishment move forward?
3. How did you decide to accomplish this?
4. What action will you take from what you observed in this exercise?

Focus: Challenging Others at Work
- Invent, by declaration, an internal separation in yourself. Divide yourself into two persons, one who acts/reacts in life and one who observes and is passive in life.
- Using the following questions, begin to observe yourself in life. Observe quietly, passively. Observe your internal states as well as what you show the world.
- At the end of each day, scan through your day and note what happened and how you reacted. You may want to write notes so you can begin to notice patterns.

1. Whom did you challenge today?
2. Why?
3. What were all the outcomes of this challenge?
4. What action(s) will you take from what you have observed in this exercise?

Focus: Insistence at Work
- Invent, by declaration, an internal separation in yourself. Divide yourself into two persons, one who acts/reacts in life and one who observes and is passive in life.
- Using the following questions, begin to observe yourself in life. Observe quietly, passively. Observe your internal states as well as what you show the world.
- At the end of each day, scan through your day and note what happened and how you reacted. You may want to write notes so you can begin to notice patterns.

1. What did you insist upon today?
2. How did you justify your insistence?
3. What were the effects of your insistence upon yourself? Upon your work relationships?
4. What action(s) will you take from what you have observed in this exercise?

6. What practices can you assign that will incorporate the new distinctions (from #2 above)?

Designing practices takes creativity. If you've done a thorough job of addressing question #2, you will have an easier time of designing practices. Practices are meant to give the client a chance to make a new distinction over and over again, and then to follow up with an action which flows from that new observation. Perhaps remembering how you learned how to do something yourself will help you out in designing practices. What did you go through in learning to drive a car? Certainly the practice wasn't simply to get in and drive around! That might sound silly, but that is what some people consider practice to be—just go and do it, rather than take the steps necessary in order to do it competently. It's as if you told the person whom you were coaching in typing to just sit down and start typing, instead of going through all of the different exercises and practices it takes to really learn how to do it.

Here is a sample of the major practices I asked Bob to do during his program:

Focus: Discovering the Concerns of Others
For each of the people listed below, answer the following questions. Do research to find the answers; don't merely speculate on your own. Remember that the answers will keep changing. You will provide baseline information for yourself by doing the exercise. Additionally, you will begin to strengthen your ability to think and observe in bigger contexts.

People
1. Your peers
2. Your boss
3. Your boss's boss

4. Your three top internal customers
5. Your three top external customers
6. Your subordinates
7. The executive managing your part of the company
8. The CEO
9. The Chairman and two other board members
10. The person holding the job you want next

Questions
1. What are the three top business concerns of this person?
2. What is the career path of this person (past and future)?
3. What does this person value in a business associate?
4. What is this person's business agenda for the next six months, twelve months, two years, five years, ten years?
5. What is this person's style—of working, of leadership, of communicating?

Focus: Building a Network of Support
Part 1
Go back to your findings in the previous section, "Discovering the Concerns of Others." For each person listed (and for the additional people noted below), ask yourself the following questions. Then take the appropriate action to expand/extend your network of support.

People
1. Your peers
2. Your boss
3. Your boss's boss
4. Your three top internal customers
5. Your three top external customers
6. Your subordinates
7. The executive managing your part of the company
8. The CEO
9. The Chairman and two other board members
10. The person holding the job you want next

Additional People
• Your counterparts in other parts of the company
• Experts in the political environment of the company
• The people you admire at work
• The people making decisions about your career

Questions
1. What concerns or breakdowns can I alleviate for this person?
2. What information, support, or guidance can I offer to this person?
3. In what other ways can I support this person?

Part 2
Make a list of people at work who can be part of your network of support. Use the questions that follow to prompt your thinking. Keep your eyes open for new people to include.

1. What concerns/breakdowns do I currently have that someone can support me in?
2. What concerns/breakdowns do I anticipate having that someone can support me in?
3. What input, information, or guidance would make my current work easier? My future clearer?
4. Whose actions don't I understand? Who could shed light on them for me?
5. What future decision/policy would I like to know about in advance? Who could help me with this?

Focus: The Big Picture
By addressing the following questions, you will have a solid understanding of the big picture at your company.

1. What are the top five specific threats to your company during the next year? The next five years? The next ten years? What ought your company do about them?
2. What specific economic or political situations will impact your company most in the next year, the next five years, the next ten years? Answer this for your company as a whole, and for each major business. Then do it by geographical area: United States and North America, Asia, Europe, South America, Africa. What will the impact be? What ought your company do in response?
3. What people, both within and outside of your company, will have the most influence upon the company? What will the influence be?

7 What are the likely potential breakdowns in your client's enacting these practices?

The breakdowns will be in both beliefs and emotions, as well as in the existing constraints of time and energy, priorities, resources, and so on. Again, it will take observation of your client over time to determine what these potential breakdowns might be.

The breakdowns I predicted for Bob were:

A. **He would become discouraged by the complexity of the changes necessary.**
B. **He would become impatient with how long the program took.**
C. **He would make the judgment that he didn't have the necessary skills or temperament to be an executive.**

8 What will these breakdowns reveal to your client? Should you allow the breakdowns to happen or try to prevent them?

Breakdowns aren't bad. In fact, in a recent survey of executives, researchers learned that it's within breakdowns that leaders learn the most. If a breakdown is too disruptive to your client, however, he may stop the coaching program. Weigh the benefits of what will be revealed against the emotional and situational impact of the breakdown.

I was very aware that I would have to keep reenrolling Bob as his program went along. Usually during breakdown I would remind him of the purpose of our program and I would point out that it was actually good news to find out in a concrete way what was hindering his forward progress. Although it may have been uncomfortable at the time when he made such discoveries, it was these insights that showed Bob what had been getting in the way so that he could take some appropriate action. It was my preparation for and sensitivity to these breakdowns that ensured that Bob would move toward his goals.

9 What support will your client require during the program, especially during breakdown?

From knowing your client, take a moment to consider this point and prepare for both the breakdowns you are anticipating and the inevitable ones that will come unexpectedly.

Bob did a lot of his processing by writing in a journal and speaking with me on the phone. These two activities seemed sufficient to support Bob.

10 Who can provide support for your client?

The point here is that others besides you can support your client. A major program such as the one we are in the middle of discussing will require challenging, difficult changes in your client's orientation and behavior. It makes a lot of sense to have other people available to provide information and emotional support. I recommend that you don't make yourself into the equivalent of a heart and lung machine for your client. Doing so will not leave your client independent and it will leave you unnecessarily constricted in your own freedom of action.

Besides me, Nancy was available to support Bob, and as he built alliances with upper management, people in those ranks also began to support him.

11 How could you structure this coaching program?

- What will be its duration?
- How often will you and your client meet? What will be the duration of these meetings?
- How much time will this program demand of your client? What other resources?
- How often will you communicate? In what form?
- How available will you make yourself to your client?

Address all these points in your design and be open to changing them according to what happens when you present the program to your client and as the program progresses.

Bob's program lasted six months. We met for six half-days and spoke with each other on the phone weekly. The exercises I asked Bob to do probably took between two and four hours a week. I told Bob I would be available to him outside of our scheduled times if he encountered something requiring our immediate attention. That did in fact happen on several occasions during his program. I didn't tell Bob that I was available 24 hours a day. I did warn him that because of my other work, I might not be able to get back to him immediately in all cases. That was fine with him.

12 What metaphor(s) could you use to show the outcome of the program to your client?

Let me simply give you some examples of this. For someone who is becoming very distracted in the completion of a project, you could say that currently his work is like a pipe full of steam that has loose joints that allow the steam to escape and therefore diminish the power of the apparatus. After the coaching, the client's work would be like a pipe with no leaks, so that the full heat and pressure of the steam can be applied to the machine. For someone who is disorganized and has to reorganize himself each day or even each hour, perhaps you could use the metaphor of reading a book, so that being disorganized is like having to begin at page one again and again, while being organized allows one to pick up where one left off without any loss of time or effort. For a client who is not being assertive, perhaps you can use the metaphor of a diamond that is covered with dust, alluding to the fact that there is nothing wrong with the diamond and that it's simply a matter of cleaning it off so that its true brilliance can shine—the connection being that overcoming nonassertiveness is not a matter of the client being adequate but of there being something in the way of his adequacy coming across to others. Metaphors can be very memorable for your clients and can be used to give them an intuitive feel for what success in the program will be like.

The essential metaphor I kept returning to with Bob was that his executive potential was like oil buried deep beneath the ground, which would only become valuable when it was brought to the surface. Given that he worked for an oil company, this was an apt description for the task of showing his aptitude for leadership to the people who could promote him.

13 What paperwork (calendars, worksheets, etc.) would support your client?

The more support you can give to your client the better. What have you used to remind yourself, to keep yourself organized, or keep yourself focused on your work?

I gave Bob all of the practices and self-observation exercises in printed form so that he did not have to remember them. I also provided him with a loose-leaf binder with tabs for the purpose of the program, his journal, current self-observation, current practice, and notes.

14 How can you present this program to your client? What questions is your client likely to have? What concerns? What objections? How can you address these?

Sometimes I wonder if the food tastes better in a restaurant that has beautiful furniture, or if we really do trust a salesperson who is well dressed. In any case, take as much care in the presentation of your program as you did in designing it. That way you'll ensure an open acceptance by your client.

From my understanding of Bob, I guessed that the most important aspect of enrolling him in doing all of this work was establishing my credibility. It was important for him to know that I had coached other people successfully in accomplishing what he was setting out to do. I did this by telling him stories of other coaching programs and reminding him of these stories from time to time.

In developing yourself as a coach, I recommend that you begin with Type One conversations, then move to Type Two and Type Three as you grow more competent. Don't try brain surgery before you know how to administer first aid.

ASSESSMENT EXERCISE

Use these questions to prepare for Conversation Number One. Base your assessment upon *actual observations*.

1. What opening did you observe for coaching?
    *   breakdown (specify)
    *   enhancing a competence (specify)
    *   new possibility for client (specify)
    *   threat to social identity (specify)

2. What new competence or quality must your client have to address the situation described in #1 above?
3. What is your potential client's current competence in doing this? Write down at least three examples of behavior that verify your assessment.

Using at least one model, determine the structure of interpretation of your potential client.

- Five Elements Model
  - Immediate concerns
  - Commitments
  - Possibilities
  - Mood
  - Current history
- Domains of Competence Model
  - Facts and events
  - Relationships with others
  - Self-management
- Components of Satisfaction/Effectiveness Model
  - Intellect
  - Emotion
  - Will
  - Context
  - Soul

SELF-OBSERVATION EXERCISE

Use these questions to design an observation exercise to present to your client at Conversation One. A sample exercise follows the questions.

1. What is to be observed?
2. What is the duration of the exercise?
3. What is the frequency of observation?
4. What are the exact instructions for this exercise?

Sample Self-Observation Exercise

Beginning Date: (Today)
End Date: (Ten days from today)

1. Invent, by declaration, an internal separation in yourself. Divide yourself into two persons, one who acts/reacts in life and one who observes and is passive in life.
2. Begin to observe how you react in life. Observe what happens (life) and then what you do, say, feel, think, your reactions, etc. Observe quietly, passively. Keep noticing your judgments about yourself, about others, about life. Observe your internal states as well as what you show the world.

Continued

Sample Self-Observation Exercise—cont'd

3. At the end of each day, scan through your day again and note what happened and how you reacted.
4. Do this exercise for ten days.

PRACTICE EXERCISE

Use these questions to design a practice to present to your client for Conversation Two. A new practice exercise is a combination of action and reflection which captures learning and connects it back to action so that competence improves. An example of a practice is on the following page.

1. What repeated behavior can your client do that will improve his competence?
2. How will your client know if the action(s) is successful? What are the standards?
3. What specifically will you ask your client to reflect upon while doing this practice?
4. What will be the duration and structure of the practice?
5. What are the exact instructions for this exercise?

Sample Practice Exercise for Business

Objective

To establish and maintain management practices that enable you to identify your priorities and manage your time more effectively.

Directions

1. List all of the activities that you actually do at work.
    a. Divide them into categories A, B, and C, with A being the most important for the success of the business and C being the least important.
    b. Within each category number the activities, with #1 being the most vital.
    c. Write next to each activity how much time you spend doing it each week or, in some cases, each month.
2. Then ask yourself:
    a. Can I allocate my time more effectively? How?
    b. What activities can I give to someone else?
    c. What is my job at the company, really?
3. List all of the activities you wish you were doing at work, but that you never get around to doing. Be exhaustive in your listing.
    a. Divide the activities into categories and prioritize them as above.
    b. Write next to each activity how much time each week/month it would take you to complete.

Sample Practice Exercise for Business—cont'd

4. Then ask yourself:
   a. What would be the benefit of doing this activity?
   b. What recurring breakdowns could I avoid by doing this activity?
   c. What is my job at this company really?
5. Have your staff do steps #1 through #4. Then, having shared what you wrote and having read their responses, ask them for ways to reorganize and/or redesign your department's work systems, accountability procedures, management systems, reward systems, and training and development of staff.
6. What did you learn by doing this?

SUGGESTED READING

The listed books offer many different approaches to coaching. None is applicable to all clients. Each is useful for particular clients. By becoming familiar with many of them, a coach will be able to work successfully with a wide array of people. If you're interested in reading only a few, I recommend the following in the order listed:

1. Educating the Reflective Practitioner, Donald Schön
2. The Path of Least Resistance, Robert Fritz
3. Shambhala, Chögyam Trungpa

Adams, & James, L (1986). *The Care and Feeding of Ideas*. Reading, MA: Addison-Wesley Publishing Company.
   A primer in fostering and supporting creativity and innovation.
Anderson, & Nancy. (1984). *Work with Passion*. New York: Carroll & Graf Publishers, Inc.
   A practical guide, replete with exercises and examples, that directs the reader in finding a career of passion and purpose.
Argyris, & Chris. (1990). *Overcoming Organizational Defenses*. Boston: Allyn and Bacon.
   The author is a founder of the organizational development discipline. He explains how it's possible for very intelligent people to come together in a group and have their intelligence cut in half. Additionally, he presents many examples of how organizations populated by well-meaning people "protect" themselves from change. From his own experience, he recommends ways to overcome the defenses.
Beckett, Liana, & Stephanie Covington (1988). *Leaving the Enchanted Forest*. San Francisco: Harper & Row.
   A text intended to break the spell that romantic love has cast over many people in our culture. Contains useful exercises. (See also Solomon: About Love.)
Bradshaw, & John. (1988). *Bradshaw On: The Family*. Beach, FL: Health Communications, Inc. Deerfield.
   Proposes that many emotional/psychological problems have their sources in the dynamics of family relationships. The patterns of response and reaction learned in the family will likely appear at some point in an extended coaching program. The book's distinctions can help you recognize these patterns for what they are.

Burns, & David, D. (1980). *Feeling Good.* New York: Signet Classics.
An introduction to cognitive therapy, which is based upon the premise that thought initiates feelings and moods. Can be helpful in designing self-observation exercises, and as a framework for dealing with troubling experiences.

Dail, & Lee, Hilda (1983). *The Lotus and the Pool.* Boston: Shambhala Publications.
Presents a process for finding a suitable career (based upon long experience). The approach is based upon profound human values. The book has useful exercises and practical advice.

DePree, & Max. (1989). *Leadership Is an Art.* New York: Doubleday.
Reading this book is like sitting under a palm tree in a beautiful oasis while a cool breeze caresses your face. Deeply human. Credible because of the undeniable success of the author. Inspiring.

Fournies, & Ferdinand, F. (1978). *Coaching for Improved Work Performance.* Blue Ridge Summit, PA: Tap Books, Inc.
Not a book on coaching as presented in this text. Rather, it's a tract on how to use the tenets of behaviorism to manipulate the behavior of others. Why would professional people tolerate being treated the way the author recommends?

Fritz, & Robert. (1984). *The Path of Least Resistance.* New York: Ballantine Books.
Proposes a methodology for creating goals and a structure that supports their fulfillment. Especially useful in preventing the excuses, justifications, and self-defeating behavior people engage in around goals. Valuable background for any coach.

Goldstein, Joseph, & Kornfield, Jack (1987). *Seeking the Heart of Wisdom.* Boston: Shambhala Publications.
How to work skillfully with our human condition. Full of exercises and recommended practices that can be taken on for life. Well written, friendly, and nondogmatic.

Kinlaw, & Dennis, C. (1989). *Coaching for Commitment.* San Diego, CA: University Associates, Inc.
A collection of some of the best techniques of reflective listening, open-ended questioning, supportive speaking, and so on. Based upon the varied and extensive experience of the author. The presentation is clear and well organized.

Kornfield, & Jack. (1993). *A Path with Heart.* New York: Bantam Books.
Written by a meditation teacher who is also a clinical psychologist, the text is a compassionate sharing of what he's learned of the spiritual path through personal experience and working with thousands of students. Thorough, understandable, and unflinching in dealing with pitfalls on the path, from students using it to deny/avoid psychological pain to teachers who exploit students. Each chapter has suggested exercises and practices. A valuable resource.

MacIntyre, & Alasdair. (1981). *After Virtue.* London: Gerald Duckworth & Co.. reprint, Notre Dame, IN: University of Notre Dame Press, 1981.
An examination of morality in an historic, philosophical context. Very useful for coaches in showing the fundamental importance of practices in determining who we are.

Schön, & Donald, A. (1987). *Educating the Reflective Practitioner.* San Francisco: Jossey-Bass, Inc.
This book (and The Reflective Practitioner, *which follows) reveals the way professionals actually work, not by applying formulae, but by learning and correcting as they go. By studying diverse disciplines, the author shows how one can reflect-in-action and how a coach can contribute. Useful, readable, and realistic.*

The Reflective Practitioner 1983. New York: Basic Books, Inc.

Solomon, & Robert, C. (1988). *About Love.* New York: Simon & Schuster.
A book that presents a new way to understand and create romance beyond the self-defeating narratives perpetuated by songs, novels, movies, and television. Written by a philosopher with wit, insight, and gentleness. (See Beckett: Leaving the Enchanted Forest.*)*

Starcevich, Matt, M., & Stowell, Steven J. (1987). *The Coach*. Salt Lake City, UT: The Center for Management and Organization Effectiveness.
A form of coaching based upon research of successful managers. Straightforward. Applicable to boss/subordinate scenarios at work.
Trungpa, & Chögyam. (1984). *Shambhala*. Boston: Shambhala Publications.
Makes available the ancient, powerful approach to personal transformation in the Tibetan tradition. Full of wisdom and practical solutions to difficult problems. Shows how to develop compassion, generosity, and acceptance and still lead a day-to-day, in-the-world life.
Woodman, & Marion. (1982). *Addiction to Perfection*. Toronto: Inner City Books.
A challenging, dense essay written from a Jungian perspective that unravels the inner forces that drive many women to desperate attempts to be perfect in body and behavior.

10

Stuck

Stuck: By calling the chapter this, I want to address two topics. The first is when the focus of the coaching is the client being stuck in his or her job or life, and the second is what to do when our coaching (which to us seems, of course, brilliant) is somehow leaving the client stuck.

CLIENT BEING STUCK

Probably the majority of our clients come to us because they feel stuck in their life. Of course, the word "stuck" describes a wide variety of phenomena. Clients can mean that they are bored, not learning anything, and don't see a future for themselves. They could also mean that they are attempting to accomplish something and can't get it to happen. Alternately, they might mean they are seeing the same cycles of behavior return again and again, at their work or in their relationships or in how they take care of themselves. It is even used to describe existential dread or angst, the experience when clients feel no grounding or support or meaning in their life.

Our initial questioning will quickly clarify for us what the client means. The central distinction with clients who report that they are stuck is the same, regardless of the content of the experience. My feeling is that they all share a common root. The root is feeling unheld by the world. By this I mean that they do not feel in their body—and consequently in their emotions and thinking—that they have a place in the world.

In this state, they find themselves working frantically to resolve the anxiety and frustration that invariably accompany this experience. Their actions become unskillful, self-defeating, and sometimes destructive. Frequently they judge themselves negatively, disparage others, and cynically turn away from whatever support is offered. They are certain that their situation is unique and complex and that what they are going through has never happened to the same extent to anyone else. They simultaneously feel that they have to get out of the experience and that somehow there is no way to get out of it (because if there were a way, they would have figured it out by now). This cognitive/emotional dilemma gives rise to the frustration I just mentioned, which is quickly followed by anxiety as they begin to worry that this may go on forever.

All this may sound terribly difficult and dramatic but that is because we make it into that. As I said, I am proposing that the root is feeling unheld by the world, so let me lay out what I see to be how this experience (for the most part) unfolds. (It is because the phenomenon unfolds in this way that it becomes complicated, and as coaches, we can get caught in this web if we don't know to work on the root instead of its manifestations.)

Once we feel the searing pain of not being held, we immediately, reflexively look for who did this to us. We blame others, which leads to our then acting cynically toward them. Or we blame ourselves, which amplifies our inner voice of negative self-assessment. We do not know to explore the pain—it seems too much and we want to move quickly away from it—and that is where the frantic actions begin.

As coaches, instead of trying to fix all of the difficulties that arise from the frantic activity, it is more helpful to invite the client to investigate what the experience of being unheld is like (which will alternately be described as lonely, misunderstood, out of place, unseen, unloved, and abandoned). I am not talking about a psychological state that is a product of trauma or abuse. Rather, I am pointing to a way of looking at life that seems totally true and valid. The key to undoing it is knowing that there is a lot of truth in the point of view but it is only looking at life from one angle.

There is no use in arguing with our clients into seeing the partiality of their view. They'll have to discover that what they are seeing is not the whole story even though at the time it feels like it is. So it is true, in a way, like the existentialists say, that we are alone. No one can feel what we are feeling, or go through what we have to go through, or live with the consequences of the choices we make. These points seem to me to be unarguably the case but it is also true that we are conjoined with others.

The food we eat, the water we drink, the clothes we wear, the homes we live in, and the roads we drive on link us inseparably to everyone who has ever lived. Our very body is a gift from the ancestors, as is the language that we speak, which gives rise to the thoughts we have. It is not possible to step out of the world and, in fact, every moment the world is holding us. We are given air to breath, gravity that holds us, trees that shade us, and the possibility of relationship with the next person who walks by. We forget all of this in the moment of being tripped by pain, searching for whom to blame for it, how to escape it.

With all that as background, here is what we can do as coaches.

- First, keep in mind all that I said.
- Second, design practices that support the client to build exquisite self-care for himself. Explore together different domains of concern he has and how his needs in each of these can be realistically met. The phenomena of being

stuck is frequently started by a person who is neglecting sleep, food, companionship, self-expression, exercise, encounters with beauty; and then wonders why he feels dried up and abandoned.

• Third, design a series of exercises that help the client to scale his expectations. People in our culture watch too many movies and look at too many magazines that have images of people whose lives are "perfect." Along with the mighty support of marketing, we conclude our life ought to be, should be the same as we see on the screen or in the magazines. We even conclude that we deserve it to be.

We've been fooled: no one's life is like that. Movie stars have to do two hours of makeup and have three hours of special lighting arranged so that they can look like that. The lives of people who have great wealth and power aren't especially happy, in case you haven't been noticing.[1] Our client's expectations on this become realistic when he sees through this mirage to how life really is. A client who watches the Olympics and then says "I ought to be able to do that" will likely severely damage himself when he jumps off the 10-meter diving platform attempting a triple-twisting double somersault. That example is an obvious one, but people ruin their lives trying to have the wealth of Bill Gates or the body of Michael Jordan. You see how this goes when we have unrealistic expectations that aren't fulfilled. We feel that the world has let us down and the whole syndrome that I've described above kicks in.

Once our client has taken care of his genuine needs and has set realistic expectations, life begins to flow effortlessly and he begins to harmonize with the people around him. Suddenly the world is there with all its stark beauty and intimate tenderness. Stuckness is gone—by dissolving its roots.

PROGRAM BEING STUCK

Sooner or later, one of our coaching programs will become stuck. Our client who seemed clear, engaged, and committed during the last session hasn't done his practices and seems to have forgotten everything he has learned. We try everything we know and the same or similar keeps happening over and over. Since there is a time limit for our coaching, we begin to feel some pressure, which further clouds our creativity. At this point, it is easy for us to blame our client and many coaches, in fact, do just that. They categorize the client as "uncoachable" or "uncommitted" or "not in enough pain yet" and stop the coaching. My view is that this juncture is the ultimate moment for coaches to learn something, and maybe the biggest chance for our clients to have a developmental breakthrough.

It is always possible to end the coaching, but there is a lot to try out first. Here are some suggestions. (Careful readers will notice that the coach's response to

---

[1] See the work of Martin Seligman in *Authentic Happiness* for more on this.

program stuckness is an example of the events written about immediately above.) I am not going to attempt to list all of the possible reasons why a coaching program might be stuck. Instead, I am going to list a series of actions you can take to move the program forward and learn something about yourself.

1. Reexamine your initial interview of the client. What assumptions did you make and how did you come to these? How grounded was your assessment? What in the client's actions are not accounted for in your assessment? Consider redoing the intake interview, including speaking to people who work with and live around your client. It is likely that you missed something or misunderstood it.

2. Examine whether the client is acting in ways consistent with your own "shadow." Your shadow is a collection of unwanted qualities that you have pushed out of your own awareness. We usually find out about our own shadow by seeing it projected onto others. When clients act in ways consistent with our shadow, we have a very difficult time understanding it and an impossible time intervening in it. You can know for sure if you find yourself having a strong emotional, personal response to your client's actions. This usually indicates that someone is taking actions we are afraid that we ourselves might take and, therefore, our emotional guardians are screaming. Speak with someone who knows you well, who is a good observer and is candid. Ask your friend if the behavior you are seeing (remember to maintain confidentiality of your client) is something that could be your shadow. If it is, seek some support yourself in working with it before you address it with your client.

3. Investigate whether your client has the wherewithal in his life to go through with the coaching program. Does he have enough physical energy, emotional reserves, and relational support? If not, address these topics before continuing with the rest of the coaching program.

4. Change the venue where you are doing the coaching. Go for a walk outside. Sit at the beach. Stroll through nature. Shifting the environment often brings new topics to awareness. Moving the body also frees people from typical thought patterns.

5. Do the coaching work in the session itself. Instead of assigning a body scan, do it during the session. Instead of asking your client to go to the gym to do weightlifting, have your next session at the gym. Frequently, once the pump of practice has been primed during the session, it is easier for it to continue outside the session.

6. Form a partnership with the client and do a forensic review of all the work you've done together. Methodically go through each conversation, each meeting, each assignment looking for what was unsaid, unheard, misunderstood, not addressed.

7. Has your coaching somehow brought to the surface abuse in the client's background? It is difficult to describe on paper, but there is a unique sense

that is somehow emotional and somatic when such abuse is in the atmosphere. If you get any inkling of this, refer your client to a competent, trusted therapist who specializes in abuse. Your coaching may have to be postponed for a while or you may be able to form a partnership with the therapist and do both simultaneously. If you are not sure, find a delicate, spacious way to ask your client about it.

8. Study for a while through conversations and self-observations the emotions your client has connected with your coaching. Emotions are directly tied to action. Many clients habitually attempt to bypass or suppress their emotions, which makes it very difficult to take on new activities. The coaching for a few weeks might consist of the client doing some very close, possibly hourly, audit of himself emotionally.

9. Your client may have conflicting commitments. For example, he may want the promotion but be simultaneously committed to working less hours. Kegan and Lahey's book shows a brilliant exercise for revealing competing and conflicting commitments and a methodology for addressing them.[2]

10. Shift the content of your coaching radically. For example, if content has been primarily cognitive, move it fully into the body realm. Or, if it's been about emotions, for a while make it about learning new ideas. Open your creativity and expand your palate of practices. Invite your client to do art, visit museums, travel, listen to different music, anything that will require him to stand in a new identity at least while doing the practice.

That list is a beginning. I intend it to spur your own creativity. As I said previously, when clients are stuck, it is the supreme moment to learn something. If you only have clients who move along readily, you will easily become complacent, maybe even arrogant. It is important for our development to have our best efforts defeated from time to time and remake ourselves. Isn't that what we are asking our client to do?

The most important job we have as coaches is to keep ourselves in a fluid state, never landing on a solid understanding of ourselves, others, or life. In 500 bc, an ancient Greek philosopher, Thalus, said "Life is water." Most moderns think he got his physics wrong. He was really saying that life is moving, life is flowing, life is a process. When we are fluid ourselves, we harmonize with life, and as soon as we settle on an idea we begin to harden and become less responsive. Getting stuck in our coaching work shows us where we have become hardened and is a red flare pointing to exactly where our work is. Will you take it up?

The longer you coach, the more you will develop your own large array of practices and exercises. Keep working to reveal your own blind spots and keep learning new methodologies to work with people. Even if you are at the moment fabulously successful at your coaching work, sooner or later, as I've said before, you'll find yourself in a stuck place with a client. At that point, you

[2] This exercise appears in the book *How the Way We Talk Can Change the Way We Work*.

will be glad that you've done your own work and have kept educating yourself. The books at the end of this chapter take up this theme and encourage readers to expand their view of people and the world.

SUGGESTED READING

These books will show you many angles on how to work when you or your client is stuck.

Gerrish, Michael. *When Working Out Isn't Working Out.* New York: St. Martin's Griffin, 1999.
 Unique book written by a psychotherapist and exercise physiologist that shows many methods for overcoming obstacles to our development.
Kegan, Robert and Lisa Laskow Lahey. *How the Way We Talk Can Change the Way We Work.* San Francisco: Jossey-Bass, 2001.
 Brings (among many other gems) to the world a phenomenally clear, complete, and powerful process for uncovering and dissolving competing commitments. A skillful razor for cutting through stuckness.
Lasater, Judith. *Relax and Renew.* Berkeley, CA: Rodmell Press, 1995.
 The author presents gently, peacefully to the world a yoga that brings profound rest, slowing the nervous system and rejuvenation. Many photographs, clear instructions, beautifully laid out. Classic handbook for the harried.
Loeb, Paul Rogat. *The Impossible Will Take a Little While.* New York: Basic Books, 2004.
 Inspiration from contemporary, heroic people who speak directly to our heart and mind. Shows the emotional, cognitive approach they took to seemingly immovable forces (segregation, communism, and apartheid). Electrifying and enlightening.
Mellin, Laurel. *The Pathway.* New York: HarperCollins Publishers, 2003.
 A book that could only be written by someone who has worked with the most "stuck" of people (who overeat, overwork, overspend, etc.) for more than 20 years. Cuts to the root of self-defeating, obsessive, stubborn behaviors with a proven methodology based upon solid research and practical experience. Indispensable.
Schwartz, Barry. *The Paradox of Choice.* New York: HarperCollins, 2004.
 Helps untie some of most perplexing mental knots by challenging some of our most cherished beliefs—that more choice is better, that we know what will make us happy, etc. Brilliant tool for illuminating the benefits of simplicity in thought and action.
Wilson, Timothy D. *Strangers to Ourselves.* Cambridge, MA: Harvard University Press, 2002.
 The book clearly, convincingly shows us how much of ourselves we do not know (and perhaps cannot know). The culmination of more than 30 years of study, research, and experimentation, yet jargon-free and readily accessible. A book you'll never get over and one you'll want everyone to read.

11

Getting in Condition
for Change

Coaching can be a hugely effective and a relieving intervention in someone's life. When it's not, that's often because the client is not in the condition to take the coaching on. It's not new to say that our lives are full, our bodies are stressed, our relationships are frequently neglected, and we have endless amounts of input from sources everywhere in the world. We can easily avoid frustration as a coach and make the experience smoother for our clients if we attend to the client's capacity for change as coaching begins. This chapter makes the case for attending to these conditions, provides assessment questions for determining a client's capacity for change, and suggests remedies so that readiness can be improved. By the way, these remedies can be taken on by coaches who can find their lives in the same condition as those of their clients.

Anyone who's coached for a period of time knows that it is rarely a matter of clients discovering what they want and coaches laying out a path to get there. There are unexpected and complex and stubborn obstacles that can be frustratingly difficult to resolve. When this occurs, we take one of three steps. First, there are numerous explorations about whether the client really wants the goal and wants it sufficiently (the notion here is that clarity and strong desire are the engines of success). Second, the coach will question the path that was designed. Was it too steep, too boring, out of step with the client? Third, the coach and client together might talk about incompatibility. Maybe there is not sufficient chemistry for the coaching program to be powerful.

There is another category that takes in elements of the other three. In this situation, the coach says that the client is "uncoachable." Most clients hear this as something that is personally wrong with them. The additional trouble with such a characterization is that the client never knows how to respond. The client asks herself, "What can do I to get coachable?" In sum, it is not a fruitful end of a coaching engagement.

This chapter is meant to alert coaches to another possible factor—and a very common one—for the program not getting traction. When you read it you might say, "Well, that's obvious." Nonetheless, it is rare for coaches to attend to it.

WHAT'S NECESSARY FOR CHANGE

I propose that the first design step for a coach (an initial meeting, an intake session, and a time of analysis precede design) is to determine the client's *current capacity* for being coached. Clients come to us with very full lives, competing commitments, stressful pressures, and often in the middle of a breakdown that initiated the coaching itself. Anything we say or bring to a person in such a condition likely won't help for long. Even if the client is in acute distress and flies into action, embracing all elements of the program, she'll soon end up with more stress, less wherewithal to lead her everyday life and may be even a bleaker view of her future. Coaches who attempt inspiring the client to "be bigger" than the current situation similarly set the client up for a very hard landing when the coaching program is concluded.

Recollect please that the outcomes of coaching are a client who is excellent in a long-term way and can self-correct and self-generate. Reflecting upon this for a moment, you'll see that fundamental to these three elements is that the client has built more capacity, not wrung more performance out of herself in order to sprint to an immediate goal.

One of the important contributions coaches make is having a wide perspective on the client's situation. The perspective includes taking into account not only as many circumstances and conditions in the client's life as possible but also a longer time horizon, backwards and forwards, than the client brings. This becomes especially important when the situation in question has lasted a long time already, or when building the client's lasting competence will take a long, sustained commitment. Yes, it is important to have immediate or near-immediate results so that some pressure is lifted from the client, but let's not conclude that the whole point of the program is that initial relief.

Bringing this perspective allows the coach to realistically view and appreciate the life condition of the client. Such an examination frequently reveals that the basics necessary for initiating and sustaining change are not present. It is as if we are attempting to load a large cargo onto a ship with many leaks, even gaping holes, or trying to drive a multi-ton truck across a decrepit bridge. Either effort might look fine at first but will soon show its true limitations.

Being in condition to change means that clients have reserves of attention, physical and emotional energy, and social support. The way we live our lives in the twenty-first century makes the building of these reserves extremely challenging. Many of us feel pressed in our personal, business, relational, and financial domains. When not pressed by external circumstances, we usually feel compelled to maximize our activities so that at the end of the week or the end of the month, nothing is left. Then something goes amiss, or a potential new possibility fascinates us, and we consider working with a coach. Somehow we imagine that the coach knows something that will make this unworkable situation turn out just fine.

As coaches we mis-serve our clients when we pretend (unfortunately, some coaches do believe that they can—by force of personality, clearness of insight, or through clever motivation—shift reality) that our coaching will work and bring about the intended outcomes, regardless of the client's current capacity for change. Rather than pretense, the first design step is asking: what activities does it make sense for the client to end? What relationships are best altered? What about the client's self-care must be addressed? And, what additional support must be in place so that sufficient reserves can be built (See Figure 11.1.)

Some coaches might find this approach too slow, cumbersome, or boring. Still it is practical, realistic, and necessary. The step will also save you from blaming the client or blaming yourself or falling into frustration when the client doesn't progress as planned. Clients cannot long sustain an effort beyond their current capacity without doing damage to their health, mental state, mood, or relationships. All these factors must be included when we are bringing the perspective I've been speaking about.

Nothing long term can take root unless all those conditions are harmonized. For coaches it can be personally challenging to have the patience to slowly begin the program by attending to the basics. But it is like training in karate: for the first day, week, month, or year, the student isn't breaking bricks or repelling the attack of three people simultaneously. She is stretching her hamstrings, opening her hips, learning to focus, and slowly building strength by engaging in exercises over and over again. Bruce Lee wasn't built in a day.

Readers might protest that clients don't have the necessary determination to persist in these basic activities. And, therefore, coaches must go along with the impatience. Instead, coaches can use this initial step to talk about and educate the client in what sustainable change requires. Probably too many of us have watched movies that start with someone being 300 pounds overweight and end up with her being the Olympic diving champion. Here in the real world, where we live, a change like that is possible but it would take a long time and a full life change for the diver.

To be honest, truthful, and authentic, we coaches have to base our work on solid principles and not on salesmanship. Even those of us who find ways of putting our clients in such a pressurized situation that she does in fact perform—and that the results do consequently happen—are neglecting the long term, are forgetting in this scenario that the client didn't become self-correcting and never discovered her own source of inner power or outer support and, consequently, never became self-generating. In a world where so much seems to be going faster and faster, let's not forget our humanity and that we are biological beings and not electronic ones.

ASSESSING THE CLIENT'S READINESS

How do you assess someone's readiness for change? Being clear and precise is helpful, as is being energetically committed; they are just not sufficient. Have you ever seen people at the end of a marathon, even very committed people, who cannot continue once their physiology gives way? And even people who somehow force themselves to complete the race are not in good shape for quite a long time afterwards. There is no substitute for long-term training in such a situation. Our everyday life circumstances are much more complicated than completing a marathon because the running course keeps changing, the distances keep morphing, and who is supporting us or thwarting us keeps shifting as well.

Depending upon the degree of your client's openness, the depth of mutual relationship, and the length of the engagement, you can customize the following instrument to get a feel for your client's readiness for change. There is more information and resources on all these topics in the bibliography at the end of this chapter.

Client's Self-Assessment

- How stressed and stretched does your client say he or she is? (Does this feel accurate to you from being with them?)
- Is your client feeling financial, relational, or employment pressure?
- Does your client feel satisfied in her or his work?
- How complex and unstable is the client's work life? Personal life?
- How much available non-assigned attention, energy, and creativity does your client say he or she has?
- What's your client's overall report of their emotional state?
- How does the client assess her/his overall sense of health and well-being?

General Well-Being

Here are some questions to work with in determining how well your client is taking care of herself/himself.

- How many hours of sleep does she or he get per night?
- How many hours of exercise per week?
- What does she or he typically eat for breakfast? How long is taken for this meal? For lunch? Dinner?
- How long is the average workweek? How long is the average workday? How many days does she or he take off per week? Length and frequency of vacations? What does she or he do to refresh and renew herself/himself? (This is different than decompress, unwind).
- Does your client smoke?
- How many ounces of alcohol does she or he drink each week?
- What is your client's intake of caffeine?
- How much external stimulation does she or he take in during the day? (For example, email, texts, twitters, music, meetings, internet, or other media).

- How many hours per week does your client spend per week commuting?
- When was the last comprehensive physical exam? When was the last dental checkup?
- How many nights per month does your client spend traveling away from home?

Relationship

- How deep and close in is your client's network of support?
- Whose well-being does she or he feel responsible for?
- How much time is spent each week in non-work-related conversations?
- Who are the specific people the client feels she or he can be open, vulnerable, and undefended with?
- Who are people who are toxic for the client? What can she or he do to reduce or eliminate contact with this person?

Others Sources of Stress/Renewal

- How often is your client in nature? (Golf courses do not count.)
- When does she or he encounter beauty? (This could be natural or artistic expression.)
- How much chaos or disorder does your client have in her/his work or personal environment?
- What does she or he do to stay educated beyond business-related reading?
- To whom or to what is your client dedicated beyond the survival of herself/ himself and her/his family?
- What activities does your client have to cultivate creativity?
- What organizations (churches, community groups, etc.) does your client belong to that are a source of support and renewal?

WHAT TO DO WITH WHAT YOU FIND

Here are some overall principles to use in assisting your client in having a strong foundation upon which coaching can succeed.

- Simplify life as much as possible (practically, this means taking as much support and nurturance in and eliminating as much disorganizing, toxic input as possible);
- Strongly support your client in establishing regular routines of sleep, eating, and exercise (This will improve your client's ability to concentrate, deal with the disorder of starting something new, and stay resilient in the face of challenges).

FIGURE 11.1   Getting in condition for change.

- Collaborate with your client in establishing a strong network of support. If none exists, start with an inventory of current associates, colleagues, and friends and ask your client to reach out to each person and set up a situation in which support can be made available as necessary.
- Remember that your client is more than a physical body. Consequently, strongly suggest that she or he take up activities that renew his or her mind, heart, and spirit. Being in beautiful nature, listening to music are

renewing (classical music, especially Mozart and Bach, have been shown to integrate brain activity, so these can be especially helpful).

- For folks who are overstimulated, reducing chemical and electronic stimulation will be of great assistance. Even though your client might feel uncomfortable when the world becomes quieter and her/his body less jumpy, be encouraging through the transition so that she or he can come to a place of greater calm and resourcefulness.
- Helping your client with mental hygiene can be quite important. This means releasing from patterns of recurring anxious thought, second-guessing, or engaging in worst-case scenario thinking. No one needs to be a therapist to ask clients to observe thoughts and redirect them.
- Ask your client during an early conversation what she or he will give up or cut back on in order to make time and space for the coaching to occur (other than sleep, meals, time with important relationships or renewal time).
- Ask your client to display physical props to remind her/him to return to what's important and so that beauty surrounds her/him; for example, pictures of nature, or live plants or flowers, or pictures of loved ones, or reminders in the form of cards or screen savers, or another object that reminds her/him of a deeper, larger world outside the immediate activity.

Examples

Example 1

I worked with the managing partner of an international architecture firm based in San Francisco. He was working on projects throughout the States, in Paris, and in Japan. New technology was constantly being brought onto the scene, outdating the skills he had honed during his 30-year career. He was being groomed to be the CEO and he had no time or available attention to develop himself in the necessary ways.

This fellow was warm, open and friendly, as someone from the Midwest of the United States can be. Balancing those fine qualities, it seemed to me, was an exaggerated sense of responsibility for everyone and everything in any way associated with the firm. I could tell right away that for this leader to take on the next level of his career, he had to free up his life for generating a new vision, renewing his enthusiasm, and building different relationships with customers, vendors, and employees.

The usual dilemma with a busy person was present: how to start something new when there was no room for it to exist? My solution was to start with two very small, but—it turned out to be—pivotal practices. I asked him to take a 10-minute walk every day outside the building into the neighborhood where he worked in downtown San Francisco. On this walk, he re-found his love for architecture and urban environments and, even in this brief period of time, his head cleared a bit and he could look beyond the crisis of the day.

The second practice was to go to lunch twice per week with someone from the office, starting with the younger people whom he didn't know very well. From this simple exercise, he got away from the office and built a new appreciation for the talent and commitment of the people with whom he worked. He also discovered underlying forces of friction and untapped pools of creativity. He came away from each lunch with renewed eagerness to engage with people and a freshened commitment to the future of the firm.

After a month or so of doing these activities, along with a few others, he began to have enough available attention and energy to tackle the more challenging aspects of his upcoming new role. He was able to do that without adding any additional stress to his life or feeling that he was neglecting important people.

Example 2

The client came to me from the high-tech world of Silicon Valley, close to where I live. He was a high-level operations manager in a semiconductor firm. He was such a technical expert and virtuoso in solving technical problems that he'd been stuck at his current level, high though it was, for 12 years—a very strange occurrence for an organization used to rotating people every 3 years.

Other coaches reading this can probably predict the situation. My client was so embedded in the day-to-day that he didn't have enough vision or a long enough time horizon to be considered for advancement to the executive ranks where he wanted to be. He considered it a virtue to storm in at the last moment and dramatically solve problems that were holding up a new product line. His company worked on short, unpredictable, never-ending product cycles, so that the combination of his personal inclinations and the financial, technical, and time pressure surrounding him made even the start of a coaching program very problematic.

The first steps in freeing up time and energy were basic but essential. I asked him to list all the meetings he was going to every week and then had him say why he was attending. Fully 40% of the meetings were "just in case." Behind this phrase was his lack of trust in his team and his exaggerated sense of his irreplaceability.

For 2 weeks he experimented with not attending these meetings, consequently freeing up 10–12 hours on his schedule each week. No crisis occurred, his team members were competent in capturing important information and impending crises and reporting back to him about them.

In the freed-up time, my client began to formulate a vision of where his organization could go, how recurring process glitches could be resolved, and expanded his time horizon beyond the typical product cycle. He got himself educated in the edgier, emerging technical aspects of his job and worldwide business trends. He began to show up at meetings bringing up new topics, making new suggestions, and having a grounded background in topics that were germane to upper leadership.

Meanwhile, his organization continued to run very smoothly and he found out on his own how disempowering it was for his team to have him rush in and save them. To his chagrin and delight, he discovered that his team didn't need to be saved. Additionally, my client built a stronger internal network of support and began to reach out more deliberately to the vendor community and discovered what new technologies were emerging there. He even began to gradually and methodically began an exercise program, which reduced his stress and let him concentrate more clearly on the job.

All these changes registered on the C-level leaders and he was seen as an extraordinarily capable, insightful, and energetic addition to their ranks.

Example 3

I was hired by the founder of a technical search firm in San Francisco. She had started the company 20 years ago and had built it to a large and flourishing enterprise. She'd been smart enough to easily weather the downturn of the 2000 dot-com collapse. But the economic downtown that began in 2008 was a different matter. There didn't seem to be any company or sector that was left unaffected. Long-term clients were shifting their business model, requiring quicker turnarounds of job orders, tighter management of the process, while simultaneously paying lower fees. She felt squeezed from every direction.

Besides all that, my client had a busy, complex social world of friends, charity events, and dinner parties. She could find no mental or emotional space to address directly the situation that confronted her. All of her seemed to be swept up in day-to-day operations, solving the crisis of the moment, or preparing for the next social occasion. She felt no room to back out of anything. Everything that she was doing seemed vitally important and interesting.

For the longest time, she held onto the ardent hope that—because things had always turned out before—something wonderful and yet unknown would occur and turn the situation around. When this did not occur, she became more anxious and threw herself more fully into activities, leaving her less room to creatively respond.

Two small interventions assisted her greatly in freeing up her attention and energy to take on the huge challenge she was facing. She took up a modest but sustained exercise program. She found that walking in her neighborhood and walking on the treadmill at the gym put her body in a rhythm that disrupted her anxiety patterns. Elevating her heart rate and exercising her muscles also put her into a more positive mood. The combination of these two gave her the possibility to easily put down some of her long-held views and open up two new lines of business that were not so competitive with other firms and that were still paying good rates for the searches.

The second activity she took up was shifting the people she spent time with. In all instances, she reduced the amount of time she spent with people she felt were toxic for her and, in some other cases, ended the relationship fully. By toxic relationships, she meant people who increased her anxiety, undermined her confidence, and left her physically and emotionally drained at the end of their time together. Taking these people out of her schedule left her with more time—part of which she dedicated to exercise, but the other part towards research into the new markets she was entering, and the rest into building new client relationships, which she was excellent at doing.

As in the other examples, she took up these new activities with eagerness and ease. She didn't have to force herself. Her company came to a place of greater financial stability and she became realistically confident in the future of the company she'd spent 20 years developing.

Some Concluding Remarks

Some readers may remain unconvinced by what they've read here. Of course, it is not possible to convince people, but I invite those of you who find yourself in this frame of mind to experiment with what I'm suggesting here. Perhaps you could start with yourself and see what happens when you attend to your well-being in all dimensions pointed to in this chapter. Then you could try these recommended initial steps with a client that you find open and willing to try the unexpected.

Lastly, I would like you to consider the kind of person you would want at your side in the middle of a crisis or in the midst of a stressful situation. Would you want someone calm, present, in touch with her capacities and confidence, or someone who was worried and anxious to distraction? What frame of mind and emotion would you want the paramedics to be in when they rush to an accident you are in or the pilots when a red light starts flashing in the cockpit? The economic crisis of 2008 and 2009 for me is evidence enough that people making decisions under extreme pressure after years of living in stress leads to bad outcomes for large numbers of others.

Bob had long neglected his life outside of work. He had long ago taken the stressful, agitated buzz of his everyday life for eagerness and ability to take on more tasks. Yet, when he took on something new, he found himself to be stressed, not focused, sometimes guilty, and even resentful. At such moments, the only thing Bob knew to do was to work longer hours and internally berate himself for slacking off. Bob's solution was to apply more pressure to himself in order to meet the pressure he was feeling from his situation.

We all do this. Our usual solution to problems is doing the same things that brought about the problem in the first place. Here's where the intervention of a coach can be very helpful. When we look to our own experience, we all too readily repeat what has worked before even though the present is different from the earlier time when those actions succeeded.

My main task with Bob was asking him to re-enter his friendships outside of work that he had neglected for a long time. Through many promptings and reminders and promises from him, he eventually reached out to some old college friends and parents of his children's friends. Going out to dinner, attending some sporting events, taking walks, playing golf with these folks refreshed and renewed Bob in a way that he hadn't felt in a long time.

Creativity, curiosity, and focus on his work naturally and easily flowed back into his life. Bob was amazed that—by taking the pressure off and letting himself have fun, be concerned about others, and relax—he did a much better job at his work. Being a smart and adaptable person, Bob quickly routinized these activities and made them an essential part of his life going forward. He thereby assured that he would have the necessary support and elements of self-care required for his new level of engagement at the executive level.

SUGGESTED READING

Chek, Paul. *How to Eat, Move and Be Healthy!* San Diego, CA: Chek Institute, 2006.
This book presents all the elements of a healthy lifestyle. The author is a world-renown physical trainer and he provides exercises and routines that can strengthen and center us for our stressful lives. Just the right amount of challenge.

Eliot, T.S. *The Four Quartets.* San Diego, CA: Harcourt Brace & Company, 1971.
The reflections of a deeply wise poet near the end of his life, summarizing what he's learned about how our lives unfold. Many memorable lines and deeply moving images. Simple words and endless depth.

Kodish, Susan Presby, and Bruce I. Kodish. *Drive Yourself Sane: Using the Uncommon Sense of General Semantics.* Pasadena, CA: Extensional Publishing, 2001.
Often our thinking drives us crazy. We imagine what could be, worry about what wasn't, and second-guess ourselves endlessly. The authors show us how to have good mental hygiene so that our cognitive processes and habits support our well-being, our relationships and our intentions. Surprisingly immediate in its effects.

Lesser, Marc. *Less: Accomplishing More by Doing Less.* Novato, CA: New World Library, 2009.
The book plunges into the middle of our modern life, in all of its complexities and speed, and then shows us a way to bring some calmness and serenity to it. Paradoxically, the move towards doing less is convincingly shown to be a useful method for accomplishing more while keeping our life intact. Easy to read, full of practical know-how, deeply grounded in experience.

Lowen, Alexander. *Fear of Life: A Therapy for Being.* Alachua, FL: Bioenergetics Press, 1980.
The title is Lowen's definition of neurosis. His case studies show us the many ways we humans defeat ourselves by holding back from engaging in life. The book is an invitation to courage and an inspiration to what's possible to overcome.

McCall, Timothy. *Yoga as Medicine*. New York: Bantam Books, 2007.

We don't have to reach into the medicine cabinet when we have aches and pains, or even fatigue or a low mood. Instead we can draw on the 5,000 years of collected wisdom in the yoga tradition. The author is a Western physician who has filled his book with beautiful illustrations, clear instructions, and useful categories for addressing the physical and emotional ailments of our time. A treasure trove for all of humankind.

Mingyur Rinpoche, Yongey. *The Joy of Living: Unlocking the Secret & Science of Happiness*. New York: Harmony Books, 2007.

The author is a Tibetan monk who has studied neuroscience. He blends what he's learned in both traditions into a method that facilitates our bringing happiness to our life. Warm, friendly, and convincing.

Putnoi, Johanna. Senses Wide Open: The Art & Practice of Living in your Body. Berkeley, CA: Ulysses Press, 2000.

Telling ourselves to relax doesn't work. Inviting our clients to do the same is equally pointless. This book has many exercises and guidance so that we can learn how to attend to our body, conduct our life with greater ease, and stay buoyant in the midst of turmoil. Immediately accessible.

Roizen, Michael F., and Mehmet C. Oz. *You: The Owner's Manual*. New York: HarperResource, 2005.

The authors are two eminent physicians who present in a humorous way the cutting edge of what's known about human physiology and well-being. They've sprinkled quizzes, factoid boxes, and amusing illustrations everywhere so that the book is captivating as well as informative. An indispensable guide to anyone having a human body.

—. *You: On a Diet*. New York: Free Press, 2006.

The world of nutrition, diet and exercise is full of contradictory information. The authors base everything they say upon research, findings, and actual practice with patients. They find a way to keep the rigor of the science and at the same time make it understandable for the general reader. Everything physiological or psychological we need to know about food is here in one volume.

Siegel, Daniel J. *The Mindful Brain*. New York: W.W. Norton & Co., 2007.

The author, a psychiatrist and graduate of Harvard Medical School and a researcher into brain science, presents all the findings about how mindfulness—paying close attention to what we're doing—shifts our brain chemistry and physiology. These effects permanently shift our sense of well-being, our attentiveness to others, and our everyday happiness. Written in a clear style with wondrous examples.

12

Track Two: Working with Ourselves

> *Here's a chance to assess your coaching skills and qualities and design a program to improve them. Also, you'll find a series of questions that can direct you in capturing your learning and continuously improving as a coach.*

In the first chapter we spoke about the importance of continuing to develop ourselves while simultaneously coaching our clients. By doing this, we stay out of the temptation to become experts, dispensers of advice and opinion who have no experience about what it really takes to change. We also stay grounded in the fact that when our coaching efforts fail, it can be because of our own lack of competence, as well as limitations with the client. Also, clients will continue to present new questions, breakdowns, and challenges to us as coaches, and if we are going to be of use to them it is important that we continue to become more skillful. Besides all that, staying involved in Track Two will keep our coaching alive, vibrant, and nurturing for us instead of becoming a rote, mechanical, deadening repetition of what we've done dozens of times before.

I haven't found this aspect of coaching in any other text on the topic, but self-development seems to be a self-evident component of coaching. Besides working with yourselves, I recommend you find colleagues, friends, and yes, a coach, who can support you as you coach. Psychiatrists, physicians, teachers, and lawyers all confer with peers and mentors in difficult cases. Coaches are, it seems to me, no exception to this practice.

In this chapter, I'll present a way for coaches to continually improve. First will be a series of questions to ask yourself while you're coaching so that you can capture what you are learning and improve as you go. Next will be the creation of an action plan to improve your competence in the skills and qualities it takes to be a successful coach.

TRUING QUESTIONS

Below is a list of questions I suggest you ask yourself while you are engaged in coaching. The questions are listed in a kind of chronological order. The earlier ones are most appropriate early in the coaching program and the later ones make the most sense near or at completion of the program.

1. What am I learning about myself and others in coaching?
2. What makes my coaching most potent?
3. What in coaching makes me most uncomfortable? (Probably the most growth can happen here.)
4. From my coaching work, what is becoming more mysterious about people?
5. What am I discovering about the relationships I form with people?
6. What ideas of mine are being challenged in the coaching program?
7. What mood of mine seems to work best in the coaching program?
8. What don't I understand about my client? What does this show me about myself?
9. Am I modeling what I am coaching? If not, how am I justifying this?

Questions to ask at the end of a coaching program:

10. What did I learn about coaching?
11. What did I learn about my competence as a coach? What are my strengths? In what can I improve?
12. What surprised me?
13. In what was I flexible? In what was I rigid? What does that show me about myself?
14. What can I take to my next coaching program?

SELF-DEVELOPMENT PROCESS FOR COACHES: SKILLS AND QUALITIES

Following, you will find a process you can use to continually improve the skills and qualities you'll need as a coach. It's also an example of a methodology you can employ in working with clients. It's simple and it's a process you can use over and over with yourself.

First I'll describe each of the skills and qualities and, second, I'll present a simple way you can do a self-assessment. Lastly, I'll give you a structure that you can use to design a coaching program for yourself. As in any coaching program, it's probably best done in partnership with a coach, and at some point as you work in Track Two you may want to call upon the assistance of someone else. The process has proven to be powerful and useful and I recommend that you get started with it.

Skills

Speaking

As I said earlier, the primary act you'll do as a coach is speak with your client. Speaking means to point out to your client new distinctions that will allow him to make new observations. Also at times the coach must speak in a way that inspires the client to see some new possibility, overcome some obstacle, or stick with a program that is moving more slowly than anticipated.

The form of your speaking doesn't matter as much as does your clarity about what you are intending. You may find yourself telling stories, you may cite examples, you might reveal something about yourself. As you continue to coach, you'll find your own voice. What's important is that you develop your competence in making new distinctions and inspiring your clients.

Listening

Sometimes people have the notion that listening means being a human tape recorder, that they've been really good at listening if they can repeat back what's been said to them—and for some people that might be a useful initial step in learning to listen. Although listening as a coach includes hearing what's said, it goes well beyond that.

The two main intents in listening are to understand the uniqueness of the client and situation, and to discern the root cause. Perhaps the biggest obstacle in listening well is being quiet enough and open enough ourselves so that we can sensitively be affected by what our client says and does. Our understanding is affected not only by the words the client says but also by the whole array of actions one can take while speaking, including posture, intonation, and facial expression. Besides all that, a coach must take on the openness of listening whenever observing the client.

Resolving Breakdowns

If you're going to coach people, you're going to have to deal with breakdowns. The main task in resolving breakdowns is to stay out of emotional reaction yourself. Allowing yourself to become upset, frustrated, angry, or regretful does not add anything useful to your work to resolve the breakdown.

Can you imagine visiting an emergency room and having the physician become as upset as the parents of an injured child? At such moments, it's the calmness of the physician that is most important. Otherwise, judgment will become clouded and scattered. The second important task is to generate many possibilities—the more, the better—because many of them may already have been entertained and disregarded by the client.

Assessing

Assessing means observing with distinctions in mind. To be competent as an assessor, you must take time to observe, know what the standards are, and keep out your own prejudice as much as you can. It's a delicate matter to keep separate what we observe from our interpretation of the observations. For example, when we see a loud conversation between two people, we might add the interpretation that he was bullying that clerk or she was abusing that secretary. Without a lot of comprehension of the whole context of the situation, we can't come to a conclusion like that. On the other hand, just saying "I observed someone speaking loudly" usually will be useless in terms of coaching.

In order to make a coaching assessment, we have to understand what the person being observed was attempting to accomplish, what it means to succeed at that accomplishment, what action she took, and the outcome of that action. By addressing these four points precisely, you will keep your prejudice at a minimum and you will be able to present your assessment in a fair way to your client if necessary.

Designing

Designing means making the connection between current reality and the desired outcomes in the coaching program, even when the program consists of only one conversation. The first step in design is to understand the current reality of the client, thus the importance of assessment. Next, describe what competence the client will have at the end of your coaching. For example, what new action will he be able to take, what better decisions will he make, in what way will his sales efforts improve? Describe the outcomes in a way that can be observed by both client and coach.

The last element is designing the path between understanding the client and achieving the desired outcomes. The path will consist of three elements: practices the client does, a network of support the client can call on, and a time frame by which the outcomes will occur.

Qualities

Rigor

Being rigorous means upholding the highest standards of a tradition and applying them fairly. Mathematicians and scientists are examples of people who must be rigorous in order to succeed. In those disciplines, the standards of excellence are well established and they are applied without exception to any and all new discoveries. Mathematicians and scientists don't change the standards according to whether or not they are friends or enemies with the person whose work they are assessing.

As coaches, it's necessary that we be rigorous so that we are seen as scrupulously fair and as dedicated to the highest standards. If we're *only* rigorous as a coach, however, we will dissuade many potential clients from working with us. If we're the best coach of a particular discipline, then our clients may have to put up with a high level of rigor. If, for example, we are the best violin teacher in the world, clients, usually called students in this tradition, may even have to audition to work with us, but in most situations you will find yourself in as a coach, you won't have this luxury.

At work, you'll find that you've inherited a team of people. If you are a parent, you don't get to select your children from a pool of eager applicants. And as a school teacher, your class each year is randomly assigned to you. Consequently, most of us must balance rigor with the other qualities listed, such as patience and flexibility. As you assess yourself, see which side of the equation most needs balancing. Are you too rigorous and perhaps even harsh, or are you too patient and sometimes even wishy-washy?

Patience

Patience is waiting without complaining. In coaching, it's important to remember that people change in biological time, not in electronic time. In these days of powerful computers, we can flip through screen after screen after screen and become impatient when it takes more than a third of a second to pull up a document. We rush through life. But no matter how quickly life moves, we are always working with a biological phenomenon when we approach people.

As was said in the chapter on openings, our habitual actions take on a neuromuscular structure within our bodies. Long-term change requires that we address this structure, and this process is not immediate. Even after moments of profound insight or transformative inspiration, it still takes time to integrate the change into your life; otherwise, the moment of change can be like a mushroom that grows mightily during one night but, having no roots, perishes during the heat of the following days.

Besides all that, complaining doesn't help your coaching effort. If you become impatient, ask yourself if the source of your impatience is your client not meeting your expectations, and how long you think it should be taking. Ask yourself how long you think it would take you to do the same thing. Most of us are not adept at being patient. But by understanding what it really takes for a human being to change, and by reflecting on our own attempts to alter a habit, we can begin to have more realistic notions. It's within these notions that patience can take root.

Self-Consistency

When we apply the same standards to ourselves that we are applying to our clients we are being self-consistent. Probably nothing will undo your credibility as a coach more quickly than being inconsistent. You probably have seen examples of this many times yourself. How often have you seen leaders of an organization instruct people to initiate a process that the leaders themselves never follow? In such cases, people disregard what's said to them and follow instead what's shown to them by actions.

In one-to-one coaching of people, there's no escaping close scrutiny by our clients. I'm not saying that we have to be taking the same actions as the client, but we must apply the same high standards to our actions just as we are applying them to the client's actions. No amount of personal force or organizational power will replace the necessity to be self-consistent.

Creativity/Flexibility

Our coaching efforts, however well designed, will almost never turn out as planned. At such moments, it's vital that we be creative and flexible, and that we find a way to have high standards somehow fit the individual client. Imagine being a Little League baseball coach and insisting that the seven- and eight-year-old boys on your team perform like big league "all-stars" because, after all, those are the standards of excellence in that tradition.

Maybe none of us would do that, but we do the equivalent when we require someone we are coaching to immediately and unconditionally perform as an expert. We do the equivalent when we only point out what's missing, what's wrong, or what's inadequate. Different people learn at different rates and in different ways, and to succeed as coaches we must find ways to have our coaching fit without diluting our commitment to the outcome.

THE PROCESS: WORKING WITH YOURSELF

Here's a way to work with yourself with these skills and qualities. First, *assess* yourself according to the descriptions. I suggest you make a scale of one to five and then take time to calibrate the scale. You calibrate the scale by describing in exact behavioral terms what a five would be or by putting a person who you know as the embodiment of that skill or quality at the five level. To make it possible for you to succeed, the goal must seem possible to you. Be rigorous with yourself but also be flexible.

If you are working on patience, for example, don't put Mother Theresa as a five on your scale, because then there is going to be either a gigantic distance between a one and a two or you're not going to be on the scale. Naturally, if you are a saint this doesn't apply to you. After you have assessed yourself on each of the skills and qualities, move on to the next step. For use in the process, select one skill or quality to work on.

The next step is to write out a description of your *current reality* regarding that skill or quality. That is to say, what are the specific actions you are taking that display your level of competence with that skill or quality? Also, what are the hindrances to your improving? What's getting in the way?

The third step is to describe your *intended outcomes*, again in behavioral terms. What actions would you be doing as an expression of that skill or quality if you were as competent as you would like to be? The fourth step is to *design the path* between current reality and the intended outcome. The path consists of practices, a network of support, and a time frame.

Practices are behaviors done again and again with standards in mind, the purpose of which is to improve a skill or quality. Only when all the component parts are present will a practice succeed. Simply doing the behavior over and over again doesn't ensure that someone will become more competent. Are you really becoming more competent in brushing your teeth? You must also self-observe your behavior in terms of standards, and continually correct your behavior so that it approximates the standard more and more closely. Even if we want to become more competent, if we are not correcting our actions according to observable criteria, we will never improve.

A *network of support* is a group of people who we can call on when we need information, emotional support, or assistance during a breakdown. No one has ever mastered anything on their own. Picasso had Braque and Eliot had Ezra Pound. At some point in your program, it's very likely that you will become stuck or discouraged, or you may even forget about what you are working on. It's at those moments that a network of support will be very useful to you.

A *time frame* puts sufficient structure and rigor in your program so that you can have a sense of forward movement. At the outset of your program give your best estimation of how long it will take. If necessary, correct your time frame by speaking to your network of support: people who have committed themselves to your success in the program. These people will make it more difficult for you to fool yourself or endlessly postpone. Below is an example of how to use this process (see Figure 12.1).

THE PROCESS: AN EXAMPLE

The selected skill is listening. On a calibrated scale of one to five, our imaginary coach Peter has assessed himself to be at level two.

Current Reality

Description of Current Reality

- Interrupting people in the middle of what they are saying
- Stop listening when I have the answer to a question that is being asked
- "Zoning out" for unknown periods of time during meetings

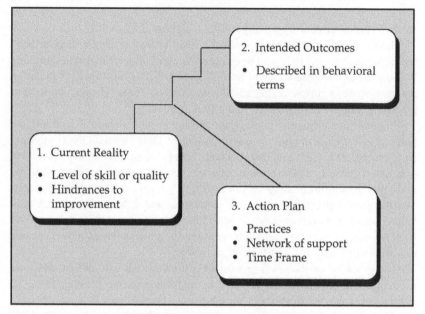

FIGURE 12.1   The Developmental Path

Hindrances

- Not enough time at work to work on this skill
- A history of social identity as an expert who must quickly solve problems and answer questions

Intended Outcome

- People who are speaking to me report that they feel that they are heard, understood, and honored.
- I stay attentive and focused during meetings.
- I continue to listen even after I have an answer to someone's question or a solution for their problem.

The Plan

Practices

- Voice echoing: saying quietly to myself what other people are saying to me as close to the moment they're saying it as possible. The standard here is to be exact in what I say, so hopefully saying it right away will make this easier. This will keep me focused during meetings.

- At the end of conversations with people, take a moment to tell my conversational partner what I understood from what she said and also that I appreciate what she said. The standard here is to continually correct my report until my conversational partner agrees that I really understood her.
- Keep a listening journal in which I record both my successes and my failures in listening. I can do that by answering the following questions in my journal several times a day:
  1. When did I listen attentively? How can I tell?
  2. When did I stop listening to the meeting or conversation?
  3. What distracted me from listening to the conversation or meeting?

In the journal, I will be able to discover patterns, such as people I stop listening to or topics that I don't listen to, and alert myself before entering into conversations with those people or on those topics. The standard here is to recognize the patterns and to eliminate their repetition.

Network of Support

- My network of support will be three people I trust and admire whom I will call on when I see myself unable to break a pattern, or when I don't know what to do in my program.

Time Frame

- The time frame will be three months.

I suggest that you work on one skill or quality at a time. Pick the one that you consider most urgent in your development as a coach. You can repeat the process to work on the other skills or qualities. Working with this process, along with addressing the questions in the beginning of this chapter, will allow you to stay alert as a coach. Keep coaching a learning experience for yourself and improve your competence as a coach.

Often, in the initial stages of being a coach, designing practices is a daunting challenge. Below are some questions you can use to help you design a practice.

1. What observable behavior will be part of the practice?
2. What are the standards for performance of that behavior?
3. What will you ask your client to observe so that she/he can tell how well she/he is performing?
4. How often will you have the client do the practice? How long will each session last?
5. How long will the practice itself last?
6. How often will the client stop and assess progress? What will the criteria be for assessing progress?

DEFINITIONS

Practice

Behavior done again and again with the intention to improve. It's done with standards in mind and corrected according to those standards.

Structure

Specifies the following:

- when practice will be performed
- duration of each session
- when progress will be assessed

Feedback

A time for reflection and self-assessment. Describes what it is to be self-observed in terms of standards and timeline. Corrections are then made in behavior.

Network of Support

People and organizations to call on when there's a question or breakdown.

Timeline

How long the process will take based upon the gap between current reality and intended outcomes; also includes interim goals (milestones).

HOW BOB TURNED OUT

By following the self-observation exercises and practices shown in Chapter 9, Bob was accepted into the pool of potential executives at his company after about 10 months of working with the coach. Since then he has employed his own version of these exercises to continually improve his competence.

Through his rigorous commitment to his program, Bob accomplished his goals, and beyond that, became a long-term excellent performer who is self-correcting and self-generating. He turned out to be an exemplar of the power of coaching.

SUGGESTED READING

These books are for the coach to work with herself. They introduce a level of rigor that keeps the coach alert and focused on the principles and values of coaching. If you're only selecting a few books, here are my recommendations, in suggested reading order:

1. *The Human Condition*, Hannah Arendt
2. *The 7 Habits of Highly Effective People*, Stephen Covey
3. *Care of the Soul*, Thomas Moore

Abrams, Jeremiah, and Connie Zweig, eds. *Meeting the Shadow*. Los Angeles: Jeremy P. Tarcher, Inc., 1991.
   A collection of essays examining the dark side of human nature. Educational, illuminating, and deflating of ego. A doorway to wholeness and serenity. ("I would rather be whole than good."—Carl Jung.)
Almaas, A. H. *Spacecruiser Inquiry*. Boston: Shambhala Publications, 2002.
   Accessible presentation of A. Hameed Ali's (writing as Almaas) thorough Diamond Approach work for personal transformation and development. A unique blend of depth psychology (especially object relations theory) and spirituality (especially Sufiism and Buddhism).
Arendt, Hannah. *The Human Condition*. Chicago: University of Chicago Press, 1958.
   A classic text that takes on the big issues of being a person. Many powerful insights and much brilliant analysis. Very quotable. One can work for years from the ideas presented.
Bateson, Mary Catherine. *Composing a Life*. New York: Atlantic Monthly Press, 1989.
   The author is the daughter of Margaret Meade and Gregory Bateson, a former dean of a university and an anthropologist. She writes about her life and the lives of five women friends. She beautifully shows the way they compose lives of meaning and caring without force or egotism.
Covey, Stephen R. *The 7 Habits of Highly Effective People*. New York: Simon & Schuster, 1989.
   A presentation of seven habits (which in the context of coaching would be called practices) that lead to private and public victories. Easy to follow. Many examples. Each chapter has recommendations for moving into action.
Dass, Ram, and Paul Gorman. *How Can I Help?* New York: Alfred A. Knopf, Inc., 1985.
   A practical guide for people who have dedicated their lives to service. Written with immense heart. Provides powerful context within which one can serve without either becoming the center of the activity or burning out with exhaustion and disillusionment.
Fischer, Norman. *Taking Our Places: The Buddhist Path to Truly Growing Up*. New York: HarperCollins Publishers, 2003.
   A guide to genuine maturity written by a former zen abbot, poet, father, and mentor to teens. Rich, kind, wise, and inspiring.
Goldstein, Joseph. *The Experience of Insight*. Boston: Shambhala Publications, 1976.
   A flawless gem that's an invitation to meditation practice. Clear instructions, helpful hints, and an explanation of traditional teachings.
Gutman, Huck, Patrick H. Hutton, and Luther H. Martin, eds. *Technologies of the Self: A Seminar with Michel Foucault*. Amherst, MA: University of Massachusetts Press, 1988.
   Foucault's last book. He addresses (in this text from a seminar) the traditional ways people work on their own development. Helpful in its historical perspective, rigor, and tracing of trends of thought and belief.
Levine, Stephen. *Guided Meditations, Explorations and Healings*. New York: Anchor Books/ Doubleday, 1991.
   The author provides soothing, calming, and healing passages and meditations that address many occasions of suffering: death, illness, pain, addictions, etc. Indispensable for working skillfully and compassionately with the human condition.
Mezirow, Jack, and Associates. *Fostering Critical Reflection in Adulthood*. San Francisco: Jossey-Bass, Inc., 1990.
   This book is a collection of essays in which the authors present many different ways to realize the goal expressed in the book's title. By taking on one or more of the suggested practices, coaches can become more skillful in self-reflection and critical thinking.

Moore, Thomas. *Care of the Soul.* New York: HarperCollins, 1992.
  A lyrical, metaphor-rich book about how one can bring depth and meaning to everyday activities and circumstances. The soul has its own language. This book alerts readers to that fact and invites them to listen.

Nicoll, Maurice. *Psychological Commentaries on the Teaching of Gurdjieff & Ouspensky, Volumes 1–5.* Boston: Shambhala Publications, 1984.
  Fabulous introduction into the importance of self-observation in bringing about personal awakening. Unflinching, opinionated yet deeply compassionate.

Nozick, Robert. *The Examined Life.* New York: Simon & Schuster, Inc., 1989.
  A collection of essays (that form one argument by book's end) addressing in a Socratic fashion important issues in human life, such as what is love, emotion, happiness, and so on. The author is a philosopher and the book is hard-selling from time to time. Useful in examining one's own views and probably not so useful in adapting those of the author.

Palmer, Parker J. *Let Your Life Speak.* San Francisco: Jossey-Bass, Inc., 2000.
  Very good introduction to uncovering our vocation by quietly, patiently listening to what we are called to do with our one precious human life, the one that's unfolding right now.

Riso, Don Richard, and Russ Hudson. *The Wisdom of the Enneagram.* New York: Bantam Books, 1999.
  Fabulous presentation of a powerful, comprehensive, coherent traditional method for understanding and developing ourselves. Full of useful charts, questions, and practices. First rate.

Trungpa, Chögyam. *Cutting through Spiritual Materialism.* Boston: Shambhala Publications, 1973.
  A death blow to using spiritual values or powers to get ahead in life. A razor for separating the egotistical from the compassionate.

Zimmerman, Michael E. *Eclipse of the Self.* Athens, OH: Ohio University Press, 1981.
  A philosophical examination of Heidegger's notions of authenticity. An opportunity to investigate one's own values and explore the basis of one's life.

Conclusion

Instead of attempting to summarize the content of this book, I'll attempt here to summarize my intent in writing the book.

My view is that our life is mostly about finding a way to contribute. Many of us have been deterred from this path early on in our lives. Additionally, some of us have concluded that it is not possible to contribute as we want to in business. Over more than a decade I have found this not to be the case.

In fact, this book is meant to answer the question, "How can I contribute?" It is by continually asking this question that our identity and competence as coaches will continue to unfold. Your openness to allowing this book to contribute to you is a gift to me and for that, I thank you.

Appendix A

Self-Observations

All change begins with self-observation. People confuse self-observation with self-judgment. Judgment includes a critical element that is absent from self-observation.

Many people feel as if they are quite good at self-observation because they have an internal voice that is continually jabbering at them: "Oh that was stupid," "You can do better than that," "I don't like this," and so on. To self-observe means to not become attached to or to identify with any content of our experience, but to watch alertly, openly, passively. Many Americans hate the word *passively*—especially authors and advocates of self-help. Not acting allows self-observation to occur. We are already taking enough actions, be they physical or mental. The point in being passive is to have some power in intervening in the mechanicalness of thought, action, and speech.

The general instruction for self-observation is to divide yourself into two people, one who acts in life and one who watches. Maybe this sounds simple to you, but you'll find in practice that it is quite difficult. At first, almost everyone forgets to self-observe. That's why it makes sense to leave reminders around, maybe notes on your mirror or computer screen to keep bringing you back to your self-observation. Below, you'll find examples of self-observation exercises that clients have done over the years. They are divided into three main categories: business, relationship, and personal. It's not that I don't think these domains influence each other; it's more that by dividing a person's life into three categories, it is easier to observe. I recommend that you use self-observation in almost all of your coaching efforts. It will provide powerful insights for your client, give you more information from which to conduct your coaching, and will keep showing you the importance of the coaching program.

Examples given are meant to illustrate a form you can use and to trigger your own creativity. If you find a client for whom the questions seem to apply, feel free to use them. The objective listed at the top of each exercise is an explanation for the reader. The client's exercise would omit this and begin with the instructions.

SELF-OBSERVATION SAMPLE 1: BUSINESS

Objective

To become more aware of the present status of my life.

Daily Journal Questions

Please take 15–20 minutes each day and address the following questions.

1. In what ways is my life balanced (or not) today?
2. How did I take care of myself today?
3. How did I take care of my spouse today?
4. What is my attention on today?
5. What are my current breakdowns? What action will I take to resolve them?

Weekly Journal Questions

Please take 15–20 minutes each week and address the following questions.

1. What did I learn about myself this week?
2. What did I accomplish this week?
3. What part of my life did I ignore/avoid this week?
4. At what did I become more competent this week?
5. What part of my accountability did I give away this week? What did I learn by doing this?

SELF-OBSERVATION SAMPLE 2: BUSINESS

Objective

To become more aware of how I feel during the workday, and what I accomplish on a daily basis.

Instructions

Stop twice each day—at midday and at the end of the day—and ask yourself the following questions. I suggest that you anticipate this exercise by observing yourself throughout your day. You may wish to record your responses in your journal.

1. What energized me most at work today?
2. What discouraged me most at work today?
3. In what ways did #1 and #2 above affect how I spent my time? What did I accomplish?
4. What patterns do I see emerging from what I am observing in this exercise? What action will I take about what I have observed?

SELF-OBSERVATION SAMPLE 3: BUSINESS

Objective

To become more aware of how I feel during the workday.

Instructions

Stop twice each day—at midday and at the end of the day—and ask yourself the following questions. I suggest that you anticipate this exercise by observing yourself throughout your day. You may wish to record your responses in your journal.

1. What did I feel uncomfortable about doing? About saying? Why?
2. What emotions or feelings were most present for me?
3. When did I experience fear?
4. What thoughts did I have while I was feeling fear?
5. What action will I take from what I observed?

SELF-OBSERVATION SAMPLE 4: BUSINESS

Objective

To become more aware of what I am and am not accomplishing during my workday, why I may not be accomplishing, and how I justify breakdowns.

Instructions

Stop twice each day—at midday and at the end of the day—and ask yourself the following questions. I suggest that you anticipate this exercise by observing yourself throughout your day. You may wish to record your responses in your journal.

1. What specific, observable outcomes did I produce?
2. What excuses, stories, or justifications do I have for not producing the outcomes I said I would produce?
3. What events, people, or personal limitations got in the way of these outcomes?
4. How do I feel about what I have observed here?
5. What action will I take from what I observed?

SELF-OBSERVATION SAMPLE 5: BUSINESS

Objective

To become more aware of my challenging behaviors and their consequences.

Instructions

Stop twice each day—at midday and at the end of the day—and ask yourself the following questions. I suggest that you anticipate this exercise by observing yourself throughout your day. You may wish to record your responses in your journal.

1. Whom did I challenge today?
2. Why?
3. What were all the outcomes of this challenge?
4. What actions will I take from what I observed?

SELF-OBSERVATION SAMPLE 6: BUSINESS

Objective

To become more aware of what I am insisting upon and how it affects my work and my relationships at work.

Instructions

Stop twice each day—at midday and at the end of the day—and ask yourself the following questions. I suggest that you anticipate this exercise by observing yourself throughout your day. You may wish to record your responses in your journal.

1. What did I insist upon today?
2. How did I justify my insistence?
3. What were the effects of my insistence upon myself? Upon my work relationships?
4. What actions will I take from what I observed?

SELF-OBSERVATION SAMPLE 7: BUSINESS

Objective

To become more aware of my feelings at work. (A different version appears earlier. Each was designed for a particular client.)

Instructions

Stop twice each day—at midday and at the end of the day—and ask yourself the following questions. I suggest that you anticipate this exercise by observing yourself throughout your day. You may wish to record your responses in your journal.

1. What was my strongest feeling at work today?
2. What triggered this feeling?

3. How did I respond/react to this feeling?
4. What actions will I take from what I observed?

SELF-OBSERVATION SAMPLE 1: RELATIONSHIP

Objective

To become more aware of my judgments of men and the reactions I trigger in them.

Instructions

A. Do the exercise twice each day: once at midday, using the first set of questions, and once at the end of the day, using the second set. I suggest that you anticipate this exercise by observing yourself throughout your day.
B. Ask yourself the following questions. You may write your responses in your journal if you wish.

Questions: Set #1

1. What judgments did I make of others, especially men?
2. What was the basis of my judgment?
3. How did my judgments shape my relationships with people, especially men?
4. What action will I take from what I observed in this exercise?

Questions: Set #2

1. What reactions/responses did I trigger in men?
2. Did I intend to bring about these reactions/responses? If yes, for what purpose?
3. What did I do to trigger these reactions/responses?
4. What action will I take from what I observed in this exercise?

SELF-OBSERVATION SAMPLE 2: RELATIONSHIP

Objective

To become more aware of my relationships.

Instructions

A. Do this exercise twice each day: once at midday, once at the end of the day.
B. Ask yourself the following questions. You may write your responses in your journal if you wish.

1. What specific expectations did I have of other people?
2. What was I not able to fully communicate to someone?
3. Who currently feels loved, appreciated, and nurtured by me?
4. What current situations, worries, circumstances, relationships, or breakdowns am I not able to resolve?
5. How do I feel about myself right now?

SELF-OBSERVATION SAMPLE 3: RELATIONSHIP

Objective

To become more aware of how I interact with myself and in relationships.

Instructions

A. Do this exercise twice each day: once at midday, once at the end of the day.
B. Ask yourself the following questions. You may write your responses in your journal if you wish.
   1. What judgments did I make about myself?
   2. In what ways did I disappoint myself?
   3. When did I stop listening to someone?
   4. In what ways was I better than other people I've encountered?
   5. In what ways did I mistrust myself?
   6. What did I learn from these observations and what will I do about it?

SELF-OBSERVATION SAMPLE 4: RELATIONSHIP

Objective

To become more aware of the status of my primary relationship.

Instructions

A. Do this exercise twice each day: once at midday, once at the end of the day.
B. Ask yourself the following questions about your primary relationship. You may write your responses in your journal if you wish.
   1. What is not complete? What will it take to complete it?
   2. What do I regret?
   3. What do I resent?
   4. What do I wish I did more of? What do I wish I did less of?
   5. What judgments have I made about this person? About myself?
   6. What do I secretly hope will happen?
   7. What am I angry about? Sad about? Unresolved about? Fearful about?
   8. What have I been unwilling to forgive?

9. What am I holding on to?
10. What am I resisting?

SELF-OBSERVATION SAMPLE 5: RELATIONSHIP

Objective

To locate and study the connection between our body and how we listen.

Instructions

A. Please observe yourself on the following points at midmorning, noon, mid-afternoon, and the end of the day.

B. Please take some notes so you can begin to notice patterns. During this period of time:
1. Whom did you resist listening to?
2. How did this happen in your body? What tension or holding did you feel?
3. What did your breath feel like?
4. What action(s) will you take from what you learned in this exercise?

SELF-OBSERVATION SAMPLE 6: RELATIONSHIP

Objective

To locate and study the connection between our body and how we speak.

Instructions

A. Please observe yourself on the following points at midmorning, noon, mid-afternoon, and the end of the day.

B. Please take some notes so you can begin to notice patterns. During this period of time:
1. What did you want to say that you didn't say?
2. How did this happen in your body? What tension or holding did you feel?
3. What did your breath feel like?
4. What action(s) will you take from what you learned in this exercise?

SELF-OBSERVATION SAMPLE 1: PERSONAL

Objective

To become more aware of my thoughts and judgments, and how they affect my clarity and actions around goals.

Instructions

A. Read *Bradshaw On: The Family*, by John Bradshaw (1988).
B. Stop twice each day—at midday and at the end of the day—and ask yourself the following questions. You may wish to record your responses in your journal.
  1. What is occupying my thoughts?
  2. What judgments have I made about myself?
  3. Whom do I feel close to now? Why?
  4. What is my most important goal right now? Why?
  5. What did I learn from this exercise? How will I take what I learned into action?

SELF-OBSERVATION SAMPLE 2: PERSONAL

Objective

I will become more aware of my feelings, thoughts, and reactions concerning completion, and take action from what I learn.

Instructions

Stop twice each day—at midday and at the end of the day—and ask yourself the following questions. You may wish to record your responses in your journal.

1. What did I complete? Why was it important to complete this?
2. What did I leave incomplete? Why did I leave it so?
3. What do I currently feel compelled to complete? Why?
4. What will happen to me if I don't complete these things?
5. What did I learn from this exercise? What action will I take from what I learned?

SELF-OBSERVATION SAMPLE 3: PERSONAL

Objective

To become more aware of my habits.

Instructions

A. Make a list of all of the habits you wish to change.
B. Each day select a habit and answer the following questions regarding this habit. Write down your answers to the questions on separate sheets of paper.
  1. What triggers this habit?
  2. How do I feel when acting out this habit?
  3. How do others feel when I act out this habit?

SELF-OBSERVATION SAMPLE 4: PERSONAL

Objective

To locate and intervene in the precursors to a strong emotional response.

Instructions

A. Please observe yourself on the following points at midmorning, noon, mid-afternoon, and the end of the day. Please take some notes so you can begin to notice patterns.

B. During this period of time, what was happening just before you became angry (or sad, or frightened, or frozen)? For example,

   1. What conversation, what activity, were you engaged in?
   2. What thought, decision, or conclusion did you make?
   3. What body sensations, shifts of posture, changes in breathing did you observe?
   4. What action(s) will you take from what you learned in this exercise?

Appendix B

Practices

Practices naturally follow self-observation. A practice is a behavior that we do again and again with the intention of improving a quality or competence. In order to improve, we must be able to observe whether or not we are doing the behavior competently and correct accordingly. Self-observation then becomes part of every practice that we do. Here are examples of practices that clients have taken on over the years. A practice fades into the background when a person has done it enough times to be able to competently perform the action effortlessly and seamlessly. For example, many of us have practiced making right-hand turns, but probably none of us practices making right-hand turns on our way to work. We've practiced enough so that we can effortlessly turn right and the action is part of a seamless flow of driving. As you read through the following examples, remember that that is the intention of each practice. As in the self-observation appendix, the categories presented will be business, relationship, and personal. Feel free to use them as you like with yourself or your clients.

PRACTICE SAMPLE 1: BUSINESS

Objective
Establish and maintain management practices that leave you with more free time and less stress.

Recommended Actions
I urge you to begin these at once. It will take a while to have them become habits and for people to take your new actions seriously. Be patient and consistent.

Part I: Scheduling Your Time

Meetings and Appointments
1. Each Friday go over your schedule for the upcoming week with your assistant.

2. Tell your assistant at what other times you are available to meet with people. Be sure to keep 50 percent of your time inviolate to cover the rest of your job (see below).
3. Tell your assistant who you're expecting to schedule time with and how much time to allot for the meeting.
4. Ask your assistant to schedule *no one* else without your approval. They get your approval by giving you a list of requestees each day.
5. After you approve a meeting, have your assistant call back the requestee to firm up the meeting.
6. Have your assistant call the day before all scheduled meetings and appointments to confirm.

Part II: How Much of What

1. Schedule a maximum amount of time you'll work each week. Deal with breakdowns by canceling activities instead of adding hours, so that you can stay within your maximum time allotment.
2. Keep working your schedule to bring it to the following proportions:
   15% Planning
   15% Administrative activities
   50% Appointments and meetings
   20% Addressing breakdowns

Analyze your time each week and keep correcting the schedule.

Part III: Communication

1. Stay on top of major milestones in projects only and deal *only* with breakdowns that stop people dead in the water. Give all other breakdowns back quickly.
2. Stop the flow of "F.Y.I." information to you in priority form (e.g., send back voice mail that has that content ("F.Y.I.") with a message saying that you'll only accept such reports via electronic mail or memo). Use priority forms of communication, such as voice mail, one-on-one meetings, and staff meetings, only for communication of high priority.
3. Stop being a conduit for ordinary communication flow. Link people together and let them work it out.

Part IV: Miscellaneous (but Important)

Bring your lunch to work. That way you can have healthy food on hand and not be subject to whatever the vending machines provide.

PRACTICE SAMPLE 2: BUSINESS

Objective

To further your subordinates' career development plans.

Directions

Meet with each of your subordinates quarterly.

Background

Initiating and supporting career development plans for your subordinates is an important part of your managerial responsibilities. Your role is to provide feedback about performance, to suggest the next developmental step for them, and to assign work to support that development (see Figure B.1).

Preparing

1. What are the three main strengths of this person? Cite three examples.
2. What is the current greatest performance issue with this person? Cite three examples.
3. What type of assignment would most strengthen this person?

Follow-Up

Observe progress and correct your plan accordingly. Keep up with follow-up dates.

PRACTICE SAMPLE 3: BUSINESS

Assignment Management Form

The purpose of this form (see Figure B.2) is to facilitate supervision and monitoring of the work of your subordinates. Make photocopies and label each form with the name of an individual who works for you. Fill in and update the information in the columns during your weekly meetings with your subordinates.

You can also use the form as a reference when information is requested of you and when you are assigning work. Be diligent and rigorous in filling out the form and in following up.

PRACTICE SAMPLE 4: BUSINESS

Issue Inventory Form

Use this form (see Figure B.3) for support in planning, recording, and learning from your speaking up about important issues at work.

Developmental Plans

Name of Person	Competence/Quality Being Developed	Developmental Assignment	Date Assigned	Date for Follow-Up

FIGURE B.1 Developmental Plans

Assignment Management for _____

Project or Client	Current Status	Next Major Action	Action Needs Approved by	Due Date	Follow-Up Date

FIGURE B.2   Assignment Management Form

Take some time each week (15–20 minutes) and scan through events, conversations, meetings, and your reading at work. Pick out the issues that seem most important to you, your boss, peers, or subordinates. Then fill in the first and second column of the form. As your thinking around the issues clarifies, fill in the next two columns. Use the last column as a place to record what happened so that you can keep improving this process for yourself.

PRACTICE SAMPLE 5: BUSINESS

Objective

Establish and maintain management practices that enable you to identify your priorities and manage your time more effectively.

Directions

1. List all of the activities that you actually do at work.
   a. Divide them into categories A, B, and C, with A being the most important for the success of the business and C being the least important.
   b. Within each category number the activities, with #1 being the most vital.
   c. Write next to each activity how much time you spend doing it each week or, in some cases, each month.
2. Then ask yourself:
   a. Can I allocate my time more effectively? How?
   b. What activities can I give to someone else?
   c. What is my job at the company, really?
3. List all of the activities you wish you were doing at work but that you never get around to doing. Be exhaustive in your listing.
   a. Divide the activities into categories and prioritize them as above.
   b. Write next to each activity how much time each week/month it would take you to complete.
4. Then ask yourself:
   a. What would be the benefit of doing this activity?
   b. What recurring breakdowns could I avoid by doing this activity?
   c. What is my job at this company, really?
5. Have your staff do #1, #2, #3, and #4. Then, having shared what you wrote and having read their responses, ask them for ways to reorganize, redesign your department's work systems, accountability, management systems, reward systems, training, and development of staff.
6. What did you learn by doing this?

Issue Inventory

Name of Issue	Major People Involved	Actions I Recommend/My Input	When I'll Make Recommendation	Results from My Input

FIGURE B.3 Issue Inventory Form

PRACTICE SAMPLE 1: RELATIONSHIP

Dating Debriefing Exercise

Use this exercise for support in your goal to establish a lasting romantic relationship with someone.

Instructions

After going out on a date, answer the following questions:

1. What did we do on the date? How do I feel about that?
2. How do I feel about the person?
3. How do I feel about myself around the person?
4. How open am I to the person?
5. What judgments/opinions/assessments have I made about the person? Based on what?
6. What do I feel this person wants from me? What am I open to providing?
7. What support will I provide for this person?
8. What future will I bring about with this person?
9. Anything else about this date that I should consider?

PRACTICE SAMPLE 2: RELATIONSHIP

At the beginning of each day, list the actions that you will take in each domain listed below. At day's end, notice what you actually accomplished, what you learned, and what corrections to make.

1. Supporting my partner
2. Sharing my life with my partner
3. Making myself open and available to my partner
4. Having fun with my partner
5. Forwarding our life together

PRACTICE SAMPLE 1: PERSONAL

Sitting

- Sitting is a practice in observation, in acceptance, in compassion, in stillness, in discovering our true nature.
- Sitting is simple and, because of that, can be difficult to do.
- It is impossible to do wrong—if done with sincerity. And it is very tempting to continually assess and/or berate ourselves.

Instructions in Sitting

Please do this exercise for 20 minutes each day for the next three months.

How to Do It
1. Sit up straight in a chair with your feet flat on the floor.
2. Either close your eyes or gaze at a spot on the floor 6–8 feet in front of you.
3. Bring your awareness to your breathing—either on your abdomen, which rises and falls as you breathe, or to the tip of your nostrils where the air enters and leaves your nose. Select the area that you feel most. Do not change your breathing, simply begin to observe it. Do not change areas of attention.
4. Say quietly to yourself "in" when you inhale and "out" when you exhale. Between breaths bring your attention to the points where your body touches the chair, where your feet touch the floor.
5. Focus all of your attention on your breath. If you find your attention wandering, simply say "thought" to yourself and bring your attention back to your breathing. You may wish to label the thoughts as *planning*, *memory, fantasy*, and so on. You may simply use the word "thought" if you wish. If you begin to judge yourself, simply say "thought" or "judgment" and return your attention to breathing.
6. Acknowledge any sensations in your body by saying "sensation" and return your attention to breathing. Do the same with any emotions or feelings that may occur.

Moving to Action

Each week, take about 15 minutes to write out what you have learned about yourself by sitting and how you will take this knowledge into action.

PRACTICE SAMPLE 2: PERSONAL

Planning, Scheduling, and Debriefing

Use the following format to organize yourself and attend to all aspects of your life.

Weekly Overview

List what you will have achieved by week's end by consulting the following domains of concern list.

Domains of Concern
- health/body
- finance
- relaxation/leisure
- work/current projects

- marketing
- reading/studying
- maintenance: diet, education, household work, community, car, clothing, family, equipment, money, friends, others you specify

Weekly Scheduling

1. List your weekly accomplishment goals. Be sure they can be done in a week's time.
2. Check off or draw a line through items when completed.
3. Add items as necessary throughout the week.

Weekly Debriefing

Ask yourself what you actually accomplished, even if you didn't list it. Follow the daily debriefing procedure for transferring incomplete items.

Daily Overview

Each day read over the:

- List of weekly achievements
- List of domains of concern

Daily Scheduling

1. List activities and appointments for the day.
2. List actions required to complete weekly accomplishments.
3. Be sure to assign times to all activities.
4. Check off or draw a line through items when completed.
5. Add items as necessary throughout the day.

Daily Debriefing

Transfer items to future as necessary. After transferring any item three times, drop it from your activities unless it is of vital importance. If vital, ask for support in completing the item.

PRACTICE SAMPLE 3: PERSONAL

Diet Instructions

1. Eat the following each day (see *Fit or Fat Target Diet*, by Covert Bailey—serving sizes and groups are described in the book):
   - 4 servings of the fruit and vegetable group
   - 4 servings of the grain and cereal group

- 2 servings of the dairy group
- 2 servings of the meat and fish group
- Eat less than 25 grams of fat each day
- East less than 2,000mg of sodium each day
- Eat less than 2,000 calories each day
- Drink 64oz of water each day

2. Use the following form to monitor your daily food intake (see Figure B.4).

FOOD INTAKE JOURNAL

Date: _____

Using the instructions in *Fit or Fat Target Diet* for determining your diet, fill out this chart and total the columns at the end of the day.

Food	Calories	Grams of Fat	Grams of Protein	Grams of Fiber
Total				
Target				
Target Made				

FIGURE B.4   Food Intake Journal

Bibliography

Abrams, Jeremiah, and Connie Zweig, eds. *Meeting the Shadow*. Los Angeles: Jeremy P. Tarcher, Inc., 1991. (Chapter Twelve)

Adams, James L. *The Care and Feeding of Ideas*. Reading, MA: Addison-Wesley Publishing Company, 1986. (Chapter Nine)

Almaas, A. H. *Spacecruiser Inquiry*. Boston: Shambhala Publications, 2002. (Chapter Twelve)

Anderson, Nancy. *Work with Passion*. New York: Carroll & Graf Publishers, Inc., 1984. (Chapter Nine)

Arendt, Hannah. *The Human Condition*. Chicago: University of Chicago Press, 1958. (Chapter Twelve)

Argyris, Chris. *Overcoming Organizational Defenses*. Boston: Allyn and Bacon, 1990. (Chapter Nine)

Bar-Levav, Reuven. *Thinking in the Shadow of Feelings*. New York: Simon & Schuster, 1988. (Chapter Five)

Barrett, William. *The Illusion of Technique*. Garden City, NY: Anchor Press/Doubleday, 1979. (Chapter One)

Bateson, Mary Catherine. *Composing a Life*. New York: Atlantic Monthly Press, 1989. (Chapter Twelve)

Becker, Ernest. *The Denial of Death*. New York: Free Press, 1973. (Chapter One)

Beckett, Liana, and Stephanie Covington. *Leaving the Enchanted Forest*. San Francisco: Harper & Row, 1988. (Chapter Nine)

Bellah, Robert M., Richard Madsen, William M. Sullivan, Ann Sweidler, and Steven M. Tipton. *Habits of the Heart*. Berkeley, CA: University of California Press, 1985. (Chapter Five)

Bethanis, Susan J. *Leadership Chronicles of a Corporate Sage*. Chicago: Dearborn Trade Publishing, 2004. (Chapter Three)

Boss, Medard. *Existential Foundations of Medicine and Psychology*. New York: Jason Aronson, Inc., 1983. (Chapter One)

—. *Psychoanalysis and Daseinsanalysis*. New York: Da Capo Press, 1982. (Chapter One)

Bradshaw, John. *Bradshaw On: The Family*. Deerfield Beach, FL: Health Communications, Inc., 1988. (Chapter Nine)

Brown, Daniel P., Jack Engler, and Ken Wilber. *Transformations of Consciousness*. Boston: Shambhala Publications, 1986. (Chapter Six)

Brown, Lyn Mikel, and Carol Gilligan. *Meeting at the Crossroads*. Cambridge, MA: Harvard University Press, 1992. (Chapter Five)

Budd, Matthew, and Larry Rothstein. *You Are What You Say*. New York: Crown Publishers, 2000. (Chapter Seven)

Burns, David D. *Feeling Good*. New York: Signet Classics, 1980. (Chapter Nine)

Chek, Paul. *How to Eat, Move and Be Healthy!* San Diego, CA: Chek Institute, 2006. (Chapter Eleven)

Covey, Stephen R. *The 7 Habits of Highly Effective People*. New York: Simon & Schuster, 1989. (Chapter Twelve)

Dail, Hilda Lee. *The Lotus and the Pool*. Boston: Shambhala Publications, 1983. (Chapter Nine)

Dass, Ram, and Paul Gorman. *How Can I Help?* New York: Alfred A. Knopf, Inc., 1985. (Chapter Twelve)

DePree, Max. *Leadership Is an Art*. New York: Doubleday, 1989. (Chapter Nine)

Dinnerstein, Dorothy. *The Mermaid and the Minotaur*. New York: Harper & Row, 1976. (Chapter Six)

Dreyfus, Hubert L. *Being-in-the-World*. Cambridge, MA: MIT Press, 1991. (Chapter One)

—, and Paul Rabinow. *Michel Foucault: Beyond Structuralism and Hermeneutics*. Chicago: University of Chicago Press, 1982. (Chapter One)

—, and Stuart E. Dreyfus. *Mind over Machine*. New York: Macmillan, Inc., 1986. (Chapter Six)

Drucker, Peter F. *The New Realities*. New York: Harper & Row, 1989. (Chapter Five)

Durrell, Lawrence. *Justine*. Vol. 1 of *The Alexandria Quartet*. New York: E. P. Dutton, 1957. (Chapter Six)

—. *Balthazar*. Vol. 2 of *The Alexandria Quartet*. New York: E. P. Dutton, 1958. (Chapter Six)

—. *Mount Olive*. Vol. 3 of *The Alexandria Quartet*. New York: E. P. Dutton, 1958. (Chapter Six)

—. *Clea*. Vol. 4 of *The Alexandria Quartet*. New York: E. P. Dutton, 1960. (Chapter Six)

Eliot, George. *Middlemarch*. New York: The New American Library, 1964. (Chapter Six)

Eliot, T.S. *The Four Quartets*. San Diego, CA: Harcourt Brace & Company, 1971. (Chapter Eleven)

Erikson, Erik H. *Childhood and Society*. New York: W. W. Norton & Company, 1950; reprint, 1985. (Chapter Six)

—. *The Life Cycle Completed.* New York: W. W. Norton & Company, 1985. (Chapter Six)

Fischer, Norman. *Taking Our Places: The Buddhist Path to Truly Growing Up.* New York: HarperCollins Publishers, 2003. (Chapter Twelve)

Fiumara, Gemma Corradi. *The Other Side of Language.* Translated by Charles Lambert. New York: Routledge, 1990. (Chapter Four)

Flores, Fernando, and Terry Winograd. *Understanding Computers and Cognition.* Norwood, NJ: Ablex Publishing Corporation, 1986. (Chapter One)

Fournies, Ferdinand F. *Coaching for Improved Work Performance.* Blue Ridge Summit, PA: Tap Books, Inc., 1978. (Chapter Nine)

Fritz, Robert. *The Path of Least Resistance.* New York: Ballantine Books, 1984. (Chapter Nine)

Fromm, Erich. *To Have or to Be?* New York: Harper & Row, 1976. (Chapter One)

Gadamer, Hans-Georg. *Philosophical Hermeneutics.* Translated by David E. Linge, ed. Berkeley, CA: University of California Press, 1976. (Chapter Two)

Gergen, Kenneth J. *Realities and Relationships.* Cambridge, MA: Harvard University Press, 1994. (Chapter Two)

Gerrish, Michael. *When Working Out Isn't Working Out.* New York: St. Martin's Griffin, 1999. (Chapter Ten)

Goffman, Erving. *The Presentation of Self in Everyday Life.* New York: Anchor Books/Doubleday, 1959. (Chapter Six)

Goldstein, Joseph, and Jack Kornfield. *The Experience of Insight.* Boston: Shambhala Publications, 1976. (Chapter Twelve)

—. *Seeking the Heart of Wisdom.* Boston: Shambhala Publications, 1987. (Chapter Nine)

Goleman, Daniel. *Destructive Emotions: A Scientific Dialogue with the Dalai Lama.* New York: Bantam Books, 2003. (Chapter Three)

—. *Emotional Intelligence.* New York: Bantam Books, 1995. (Chapter Three)

Grossmann, Reinhardt. *Phenomenology and Existentialism.* Boston: Routledge & Kegan Paul, 1984. (Chapter One)

Gutman, Huck, Patrick H. Hutton, and Luther H. Martin, eds. *Technologies of the Self: A Seminar with Michel Foucault.* Amherst, MA: University of Massachusetts Press, 1988. (Chapter Twelve)

Hacker, Andrew. *Two Nations.* New York: Macmillan Publishing Company, 1992. (Chapter Five)

Harré, Rom. *Personal Being.* Cambridge, MA: Harvard University Press, 1984. (Chapter Six)

Havens, Leston. *Making Contact.* Cambridge: Cambridge University Press, 1986. (Chapter Eight)

Heidegger, Martin. *The Basic Problems of Phenomenology.* Translated by Albert Hofstadter. Bloomington, IN: Indiana University Press, 1982. (Chapter Six)

—. *Being and Time.* Translated by John Macquarrie and Edward Robinson. New York: Harper & Row, 1962. (Chapter One)

—. *On the Way to Language.* Translated by Peter D. Hertz. San Francisco: Harper & Row, 1971. (Chapter Two)

Hillman, James. *Suicide and the Soul.* Dallas, TX: Spring Publications, Inc., 1964. (Chapter One)

Ihde, Don. *Experimental Phenomenology.* Albany, NY: State University of New York Press, 1986. (Chapter One)

—. *Light on Yoga.* New York: Schocken Books, Inc., 1966. (Chapter One)

James, William. *Pragmatism.* New York: Simon & Schuster, 1963. (Chapter One)

—. *The Will to Believe.* New York: Dover Publications, 1956. (Chapter One)

Johnson, Mark, and George Lakoff. *Metaphors We Live By.* Chicago: University of Chicago Press, 1980. (Chapter Two)

Johnson, Robert A. *He.* King of Prussia, PA: Religious Publishing Company, 1974; reprint, New York: Harper & Row, 1986. (Chapter Five)

Johnson, Vernon E. *Intervention.* Minneapolis, MN: Johnson Institute Books, 1986. (Chapter Eight)

Keen, Sam. *The Passionate Life.* San Francisco: Harper & Row, 1983. (Chapter Six)

Kegan, Robert, and Lisa Laskow Lahey. *How the Way We Talk Can Change the Way We Work.* San Francisco: Jossey-Bass, Inc., 2001. (Chapter Ten)

Keleman, Stanley. *Emotional Anatomy.* Berkeley, CA: Center Press, 1985. (Chapter Six)

Kierkegaard, Søren. *The Present Age.* New York: Harper & Row, 1962. (Chapter One)

Kinlaw, Dennis C. *Coaching for Commitment.* San Diego, CA: University Associates, Inc., 1989. (Chapter Nine)

Kockelmans, Joseph J. *On Heidegger and Language.* Evanston, IL: Northwestern University Press, 1972. (Chapter Two)

—. *On the Truth of Being.* Bloomington, IN: Indiana University Press, 1984. (Chapter One)

Kodish, Susan Presby, and Bruce I. Kodish. *Drive Yourself Sane: Using the Uncommon Sense of General Semantics.* Pasadena, CA: Extensional Publishing, 2001. (Chapter Eleven)

Kornfield, Jack. *A Path with Heart.* New York: Bantam Books, 1993. (Chapter Nine)

Kroeger, Otto, and Janet M. Thuesen. *Type Talk.* New York: Dell Publishing, 1988. (Chapter Six)

Kurtz, Ron, and Hector Prestera. *The Body Reveals*. New York: Harper & Row, 1976. (Chapter Six)

Lakoff, George. *Moral Politics*. Chicago: University of Chicago Press, 2002. (Chapter Two)

—. *Women, Fire, and Dangerous Things*. Chicago: University of Chicago Press, 1987. (Chapter Two)

Lasater, Judith. *Relax and Renew*. Berkeley, CA: Rodmell Press, 1995. (Chapter Ten)

Lavine, T. Z. *From Socrates to Sartre: The Philosophic Quest*. New York: Bantam Books, Inc., 1984. (Chapter Eight)

Lesser, Marc. *Less: Accomplishing More by Doing Less*. Novato, CA: New World Library, 2009. (Chapter Eleven)

Levine, Stephen. *Guided Meditations, Explorations and Healings*. New York: Anchor Books/Doubleday, 1991. (Chapter Twelve)

—. *Who Dies?* New York: Anchor Books/Doubleday, 1982. (Chapter One)

Loeb, Paul Rogat. *The Impossible Will Take a Little While*. New York: Basic Books, 2004. (Chapter Ten)

Lowen, Alexander. *Betrayal of the Body*. New York: Macmillan Publishing Company, 1969. (Chapter One)

—. *Bioenergetics*. New York: Penguin Books, 1975. (Chapter One)

—. *The Language of the Body*. New York: Macmillan Publishing Company, 1971. (Originally published as *Physical Dynamics of Character Structure*. Grune and Stratton, Inc., 1958.) (Chapter One)

—. *Fear of Life: A Therapy for Being*. Alachua, FL: Bioenergetics Press, 1980. (Chapter Eleven)

MacIntyre, Alasdair. *After Virtue*. London: Gerald Duckworth & Co., 1981; reprint, Notre Dame, IN: University of Notre Dame Press, 1981. (Chapter Nine)

Macy, Joanna. *World as Lover, World as Self*. Berkeley, CA: Parallax Press, 1991. (Chapter Three)

Maturana, Humberto R., and Francisco J. Varela. *The Tree of Knowledge*. Boston: Shambhala Publications, 1987. (Chapter One)

McCall, Timothy. *Yoga as Medicine*. New York: Bantam Books, 2007. (Chapter Eleven)

McCarthy, Thomas. *The Critical Theory of Jurgen Habermas*. Cambridge, MA: MIT Press, 1978. (Chapter Four)

Mellin, Laurel. *The Pathway*. New York: HarperCollins Publishers, 2003. (Chapter Ten)

Mezirow, Jack, and Associates. *Fostering Critical Reflection in Adulthood*. San Francisco: Jossey-Bass, Inc., 1990. (Chapter Twelve)

Miller, Alice. *The Drama of the Gifted Child*. Translated by Hildegarde and Hunter Hannum. New York: Farrar, Straus, Giroux, 1983. (Originally published as *Prisoners of Childhood*. Frankfurt am Main, Germany: Suhrkamp Verlag, 1979.) (Chapter Six)

—. *For Your Own Good*. Translated by Ruth Ward. New York: Basic Books, Inc./HarperCollins, 1992. (Chapter Six)

Mingyur Rinpoche, Yongey. *The Joy of Living: Unlocking the Secret & Science of Happiness*. New York: Harmony Books, 2007. (Chapter Eleven)

Moore, Thomas. *Care of the Soul*. New York: HarperCollins, 1992. (Chapter Twelve)

Morgan, Gareth. *Images of Organization*. Beverly Hills, CA: Sage Publications, 1986. (Chapter Five)

—, ed. *Beyond Method*. Beverly Hills, CA: Sage Publications, 1983. (Chapter One)

Needleman, Jacob. *The Heart of Philosophy*. New York: Alfred A. Knopf, Inc., 1982; reprint, San Francisco: Harper & Row, 1986. (Chapter One)

Nehamas, Alexander. *Nietzsche: Life as Literature*. Cambridge, MA: Harvard University Press, 1985. (Chapter Five)

Nicoll, Maurice. *Psychological Commentaries on the Teaching of Gurdjieff & Ouspensky Volumes 1–5*. Boston: Shambhala Publications, 1984. (Chapter Twelve)

Nozick, Robert. *The Examined Life*. New York: Simon & Schuster, Inc., 1989. (Chapter Twelve)

Palmer, Parker J. *Let Your Life Speak*. San Francisco: Jossey-Bass, Inc., 2000. (Chapter Twelve)

Palmer, Richard E. *Hermeneutics*. Evanston, IL: Northwestern University Press, 1969. (Chapter One)

Perls, Fritz. *The Gestalt Approach and Eye Witness to Therapy*. Berkeley, CA: Science & Behavior Books, 1973. (Chapter One)

Putnoi, Johanna. *Senses Wide Open: The Art & Practice of Living in your Body*. Berkeley, CA: Ulysses Press, 2000. (Chapter Eleven)

Reich, Robert B. *Tales of a New America*. New York: Random House, 1987. (Chapter Five)

Riso, Don Richard, and Russ Hudson. *The Wisdom of the Enneagram*. New York: Bantam Books, 1999. (Chapter Twelve)

Roizen, Michael F., and Mehmet C. Oz. *You: The Owner's Manual*. New York: HarperResource, 2005. (Chapter Eleven)

—. *You: On a Diet*. New York: Free Press, 2006. (Chapter Eleven)

Rolf, Ida P. *Rolfing*. Santa Monica, CA: Dennis-Landman Publisher, 1977. (Chapter One)

Rorty, Richard. *Consequences of Pragmatism*. Minneapolis, MN: University of Minnesota Press, 1982. (Chapter One)

Rosenberg, Marshall B. *Nonviolent Communication*. Encinitas, CA: Puddle Dancer Press, 2003. (Chapter Two)

Ryle, Gilbert. *The Concept of Mind*. Chicago: University of Chicago Press, 1949. (Chapter One)

Schön, Donald A. *Educating the Reflective Practitioner*. San Francisco: Jossey-Bass, Inc., 1987. (Chapter Nine)

—. *The Reflective Practitioner*. New York: Basic Books, Inc., 1983. (Chapter Eight)

Schutz, Alfred, and Thomas Luckmann. *The Structures of the Life-World*. Evanston, IL: Northwestern University Press, 1973. (Chapter Six)

Schwartz, Barry. *The Paradox of Choice*. New York: HarperCollins, 2004. (Chapter Ten)

Scott, Susan. *Fierce Conversations*. New York: The Berkeley Publishing Group, 2002. (Chapter Two)

Searle, John R. *Minds, Brains and Science*. Cambridge, MA: Harvard University Press, 1984. (Chapter One)

—. *Speech Acts*. Cambridge: Cambridge University Press, 1969. (Chapter Two)

Senge, Peter M. *The Fifth Discipline*. New York: Doubleday, 1990. (Chapter Three)

Siegel, Daniel J. *The Mindful Brain*. New York: W. W. Norton & Co., 2007. (Chapter Eleven)

Sieler, Alan. *Coaching to the Human Soul*. Blackburn, Victoria, Australia: Newfield Australia, 2003. (Chapter Two and Seven)

Solomon, Robert C. *About Love*. New York: Simon & Schuster, 1988. (Chapter Nine)

—. *The Passions*. Notre Dame, IN: University of Notre Dame Press, 1983. (Chapter Six)

Starcevich, Matt M., and Steven J. Stowell. *The Coach*. Salt Lake City, UT: The Center for Management and Organization Effectiveness, 1987. (Chapter Nine)

Stone, Douglas, Bruce Patton, and Sheila Heen. *Difficult Conversations*. New York: Penguin Books, 2000. (Chapter Two)

Tannen, Deborah. *You Just Don't Understand*. New York: Ballantine Books, 1990. (Chapter Eight)

Tarnas, Richard. *The Passion of the Western Mind*. New York: Random House, 1991. (Chapter One)

Taylor, Charles. *Human Agency and Language: Philosophical Papers I*. Cambridge: Cambridge University Press, 1985. (Chapter One)

—. *Sources of the Self*. Cambridge, MA: Harvard University Press, 1989. (Chapter One)

Trungpa, Chögyam. *Cutting through Spiritual Materialism*. Boston: Shambhala Publications, 1973. (Chapter Twelve)

—. *Shambhala*. Boston: Shambhala Publications, 1984. (Chapter Nine)

Unger, Roberto Mangabeira. *Passion.* New York: Macmillan, Inc., 1984. (Chapter Four)

Vail, L. M. *Heidegger and Ontological Difference.* University Park, PA: Pennsylvania State University Press, 1972. (Chapter One)

Wilber, Ken. *Sex, Ecology, Spirituality.* Boston: Shambhala Publications, 1995. (Chapter One)

—. *The Atman Project.* Wheaton, IL: Quest, 1980. (Chapter Six)

—. *A Brief History of Everything.* Boston: Shambala Publications, 1996. (Chapter One)

—. *No Boundary.* Boston: Shambhala Publications, 1979. (Chapter Six)

Wilson, Timothy D. *Strangers to Ourselves.* Cambridge, MA: Harvard University Press, 2002. (Chapter Ten)

Wilson, William Julius. *The Truly Disadvantaged.* Chicago: University of Chicago Press, 1987. (Chapter One)

Winnicott, D. W. *Holding and Interpretation.* London: Hogarth Press, 1986; reprint, New York: Grove Press, 1986. (Chapter Four)

Wittgenstein, Ludwig. *Philosophical Investigations.* Oxford: Basil Blackwell, 1953. (Chapter One)

Woodman, Marion. *Addiction to Perfection.* Toronto: Inner City Books, 1982. (Chapter Nine)

Yalom, Irvin D. *Existential Psychotherapy.* New York: Basic Books, Inc./ HarperCollins, 1980. (Chapter One)

Zimmerman, Michael E. *Eclipse of the Self.* Athens, OH: Ohio University Press, 1981. (Chapter Twelve)

About the Author

James Flaherty founded New Ventures West (1986) and Integral Leadership LLC (2004) to bring a rigorous, compassionate, and pragmatic method for supporting human development to individuals and organizations. Consequently, his work draws upon a wide range of traditions, especially twentieth-century philosophy (Heidegger Searle, Flores, Wittgenstein, James, Rorty, etc.), somatics (e.g., Heckler and Caldwell), cognitive science (e.g., Damasio), integral studies (Ken Wilber *et al.*), spirituality (e.g., Zen, Christianity, Judaism, and Sufism), and developmental theory (Loevinger, Gilligan, Graves, Kegan, Fowles, etc.), among many others. The focus of the work is always to foster development so that competence and fulfillment improve, suffering lessens, and joy and freedom expand for everyone involved in the process.

New Ventures West, an Integral Coach® training school, offers a wide variety of programs throughout the world; Integral Leadership works primarily with organizations, teams, and leaders. Information on both can be found at www.newventureswest.com. A partial client list includes NASA, Hewlett-Packard, Ford, Boeing, Alcatel, Genentech, Cisco Systems, Capital One, Oracle, and Booz Allen Hamilton.

James lives in San Francisco with his wife and business partner, Stacy. Their beloved daughter Devin recently joined New Ventures West as the Director of Communications. James can be reached via e-mail at james@newventureswest. com.

Index

A

abuse, in client's background, 155
acceptance, 42, 103, 104
accounting method of building trust, 41–42
action
  communicative, 84–85
  conversation for, 102–5
Action Workshop, The, 62
adults, coaching, 10–11
alternative model of coaching
  amoeba theory of management, 5–6
  language in, 8
  phenomenology, 7
amoeba theory of management, 5–6
anger, 69
antireductionism, 59
anxiety, 163, 166
apologizing, 69
appreciation, 71–72
approval, 49
Arendt, Hannah, 179
assertions, 93–94
  commitment to, 93
  importance of, 94
  summary of, 95
assessment, 27–28
  of competence level, 27
  components of satisfaction/effective-
    ness model, 73, 79–80
  context, 75
  emotion, 74–75
  intellect, 74
  soul, 76
  will, 75
  context and, 172
  as conversation moves
    background knowledge and, 95–96
    experts and, 97

grounding, 96–97
  making, 96
  pitfalls of, 94–95
  summary of, 98
domains of competence model, 70, 79
  facts and events, 72–73
  relationships with others, 71–72
  self-management, 71
  exercise for Conversation One, 144–45
five elements model, 78
  commitments, 63–64
  future possibilities, 64–65
  immediate concerns, 62–63
  mood, 65–70
  personal/cultural history, 65
  flow of coaching and, 35–36
  interpretation of, 172
  models for
    applications of, 78–80
    communication and, 59
    expectations of, 59–60
    labeling and, 60–61
    using, 76–77
    validity of, 60
  of readiness for change, 159–61
  self
    client's, 160
    expectation and, 61
  skills in, 172
  structure of interpretation and, 27, 35
  of trust, 41–42
assumed competence, 88
athletic coaching, 10
Atwater, Lee, 67
Austin, John, 83
Awakenings (film), 68
awareness, 154

B

background of obviousness, 88
behavior
  expectations and, 60
  interpretation and, 7–8
  outcomes and, 7, 126–27
  structure of interpretation and, 25
Being-in-the-World (Dreyfus), 11
Bell, Chauncey, 83
body, *see* human body
body work, 21
Boss, Medard, 15, 16, 39
boundaries, declarations and, 98
breathing exercises, 21
Brown, Christy, 21

C

capacity for change, 158–59
Care of the Soul (Moore), 179
change
  assessing readiness for, 159–61
  capacity for, 158–59
  commitment to, 158
  foundation for, 161–63
  necessities for, 158–59
  relationships and, 161
characterization, self, 54
coaching
  alternative model of, 5–8
    amoeba theory of management, 5–6
    phenomenology, 7
  athletic, 10
  commitments to, 107–8
  through conversation, 101, 115–16
  creativity in, 11
  flow of
    assessment and, 35–36
    developing sense of, 31
    relationship and, 33–34
    stages of, 33–37
    structure for, 31–32, 37
  foundation for
    alternative model, 5–8
    in command-and-control organiza-
      tions, 2–3
    creativity in, 11
    learning experiences, 10
    operating principles, 9–11

  overview, 1–2
  products, 3–5, 7–8
  premise of, 7
  relationship of, 39–40, 47–48, 54
    freedom of expression in, 44–49
    social identity and, 54
  scope of, 37
  self-correction and, 158
  self-development for, 170
    process of, 174–75
    qualities, 172–74
    skills, 171–72
  self-generation and, 158
  space for, 163
  structure of interpretation and, 26
  for stuck, 152–53
  time for, 163
  in type two conversation (several
    conversations), 121
command-and-control organizations,
  2–3
commitments, 78
  assertions and, 93
  to change, 158
  to coaching, 107–8
  competing/conflicting, 155
  declarations and, 97
  enrollment and, 107–10
  in five elements model, 63–64
  mutual, 107–8
  offers and, 92–93
  promises and, 90
  requests as, 86
  speech act theory and, 84
communication
  assessment models and, 59
  coaching scope and, 37
  forces shaping, 45
  give and take in, 39
  habits in, 49
  language and, 23
  openness in, 45
  in organizations, 45
  relationship and, 33
  social identity and, 53
  structure for, 37
  style of, 49

communicative action, 84–85
competence, assumed, 88
competing/conflicting commitments,
    155
Competitive Edge Sales Course, The, 62
complaining, 173
components of satisfaction/effectiveness
    model, 73, 79–80
    context, 75
    emotion, 74–75
    intellect, 74
    soul, 76
    will, 75
conditions for satisfaction, 87–88
confidentiality, 46–47
consequences, clarity about, 57
Consequences of Pragmatism, 16
consistency, 173–74
context
    assessment skills and, 172
    in components of satisfaction and
        effectiveness, 75, 80
    historical, 93
    language as, 10, 24–25
    of speaking, 84, 86
    time as, 88
conversation
    for action, 102–5
    coaching through, 101, 115–16
    enrollment, 107–10
    listening and, 101–2
    moves in, 85
        assertions, 93–94, 95
        assessments, 94–97, 98
        declarations, 97–99, 100
        offers, 90, 92–93
        promises, 90, 91
        requests, 86–90, 91
    for possibilities, 101–2
    for relationship, 99–101
    type one (single conversation)
        outline/example, 117–20
        overview, 116, 117
    type two (several conversations)
        coaching in, 121
        first conversation, 120–25
        overview, 116–17

second conversation, 125–29
third conversation, 129–32
type three (profound, long
    conversation)
    overview, 117
    questions for, 132–44
Covey, Stephen, 179
creativity, 11, 174
cultural history, 65, 78
current reality, 175
cynicism, 67, 108

D
death, 22–23
Declaration of Independence, 97
declarations
    boundaries and, 98
    commitment in, 97
    meaning and, 98
    of outcomes, 98, 100
    possibility in, 97–98
    of reality, 98–99
    truth and, 99
    designing, 172
    exercises, 153
    practices, 152–53
Dewey, John, 115
Dickinson, Emily, 25
domains of competence model,
    70–73, 79
    facts and events, 72–73
    relationships with others, 71–72
    self-management, 71
Douglas, Michael, 67
downsizing, 2
Dreyfus, Hubert, 11

E
Educating the Reflective Practitioner
    (Schön), 147
emotion, 79
    components of satisfaction/effective-
        ness model and, 74–75
    relationships and, 72
enrollment, 36
    checklist for, 111
    commitment and, 107–10
    conversation for, 107–10

enrollment (Contd)
  difficulty of, 107
  listening and, 109, 110
  outcomes and, 36, 107–12, 117
exercise, 78, 165
exercises
  for assessing level of competence, 27
  assessment, 144–45
  for being stuck, 153
  breathing, 21
  for Conversation One, 122, 144–46
  designing, 153
  for distinctions/structures, 135
  network of support, 105
  observation, 125, 129
  practice, 146–47, 153
  scaling expectations with, 153
  self-observation, 28, 37, 122, 123, 135,
    145–46, 155
  for uncovering undiscussable, 45
Existential Foundations of Medicine and
    Psychology (Boss), 16
expectations
  for assessment models, 59–60
  behavior and, 60
  as coach, 173
  inflexibility of, 54
  scaling, 153
  from self-assessment, 61
  unrealistic, 153

F
Faulkner, William, 67
feedback, 178
five elements model, 78
  commitments, 63–64
  future possibilities, 64–65
  immediate concerns, 62–63
  mood, 65–70
  personal/cultural history, 65
flexibility, 174
Flores, Fernando, 11, 62, 83
flow of coaching
  developing sense of, 31
  relationship and, 33–34
  stages of, 33–37
  structure for, 31–32, 37

foundation for coaching
  alternative model, 5–8
  amoeba theory of management, 5–6
  language in, 8
  phenomenology, 7
  in command-and-control organizations,
    2–3
  creativity in, 11
  learning experiences, 10
  operating principles, 9–11
  overview, 1–2
  products, 3–5, 7–8
freedom of expression
  in coaching relationship, 44–49
  confidentiality and, 46–47
  cultural, 44–45
  listening and, 46
  mutual, 44–49
  openness and, 45–46
  in organizations, 45
  strengthening, 48
  trust and, 47
Fritz, Robert, 147
frustration, 68, 77
  being stuck and, 151–52
  openings and, 55, 56
future action, 87
future possibilities, 64–65, 78

G
Gates, Bill, 153
Goodfellows (film), 67
grounding, 96–97
group effectiveness, 45
guilt, 69–70

H
Habermas, Jürgen, 83
habits, 51–53
  in communication, 49
  as hindrances, 134
  physical level of, 173
  public identity and, 105
  self-image and, 105
  social identity and, 54, 55
Hatha yoga, 21
Hawking, Stephen, 21

Heidegger, Martin, 24
hindrances, 107, 134, 176
   habits as, 134
   to outcomes, 107–11, 134
   social identity as, 53
history
   context of, 93
   personal/cultural, 65, 78
Hsia Po-Yan, 59
human beings
   complexity of, 6
   defining, 15–17
   model limitations and, 60
   as possibility for relating, 18–19
   truth and, 17–18
human body, 21–22
   habits in, 173
   as locus of transformation, 21–22
   as way of being in world, 21
Human Condition, The (Arendt), 179
Hume, David, 66

I
identity
   habits of
      public identity, 105
      social identity, 54, 55
   public, 25, 105
   social
      as coaching hindrance, 53
      habits and, 54, 55
      narratives in, 54
      structure of, 55
immediate concerns, 62–63, 78
impatience, 119, 159, 173
inferior moods, 68–70
inflexible expectations, 54
innovation, 2
intellect, 79
   in components of satisfaction/effec-
      tiveness model, 74
   will v., 111
intended outcomes, 176
intention, clarifying, 118
interpretation, 10–11
   of assessments, 172
   individual behavior and, 7–8
   limits of, 76

requests and, 86
structure of, 8
   assessment and, 27, 35
   behavior following, 25
   coaching and, 26
   revealing thought process and, 118

J
Jordan, Michael, 153
Joyce, James, 25
justification, 54, 107

K
Keller, Helen, 21
Kennedy, John, 70, 97
King Lear, 69

L
labels, 60–61
laissez-faire capitalism, 67
language, 23–25
   in alternative model of coaching, 8
   communication and, 23
   context and, 10, 24–25
   listening and, 23–24
   meaning and, 25
   as orientation, 24
   time and, 19–20
learning experiences, 10
Lewis, Sinclair, 67
listening, 85
   conversation for possibilities and, 101
   enrollment and, 109, 110
   freedom of expression and, 46
   immediate concerns and, 62
   language and, 23–24
   requests and, 86–89
   self-improvement of, 175–78
   skills in, 171
   speaking and, 84–85
listening journal, 177
long-term excellent performance, 3
Lowen, Alexander, 21

M
Man in the Grey Flannel Suit, The (film),
   76
Mandela, Nelson, 97

manipulation, 107
Maturana, Humberto, 11, 93
meaning
    declarations and, 98
    language and, 25
    structure of interpretation and, 26
meetings, 164
mental hygiene, 163
Merchant of Venice, The, 69
metaphors, 143
misrepresentation, 107
mood, 20–21, 78
    five elements model and, 65–70
    inferior, 68–70
    superior, 66–68
Moore, Thomas, 179
moves in conversation, 85
    assertions, 93–94, 95
    assessments, 94–97, 98
    declarations, 97–99, 100
    offers, 90, 92–93
    promises, 90, 91
    requests, 86–90, 91
multicultural environments, 2
mutual commitment, 107–8
mutual freedom of expression, 44–49
mutual respect, 42–44
mutual trust, 40–42
Myers-Briggs type, 59

N
narratives
    interplay of, 54
    private, 54
nervous system, 52
network of support, 105, 162, 177, 178

O
observation, 25–26
    exercises for, 125, 129
    principles of, 77
    self
        exercise for Conversation One,
            122, 145–46
        exercises for, 28, 37, 123, 135, 155
    subjectivity in, 26
obviousness, background of, 88

offers
    coaching situations in, 90, 92
    as combination of request and promise,
        90
    as intersection of needs and commit-
        ments, 92–93
    summary of, 93
Olalla, Julio, 83
openings, 34, 55–57
openness, 45–46, 71
operating principles, 9–11
organizations
    command-and-control, 2–3
    communication in, 45
orientation, 24
outcomes, 107, 109
    amoeba theory and, 6
    behavior and, 7, 126–27
    clarity about, 57
    client distinctions for, 133
    commitments and, 63
    Conversation Number Three and, 129
    declarations of, 98, 100
    enrollment and, 36, 107–12, 117
    fulfillment of coaching program and,
        133
    hindrances to, 107–11, 134
    intended, 176
    language/time and, 19–20
    long-term, 158
    metaphors for, 143
    mutual declaration of, 98, 100
    offers and, 90
    operating principles of coaching and,
        9–11
    products of coaching and, 3–4, 7–8
    requests and, 86, 89
    self-correction and, 158
    self-generation and, 158
    self-management and, 71
    speaking and, 85
    structure and, 32
overstimulation, 163

P
Passion of the Western Mind (Tarnas), 11
Path of Least Resistance, The (Fritz), 147
patience, 173

personal history, 65, 78
phenomenology, 7, 64
physical props, 163
Pollack, Jackson, 96
Popper, Karl, 16
possibility
  conversation for, 101–2
  declarations and, 97–98
posture, 21
powerlessness, 25
practice, 178
practice exercise, 146–47, 153
practices, designing, 152–53
pragmatism, 9–10
premise of coaching, 7
principles of observation, 77
private narratives, 54
products of coaching, 3–5, 7–8
promises
  as commitment, 90
  individuals and, 90
  summary of, 91
public identity, 25, 105

R
reality, declaring, 98–99
Reich, William, 21
relationships, 9, 78
  coaching, 39–40, 47–48, 54
  communication and, 33
  conversation for, 99–101
  in domains of competence model,
    71–72
  emotion and, 72
  flow of coaching and, 33–34
  freedom of expression in, 44–49
  possibility for, 18–19
  readiness for change and, 161
  toxic, 166
renewal, 161
requests
  commitment and, 86
  elements of, 86–90
  summary of, 91
  time and, 88
resentment, 69
resignation, 67–68
resolving breakdowns, 171–72

respect
  mutual, 42–44
  strengthening, 47–48
rigor, 172–73
Rolf, Ida, 21
routines, 161

S
scaling expectations, 153
Scarlet Letter, The, 70
schedules, 164
Schön, Donald, 147
Sciacca, M. F., 39
Searle, John, 83
second-guessing, 163
self-assessment
  client's, 160
  expectation and, 61
self-characterization, 54
self-consistency, 173–74
self-correction, 3, 4
  coaching outcomes and, 158
self-development, 169
  for coaches, 170
    process of, 174–75
    qualities, 172–74
    skills, 171–72
self-generation, 3–5, 158
self-image, 105
self-management, 71, 73, 78
self-observation
  exercise for Conversation One, 122,
    145–46
  exercises for, 28, 37, 123, 135, 155
7 Habits of Highly Effective People, The
  (Covey), 179
shadow, 154
Shambhala (Trungpa), 147
shared background of obviousness, 88
Sieler, Alan, 83
simplification, 161
sincerity, 89
skepticism, 66–67, 108
social identity, 53–55
  as coaching hindrance, 53
  habits and, 54, 55
  narratives in, 54
  structure of, 55

something missing, 89
soul, 76, 80
space for coaching, 163
speaking
    context of, 84, 86
    outcomes and, 85
    requests and, 86
    skills in, 171
    speech act theory and, 84–85
speech act theory, 83
    communicative action principles,
        84–85
    moves in conversation, 85
        assertions, 93–94, 95
        assessments, 94–97, 98
        declarations, 97–99, 100
        offers, 90, 92–93
        promises, 90, 91
        requests, 86–90, 91
stress, 158, 164–66
    level of, 160
    sources of, 161
structure, 178
    command-and-control, 2
    communication, 37
    flow of coaching and, 31–32, 37
    outcomes and, 32
    of social identity, 55
structure of interpretation, 8
    assessment and, 27, 35
    behavior following, 25
    coaching and, 26
    revealing thought process and, 118
stuck
    client being, 151–53
    coaching for, 152–53
    exercises for, 153
    frustration and, 151–52
    practices for, 152–53
    program being, 153–56
    strategies for fixing, 154–55
subjectivity of observation, 26
superior moods, 66–68

T
Tarnas, Richard, 11
Taylor, Charles, 83

time
    for coaching, 163
    as context, 88
    language and, 19–20
    requests and, 88
timeline, 178
token, 90
toxic relationships, 166
traction, 157
transformation, human body as locus of,
    21
Tree of Knowledge, The (Maturana and
    Varela), 11
truing questions, 170
Trungpa, Chögyam, 147
trust
    accounting method of, 41–42
    assessing, 41–42
    freedom of expression and, 47
    mutual, 40–42
truth
    declarations and, 99
    human beings and, 17–18
Twain, Mark, 67
"two tracks" principle, 10
type one (single conversation)
    outline/example, 117–20
    overview, 116, 117
type two (several conversations)
    coaching in, 121
    first conversation, 120–25
    overview, 116–17
    second conversation, 125–29
    third conversation, 129–32
type three (profound, long conversation)
    overview, 117
    questions for, 132–44

U
"uncoachable" clients, 10, 157
Understanding Computers and
    Cognition (Flores and
    Winograd), 11
undiscussable, uncovering, 45
unrealistic expectations, 153
utilitarianism, 63

V

Varela, Francisco, 11
voice echoing, 176

W

walking, 163
Wall Street (film), 67
well-being, 160–61
Whitman, Walt, 25

will, 80
    components of satisfaction/effective-
        ness model and, 75
    habits of, 53
    intellect v., 111
    utilitarianism and, 63
Winograd, Terry, 11
worst-case scenario thinking, 163